Southeast Asian
Cartoon Art

# Southeast Asian Cartoon Art

## History, Trends and Problems

*Edited by* JOHN A. LENT

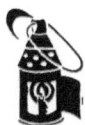

McFarland & Company, Inc., Publishers
*Jefferson, North Carolina*

LIBRARY OF CONGRESS CATALOGUING-IN-PUBLICATION DATA

Southeast Asian Cartoon Art : History, Trends and Problems / edited by John A. Lent.

    p.    cm.

Includes bibliographical references and index.

**ISBN 978-0-7864-7557-5 (softcover : acid free paper)** ∞
**ISBN 978-1-4766-1446-5 (ebook)**

1. Cartooning—Southeast Asia—History.  2. Comic books, strips, etc.—Southeast Asia—History.  3. Popular culture—Southeast Asia.  I. Lent, John A., editor of compilation.

PN6790.S65S68 2014
741.5'959—dc23                       2013048049

BRITISH LIBRARY CATALOGUING DATA ARE AVAILABLE

On the cover: "Butcher of Burma," editorial cartoon by Stephff, October 2, 2007

Manufactured in the United States of America

*McFarland & Company, Inc., Publishers*
  *Box 611, Jefferson, North Carolina 28640*
    *www.mcfarlandpub.com*

# Table of Contents

# Table of Contents

# Preface

## JOHN A. LENT

Cartoon art in Southeast Asia has been building a good reputation for many years, though it is little studied. For example, King Bhumibol Adulyadej of Thailand selected famous cartoonist Chai Rachawat to illustrate two books His Majesty wrote. The comics character Mr. Kiasu (created by Johnny Lau) fosters a Singaporean national trait called *kiasuism* (the need to be first). In Malaysia, the humor magazine *Gila Gila* for a long time topped the country's most circulated periodical list. In the Philippines, *komiks*, almost since their inception, served as the source of nearly one half of Pilipino feature film plots and as a main vehicle for social consciousness messages. In Indonesia and the Philippines, a form of graphic novel existed decades before this type of book became popular in the West.

With these and other notable accomplishments, one must wonder why Southeast Asian cartooning has been such a well-kept secret. There are a few possible answers. First, the importance given to American superhero comic books and Japanese *manga* left no room for a serious consideration of the local product. Second, in almost every Southeast Asian country, governments and the public did not think of comic strips and comic books as anything other than children's entertainment. Third, academia, nurtured by strong colonial influences as to what should be studied, snobbishly ignored comic art.

Despite these oversights, cartooning in Southeast Asia has had a long reach and a profound impact on the region's societies. Humor magazines appeared in the Philippines in the late nineteenth century; political cartoons and comic strips in some countries by the early twentieth century; and comic books after World War II. Although strong authoritarian governments were in power from time to time in each of the countries studied here, political cartoonists managed to leave their venom, usually covertly, which occasionally led to arrest, imprisonment, and other harassments. Comic books faced different problems, usually economic, but they experienced a heyday in the 1960s through the 1980s in Cambodia, Indonesia, the Philippines, and Thailand. Humor magazines thrived in Malaysia, particularly after 1978.

Almost simultaneously, at the end of the twentieth century, comic art forms suffered setbacks throughout the region: pressure from governments and corporations to stifle political cartooning; severe competition from comic strips and comic books produced in the U.S. and Japan; and new media such as television and the Internet. For myriad reasons, the comic book industry in Southeast Asia was all but buried as the 1990s approached. And then, because of the yeomen efforts of a few cartoonists and cartooning aficionados, comic books made a comeback beginning in the mid– to late 1990s. In a number of instances, what sparked this renewed interest were independent self-published comics (often crudely produced on photocopiers and distributed non-conventionally) and reprinted classics from the 1960s and 1970s. In more recent years, the Internet allowed for speedier, less-expensive production.

Additionally, other factors led to the rebirth of comic books. Manga, for all the criticisms of them as destroyers of local comics, contributed by regenerating interest in some quarters for what was a dying medium. Observing the global manga phenomenon stimulated local entrepreneurs to enter comics production, a result being that many new companies sprouted, among them Art Square Group in Malaysia; Chuang Yi, M.G. Creative, and Comix Factory in Singapore; Mango Comics, Komikero Publishing, and Sacred Mountain in the Philippines; m&c! Comics and other appendages of the Kompas Gramedia Group in Indonesia; E.Q. Plus, Typhoon Books, and New Venture Generation in Thailand; and Our Books in Cambodia. Other changes since the 1990s are:

1. The moving of sales and distribution from male-only-friendly comics shops and roadside stalls to comics and Internet cafes, comic shops, and large retail bookstores attractive to both male and female readers.

2. The demise of some genres (e.g., Philippine *nobelas*) and the rise of others such as graphic novels (e.g., E.Q. Plus Publishing's series of Knowledge Comic in Thailand; Gerry Alanguilan's *Elmer* and Budjette Tan's *Trese: Murder on Balete Drive* in the Philippines; Yuniarto's

*Garudayana* in Indonesia; or Séra's *Impasse et Rouge* in Cambodia) and underground and alternative comics (Athonk's *The Bad Times Story* and others in Indonesia; the Hesheit series in Thailand).

3. Adaptations and spin-offs of comics, such as komiks movies again in the Philippines, and television animation adaptations (e.g., Lat's *Kampung Boy* in Malaysia and *Pang Pond* in Thailand).

4. The changing role of women with an increase in their readership of comics because of Japanese girls (*shoujo*) and *yaoi* (boy to boy love) manga; more attractive rental/sales venues; female-friendly content (*Cabai*, a Malaysian humor magazine "exclusively for women," Azisa Noor's *Satu Atap* [One Roof] in Indonesia and *Mango Jam* in the Philippines); and more women practitioners (in Indonesia, most young comics artists are women working for books published by ElexMedia Komputindo).

Newspaper comic strips do not seem to have changed much in recent years. In the Philippines and Indonesia, major dailies still carry a rather large assortment of local strips in the national language, while in Singapore and Malaysia, one finds a mixture of a few local and foreign syndicated strips. Except on Sunday, when color sections of U.S. strips appear, usually Thai dailies each have one or two local funnies (sometimes political). Comic strips are rare in Cambodian and Vietnamese newspapers. The limited growth of Southeast Asian newspaper strips is attributable to economics (it is less expensive to use syndicated foreign strips), government and social pressures, and lessened importance of newspapers in light of the emergence of the Internet.

Political cartooning, as always, depends upon the type of government in power. In Cambodia, Myanmar, Vietnam, and, to lesser degrees, Singapore, Malaysia, and Indonesia, cartoonists are stifled by officialdom in dealing with political issues directly, resorting instead to covering social problems or using subtle means to get political messages across. Thai political cartoonists seem to be the most outspoken, for even historically-free Philippine political cartoonists face the perils of self-censorship brought on by the oligarchic control of the dailies. In some cases, political cartoonists have left their countries, going into exile (as with Myanmar cartoonists working out of Thailand) or seeking more lucrative financial arrangements (as with some Philippine cartoonists who went to Singapore). The latter also applies to comic book artists, particularly some from Cambodia,

Indonesia, and the Philippines, who work for U.S., Japanese, and French comics publishers, either in those countries or from their home bases.

## *Dimensions of* Southeast Asian Cartoon Art

This book brings together for the first time the various dimensions of the region's comic art, concentrating on both the history and contemporary situation, mostly from an industrial perspective. The essays are written by veteran as well as new researchers of comics and cartooning who used research techniques, solely or jointly, of historical method, interviewing, participant-observation, and textual analysis. Five of the essays are historical-contemporary overviews, justified because little is known in academia and fandom about Southeast Asian countries' cartooning; the other three, though also partly historical, hone in on cartoons' or cartoonists' relationships to issues such as the transnational public sphere in Burma, national identity in Malaysia, and chauvinism of Chinese cartoonists in Singapore.

The authors deal with different forms of comic art, including political or editorial cartoons taking a stand on societal and political issues; newspaper comic strips built around a stand-alone joke or a serialized adventure story, usually of fewer panels; comic books which come in various sizes, shapes, genres, and formats; graphic novels or book-length comics; and humor magazines containing humorous articles, illustrated jokes, and comic strips.

Though the Internet has been mentioned tangentially in some pieces, there is no significant discussion of Webtoons among these essays. The authors are very much aware of the prominence of online cartoons and comics in Southeast Asia. However, this volume concentrates on print cartooning, understandable in that much of the content predates the Internet.

Too many people contributed to the development of this book to mention all of them. Interviewees listed at the rear of the book and scores of others I interviewed since 1986 were generous with their time and information, for which I am very appreciative. I want to thank very heartedly the essay authors, Lisa Brooten, Muliyadi Mahamood, Lim Cheng Tju, and Warat Karuchit, and two other comics scholars, Xu Ying and Sueen Noh, for their technical preparation of the manuscript.

# PART I

# Historical and Contemporary Overviews

# Cartooning in Indonesia

## An Overview

JOHN A. LENT

In the Southeast Asian context, Indonesian cartooning seems to play the role of "odd man out." Surrounded by the Philippines, with its long-established komiks tradition, and Malaysia, with its internationally-acclaimed cartoonist Lat, Indonesia is virtually unknown in comic art circles. Yet, that should not be the case.

For one thing, Indonesia has a visual humor tradition rivaling most Asian countries, traceable to temple relief[1] and *wayang* characters a millennium ago. The country's first indigenous comic strip character was published in 1931, just a couple of years after Kenkoy's historic appearance in the Philippines. More impressively, Indonesia sported an already labeled graphic novel in 1962, years before this genre surfaced in most of the world. And, relative to making comparisons within the region, the "father" of Indonesia Sukarno is credited with drawing the first cartoon (a political one),[2] as Jose Rizal is thought to be the first Filipino cartoonist and Ho Chi Minh the pioneering Vietnamese political cartoonist.

Second, despite a wavering cartoon and comics presence common throughout Southeast Asia, Indonesia has held onto (sometimes barely) a culture of political cartoons, newspaper strips, humor magazines, and comic books. As this essay will show, some time periods were particularly ripe with newspaper strips, and to a lesser degree, comic books.

## The Wayang Tradition

Searching for the roots of anything contemporaneous can be problematic; the same applies to cartooning. Following in the spirit of researchers who found semblances of visual humor or narrative in Pharaoh tombs, Mayan codices, or Asian scrolls, one can make a case that Indonesia's ancient *wayang kulit* (leather puppets) carried much humor, satire, and storytelling. Though wayang had primary purposes of teaching and preserving local beliefs (see Peacock 1968), they also engaged in subtle humor, as Anderson (1990: 67) pointed out:

> In wayang of whatever sort, the punakawan (wayang clowns) appear both as comic characters *within the line* of the drama, embedded in its space and time, and as mouthpieces for contemporaneous satire directed straight at the audience, so to speak *at right angles* to the drama and outside its space and time.

For centuries, wayang clowns spoke for the common people through veiled messages about societal issues. The clowns could speak their minds in the presence of masters, because of the "obvious difference in status, the clowns' coarseness to their masters' elegance, ugliness to graceful appearance, crude to exquisite speech," allowing the clowns "to laugh at their betters but never undermine them" (Berman 2001: 24). Wayang kulit clowns were often used to perform farces as interludes within epic dramas, making fun of upper caste and class dialects and improvising biting satirical commentary (Lent 1993b: 21). Indonesia's most prominent political cartoonist, G. M. Sudarta (interview, 1992) said each clown represented attributes that were exaggerated caricature: Semar, symbol of wisdom; Petruk, frank speech; Gareng, insulting speech; Bagong, stupidity.

Wayang kulit, as well as *wayang bēbēr* (scrolled picture stories) and *lontar* (manuscripts on palm leaves), all are known for their early telling of stories with pictures. Whether these texts reflected indigenous concerns or Hindu imports is a topic of debate (Berman 2001: 36). Peacock (1968: 51), discussing wayang kulit, believed it was both. He wrote that the grotesque, uncouth, and clumsy clowns of this genre may have originated in Java "during pre–Hindu times (before 600) and therefore may be additions to the Hindu myths, from which wayang has drawn some elements of its stories of Ardjuna and the Padawas." Brandon (1967: 43) believed wayang kulit's origins were in the eleventh century. He showed a modern connection with comic books, stating, "In Java, for example, a child can read a comic book in which the *Mahabharata* story is drawn in wayang kulit style, or he can read a comic book in which Semar, Petruk, and Gareng, the traditional wayang clowns, cavort through twentieth-century adventures" (Brandon 1967: 166).

7

Sears (1996: 280), comparing wayang with comics, thought comics have advantages in storytelling, because they are meant for private reading, do away with "visible mediators between the individual and the story world," and have stronger characterization. She explained that comic book characters have more sensual bodies than leather puppets, and are not restricted to a certain type or number of body movements, adding:

> When characters move from puppet image to comic book, there is a certain release from all the bodily movements that have been associated with that character for decades and probably centuries. The amount of movement allowed comic-book characters represents a true liberation from the class positions encoded in the shadow puppet theatre and the *wayang orang*, performances with human actors, which have been structured to follow the puppet movements very carefully.

Also, according to Sears (1996: 282), stories told in comics can have sensual imagings not encouraged in puppetry.

Wayang characters find places not just in comic books, but in contemporary political and gag cartoons as well. Veteran strip cartoonist and animator Dwi Koendoro, who pointed out that in one part of wayang called *goro-goro*, satire and caricature abound, uses the "two-dimensional aspects" of its style and philosophy in his strips (Koendoro, interview, 1992). Sudarta gave an example of his use of the clown characters: "When I have a character point, it is saying indirectly that it is speaking franky" (Sudarta, interview, 1992). Extremely prolific cartoonist Johnny Hidajat said he started his popular "Djon Domino," because he was influenced by wayang's Petruk (Hidajat, interview, 1992); the character has features similar to Petruk.

## Early Comics: 1930s–50s

As would be expected, Dutch-language periodicals carried newspaper strips and editorial cartoons, such as the children-oriented "Flippie Flink" in *De Java Bode* in 1938. The strip was drawn by Clinge Doorenbosi. Of course, editorial cartoons reflected Dutch colonialist interests.

Thought to be the first indigenously-drawn comic strip was "Put On," created by Kho Wang Gie (aka Sopoiku) in 1931 (Bonneff 1976: 13). Kho was initially a trader who became interested in drawing after he

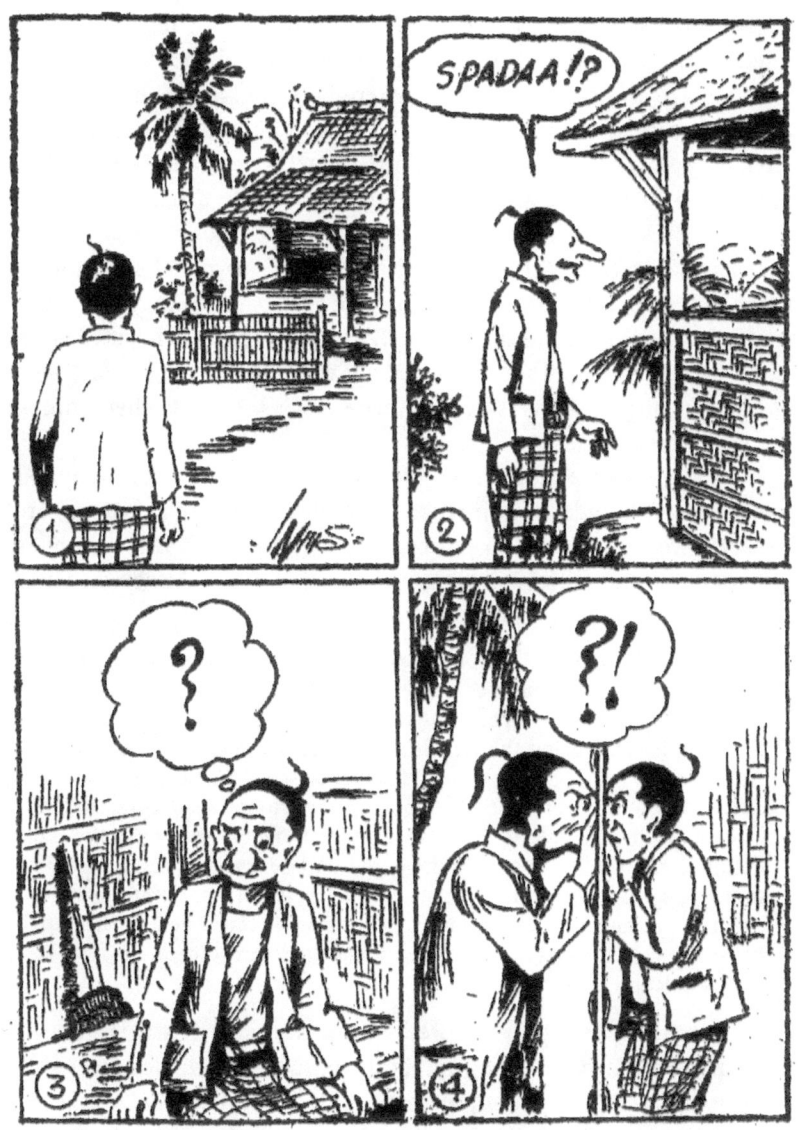

**"Put On" by Kho Wang Gie, a comic strip in *Sin Po* newspaper, 1931.**

saw a comic strip while opening a food wrap from abroad. Published in the Chinese-language daily *Sin Po*, the strip reflected the daily life of a young, single, middle-class man and his never-ending problems and foolishness while living in Jakarta. Put On lived with his disciplined, nagging mother and two teasing brothers in a "cubicle house" with a front terrace and small backyard, where he rested and had his adventures. He worked in an office under a difficult boss. The featured characters and plots resembled those of humor strips nearly anywhere (Rizal and Elsanti 2009). One writer, studying comics in an urban setting, said "Put On" presented "a view from 'down under' about the roaring and razing urbanization" (Darmawan 2009). The four-panel strip moved about as Dutch authorities closed newspapers because they did not fit the government mode (Suroto 2010: 178). "Put On," which lasted about thirty years, inspired other strips that appeared in *Star Magazine* (1939–42), later changed to *Star Weekly* (Karna 2007: 312), and other Chinese and Malay newspapers.

Through the Japanese occupation (1943–45), the war for independence (1945–48), and the immediate independence years, cartoons and poster art were often used for propaganda purposes, with strip characters even painted on walls, alongside resistance slogans. Anderson (1978: 292), in his research, found

> under the Occupation, cartoons and posters were widely used, but they appeared exclusively under the aegis of the military authorities. The targets of the cartoons were typically outside society—the Dutch, the British, and the Americans. During the Revolution, posters and graffiti were the most common and most popular form. Of forty newspapers and magazines I have checked from that period, only eight carried cartoons at all; even these cartoons appeared irregularly, and at rare intervals. Doubtless part of the explanation lies in the technical problems caused by shortages and disorders of those years. But the fact that the bulk of these cartoons were printed in papers published in Dutch-occupied Jakarta, not in towns held by the Republic, suggests that the full answer lies as much in the political-cultural as in the technical realm.

From the late 1940s, United States newspaper strips such as "Tarzan," "Rip Kirby," "Phantom," and "Johnny Hazard" found regular space in dailies and weekly supplements.[3] Their popularity spurred some local artists to convert U.S. superheroes into Indonesian characters, examples being the clones of Superman and Flash Gordon, such as Siti Gahara, Puteri Bintang, Garuda Putih, and Kapten Comet, or the imitator of Wonder Woman, Sri Asih by R. A. Kosasih in 1954 (Karna 2007: 312). American look-alikes made up some of the first comic books in Indonesia in the 1950s.

There were also sources other than American for comics stories. Beginning in the 1950s, Abdulsalam published a heroism strip in Yogyakarta's daily, *Kedaulatan Rakyat*; Teguh Santosa created "Sandhora"; "Kisah Pendudukan Jogja," about the aggression of Dutch troops in Yogyakarta, appeared as a complete series in the Bandung daily *Pekiran Rakyat*, and "Sie Djin Koei," Siaw Tik Kwei's popular comic adaptation of a Chinese legend, was started (Karna 2007: 312). But, it was R. A. Kosasih, Oerip, Otto Suastika, and Ardisoma who stood out in the 1950s. As indicated above, Kosasih created Indonesia's first superheroine, Sri Asih, while Oerip often based his comics protagonists on puppet characters. Otto Suastika was popular during this decade, particularly known for his *silat* (kungfu) strip stories which appeared in *Star Weekly*, beginning in 1954. His strips appeared for about a decade and were considered among the best in Indonesia, mainly because of their artwork. Suastika's stories were "adapted from Chinese legends, with Chinese settings and Chinese details" (Berman 2001: 19).

## 1960s–70s: Golden but Tarnished

The 1960s–70s were the golden age of Indonesian comics, as the number of titles increased greatly and sales surged. Berman (2001: 20) wrote about this time:

> Everybody was reading them! During this time, a brilliant scheme for evading the problem of economic difficulty appeared through the comic rental kiosk which blossomed throughout Java.... Many Indonesians have described for me their memories of that time through images of people sitting under trees beside the huge piles of comics they had borrowed from the rental kiosk!

Agus Leonardus, initiator of a 2004 comics exhibition, admired the work artists produced in the 1960s–70s despite technological limitations, and lauded the public respect shown for comics (quoted in Indarto 2004).

Stimulating this growth in interest for comics were their "affordability" because of rental kiosks, and their readability that resulted from more locally-relevant stories. Adaptations and copies of American superhero and other genres comics and Chinese legends still dominated, but local stories were beginning to be revived. Publishers such as Melodi (Bandung) and Keng Po (Jakarta) and culturally-sensitive writers and educators criticized the adaptations, calling for an emphasis on national culture. As a result, stories taken from wayang (shadow plays of Java and Sunda) and folktales of Sumatra became popular comics fare.

Foremost of the comics creators adding an Indonesian flavor to comics work was R. A. Kosasih. In the early 1950s, with his friend Tan Eng Hiong (Tatang Prawira), Kosasih risked bringing out his work in comic book format. His Sri Asih character appeared as a thirty-two-page comic book in 1954, and though it lasted only five issues, "its popularity launched the comic book format as a viable medium in Indonesia," according to Suroto (2010: 179). *Sri Asih* worked well in 1950s' Indonesia, blending the traditional with the modern, the Asian with the Western. As Suroto (2010: 179) wrote:

> Despite the homage to Wayang costumes, Sri Asih was seen as an expression of a Western mode of storytelling. However, by adapting Wayang stories into a comic book form, Kosasih showed comics were an accessible medium through which traditional Indonesian culture and sensibilities could be expressed.

Kosasih was famous for transferring *Mahabharata* and *Ramayana* epics from wayang to *cergam* (an amalgamation of *cerita gambar*, picture tales or comics). His *Mahabharata Series* (Seri Mahabharata) consisted of nineteen books, all but one being a two-volume set, for a total of thirty-seven volumes. Kosasih divided the rest of the stories into a whole range of new categories, some with his own spellings: *Wayang Purwah, Leluhur Hastina* (Hastina Ancestors), *Mahabharata, Bharata Yudha, Padawa Seda* (Death of the Padawa), and *Parikesit*. He also developed new characters to adapt to Islamic teachings (Sears 1996: 278).

After 1983, Kosasih did life stories of particular characters such as Sri Kresna, advisor and friend to the Pandhawa heroes. The stories of Sri Kresna were done in four volumes, employing his usual methods of combining elements from both Javanese and Indian telling of the stories and, at times, changing plots (Sears 1996: 276). Kosasih was criticized for more often giving Indian, rather than Sundanese or Balinese, twists to these classics; his response was that it was intentional to prevent regionalism. Other traits of his comics were inclusion of messages in small frames on pages, as if appearing on ancient parchment, and interruption of stories to explain differences between Indian interpretations he gave and those familiar in Indonesia (Sears 1996: 275).

Discussing Kosasih's reconceptualized accounts of the classics, Sears

(1996: 279) showed how they were similar to wayang, saying, "The flatness of comic images or, at times, the reduction of black and white of what could be more colorful drawings, is not a great leap from the flatness of leather puppets and the chiaroscuro of shadows. And the distance from puppets to human seems no greater than that between cartoon images and humans."

She explained that Kosasih's switch from imitating U.S. superhero comics to telling the classics resulted from President Sukarno's anti–West, anti-imperialist stance. In the 1960s, Sukarno accused comic book artists of subversion, calling their work garbage and a Western-induced poison, not conducive to building a national identity. As a result, schools and kiosks were raided and comics were confiscated and burned (Berman 2001: 20). Kosasih took heed, according to Sears (1996: 279), and "came up with the brilliant idea of recasting the beloved heroes and heroines of the shadow theatre as cartoons. He also decided to dress these heroes in the clothing of the *wayang orang* (human *wayang*) theatre that was flourishing at that time."

Despite the Sukarno and, later, Suharto governments' aversion to comic books, they continued to thrive, even those copying superheroes.

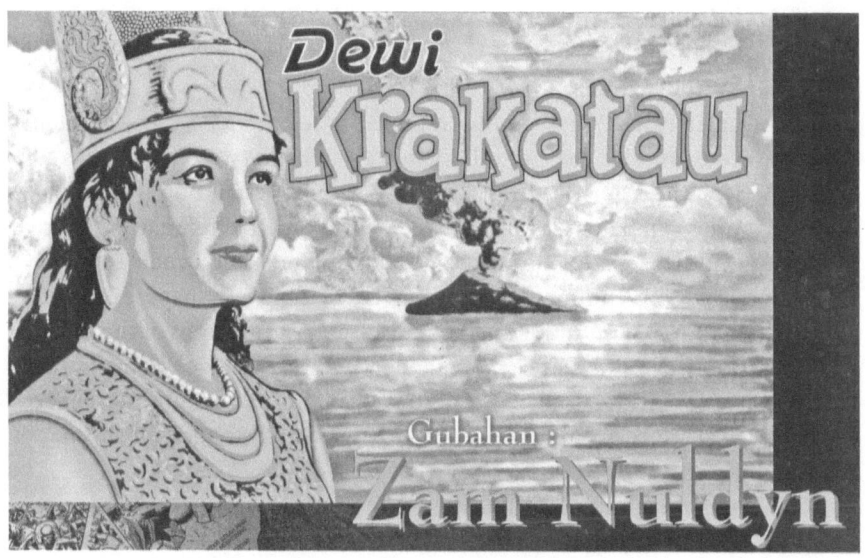

*Dewi Krakatau*, **by Zam Nuldyn, a 1950s comic book.**

13

Yogyakarta, Medan, and Bandung joined Jakarta as comic book centers. Sumatra, especially Medan, spawned important artists such as Taguan Hardjo (author of *Dolores*) and Zam Nuldyn and publishers Casso and Harris, that brought out Sumatran folktale-based comics.

Many other comics artists and their titles were popular, including, Hasmi (*Gundala*); Teguh Santosa (*Mat Pelor*); the already discussed R. A. Kosasih (*Wayang Purwah* and *Seri Mahabharata*) and Kho Wang Gie (*Put On*); Ganes Th (*Si Buta dari Gua Hantu*, or, The Ogre from Ghost Cave), and Hans Jaladara (*Panji Tengkorak*, or, Panji Skull), the latter two Chinese-influenced; Mansyur Jaman, Delsy Syamsunar, and Zaldy.

Zaldy was known for his romance comic books, a genre that sprouted in the 1960s and 1970s, but abruptly faded afterwards. Between 1966 and 1971, Zaldy created sixty romance comic books, most with stories of unrequited love and love triangles (Darmawan 2009). Among his works were *Mawar Putih* (The White Rose), *Setitik Airmata Buat Peter* (A Teardrop for Peter), *Tetesan Airmata Cinta* (Love Teardrop), and *Impian Kemarin* (Yesterday's Dream). Another romance comics creator in the 1960s and 1970s was Jan Mintaraga, some of whose titles were *Kabut di Hari Tjerah* (The Mist in the Sunny Day), *Patahnja Sebuah Melankoli* (The Demise of a Melancholy), *Tonil* (Drama), *Tertiup Bersama Angin* (Blowing in the Wind), and *Tjintanya Bakan Tjinta Kanak2* (Not a Child's Love).

Darmawan (2009) found repetitious elements in Indonesian romance comics of the period, including stylistic (western) names of characters, titles derived from western and Indonesian pop music, featured American hairstyles and miniskirts, use of visual references (films, foreign comics, posters), fully drawn backgrounds, and urban architectural styles. Also common were characters reading newspapers or magazines, a rare sight in Indonesia until the literacy campaigns of the 1980s, e.g., "Koran Masuk Desa" (Newspapers for the Village) (Darmawan 2009). A conclusion Darmawan (2009) came to is that "the romance comics, therefore, form the only genre that faithfully longed for the metropolitan city."

Romance comics continue until today, but, according to Darmawan (2009), their discussions about love are theoretical, "confined in the realm of ideas, and might be trapped in mere idealizations." He conceded that contemporary love comics are more sophisticated than those of the

1960s and 1970s, but they "fail to portray the mental complexities of their characters."

That the borrowing from the West did not subside despite government disapproval was apparent in two major works by Wid NS and Jan Mintaraga. Wid's *Godam* was a superhero akin to Superman with the difference that Godam, being a truck driver, was more mortal, closer to the common people (Indarto 2004). Mintaraga's equally favored *Sebuah Noda Hitam* (A Black Stain) featured the romance life of a teenager. Indarto (2004) said the strength of this title lay in Mintaraga's "Western images he portrayed in almost every character he created."

Cartoonist-cum-researcher Toni Masdiono (interview, 2008) thought that maybe the Sukarno government unwittingly "took part" in komiks development in the 1960s, explaining that "after 1965, you had to ask permission from the Jakarta police to do comics. That made our cartoonists creative. Censors would blacken out art work; cartoonists would purposively put typos with hidden meanings in komiks." G. M. Sudarta (interview, 1992) talked about an Indonesian indirect way of criticizing in political cartoons traceable to the days of Sukarno. Because all comics activities were scrutinized by the authorities in the 1960s and 1970s, some comic books were "driven by a particular ideology or belief," according to Karna (2007: 313). He said, "Political messages were often found in comics … messages such as nationalist vision, aspirations and hopes of the nation, and religious syncretism."

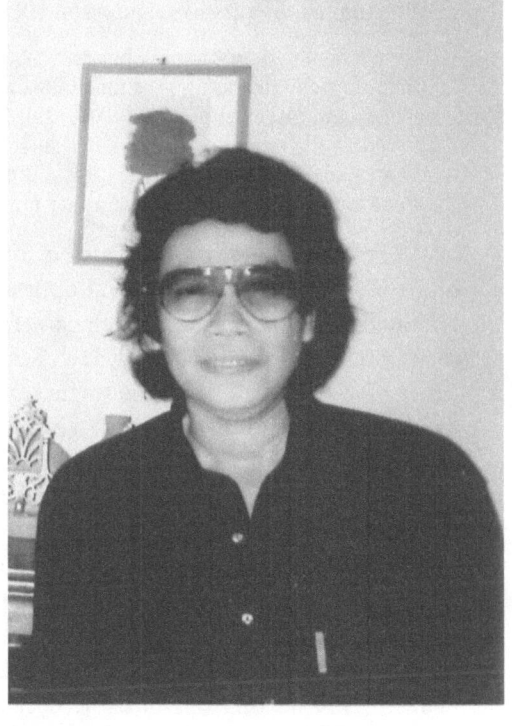

G. M. Sudarta, Jakarta, July 28, 1992 (photograph by author).

Political cartooning had serious setbacks under Sukarno, and, after a brief respite in 1967–69 (called the genre's "golden years" by Sudarta [interview, 1992]), again under Suharto. Perhaps feeling the wrath of Sukarno's suppression the most was the hard-hitting political cartoonist Sibarani, who, from the 1960s, was denied the right to draw for more than thirty years. Sibarani's fame was in the late 1950s and early 1960s when he was political cartoonist for the left-wing daily *Bintang Timur*. Analyzing Sibarani's "powerful and rough-hewn style," Anderson (1978: 292–95) identified characteristics in his cartoons as a dependence for "emotional effect on a stark charoscuro" used as "a tool for political demystification"; "iconographic density, exemplified by the conscious layering of symbolic emblems," and use of foreign languages and symbols. Sibarani's cartoons had a national quality, Anderson (1978: 295) elaborated, in that "if the landscape of his cartoons is dark and threatening, it is nonetheless a national landscape peopled by national figures." Sibarani was known for identifying his villains. As Anderson (1978: 295) said:

> They are named, not simply because Sibarani wanted, and dared, to do so, but because names assign responsibility, reveal reality, and place cartoonist, reader, and target in a clear relationship in political space. This in turn is linked to the presence of the cartoonist himself. He never appears in his own cartoon, rather it is as if he stood beside or behind them, proffering them to his readers with index finger pointed.

The "golden age" was responsible for other stimulants for the development of comics and cartoons. Importantly, a number of famous contemporary cartoonists began their careers in the 1960s and 1970s, among them, Sudarta, Johnny Hidajat, Dwi Koendoro, and Pramono. Sudarta (interview, 1992) said when he started in the 1960s, it was very difficult to criticize through cartoons. Then briefly after the mid–1960s, political cartooning thrived; there were many cartoonists using a "strong, sharp, direct style, unlike today [1992], when cartoonists are more polite, indirect, smooth."

Hidajat's career peaked during Suharto's New Order. Initially, he was cartoonist for the right-wing daily, *Pos Kota*, and a freelance contributor to a variety of magazines, particularly *Stop*, an imitator of *Mad Magazine*. From 1970 to 1975, Hidajat drew for ten magazines simultaneously. He said this was possible because he would take an event or issue and comment on it in ten to fifteen strips for a variety of magazines, and because there was an abundance of magazines full of cartoons, such as *Flamboyan, Vista, Selecta, Detektif & Romantika, Stop, Matahari,* etc. (Hidajat, interview, 1992). He took credit for popularizing cartoons with text balloons, which, he said, unfortunately, died out after 1985. He also lamented the loss of popular magazines by the 1990s, as well as lower payment for cartoonists. Hidajat (interview, 1992) said payment relative to economy was better in the 1970s than 1990s, giving this analogy: "In 1975, my pay per month was Rp500,000, and a motorcycle cost Rp125,000. Now a motorcycle is Rp3 million. I could get a motorcycle in a month then; now, it would take two years on a cartoonist's fees."

Anderson (1978: 295), in trying to determine the immense popularity of Hidajat's signature strip, "Djon Domino," attributed it to good jokes, but more importantly, to style and context. The character Djon Domino, according to Anderson (1978: 296), is, by virtue of his long nose, an allusion to wayang character Petruk, who, in the strip, unmasks figures of authority. The strip's empty space and lack of landscape recalled for Anderson (1978: 300), the cotton screen against which wayang is played out. Also characteristic of Hidajat's strips was their use of obscenity and sexuality. By his own admission, Hidajat (interview, 1992) mixed sex and politics in "Djon Domino." Anderson failed to mention one feature that Hidajat (interview, 1992) said brought many readers to "Djon Domino"—its inclusion of a number which people "played" in the lottery.

As already said, the "golden age" was noted for its plentitude of magazines, including the humor ones, *Stop* and *Astaga* (Good Lord). The latter lasted twenty numbers in 1975–76 before succumbing because of lack of funding. Chief editor Arwah Setiawan (interview, 1992) said contents were split half and half between cartoons and prose, some of the latter written by Setiawan himself, a humor writer since 1968, and founder and head of the organization Lembaga Humor Indonesia. His major problem was recruiting freelance cartoonists; he said there were "only five to ten good ones," including Koendoro, Sudarta, Pramono, Si Jon, Priyanto S., and Rahmat Riyadi (Setiawan, interview, 1992).

## 1980s–90s: Breathing Hard

The comics industry seemed destined to take its last breath during the 1980s to mid-1990s. A number of factors were blamed for the stagnation of Indonesian comics, chief of which was the huge influx of comics, first from the United States and Europe, and then from Japan and Hong Kong. *HumOr* magazine cartoonist Mahtum (interview, 1992) said that since 1987, foreign comic books along the lines of *Donald Duck* and *Goofy* and some from France were issued usually twice monthly by publishers such as Media Pustaka, Eres, Indira, and Gramedia. The latter, Indonesia's largest book chain, reported that by the mid–1990s, imported comics far outsold legal ones, with Japanese manga accounting for 90 percent of these sales.

Elex, an electronics component of the largest comics publisher, Gramedia, probably introduced manga to Indonesia. The company had the copyrights of *Akira*, *Kungfu Boy*, and *Candy Candy* about 1985, but did not publish them for fear they would not be accepted by readers. When Elex finally published *Akira* in 1989, it failed because of a premature market. After that, Elex published *Kungfu Boy*, *Candy Candy*, and *Doraemon*, followed by other firms that brought out manga, often in pirated editions. The piracy has escalated since 1990, often done by publishers that download from the Internet and print, and remain anonymous, not listing their addresses (Masdiono, interview, 2008).

Berman (2001: 21) said the industry was overrun by foreign comics despite or largely because of denouncements by Sukarno, Suharto, and other critics both inside and outside the comics community. Berman (2001: 21) wrote, that in the face of foreign comics' popularity, Indonesian comics "wallow in the dust of neglect, if, that is, they can even be found in the storage bins." Translated Western imports sometimes hid within their pages Indonesian stories. Berman (2001: 21) gave an example, "Comics such as *Musuh dalam Selimut* (Enemy in a Blanket, 1982) reveal where the local industry has gone. While the comic was sold as a western import in translation, often it concealed an indigenous (illegal) copy inside."

Other reasons were given for the comics slump. Ahmad, Maulana, and Apalanzani (2006: 74–75) pointed a finger at older artists, "from previous generations [who] never passed down his/her ability to the next generation, while at the same time they could no longer catch up with the changes and trends." A second problem they identified was the lack of attempts by publishers "to encourage artists' regeneration of local comics, many of them only seemed to care with profit rather than public benefit." Putranto and Purwanti (n.d.) weighed in with their reasons for the demise of the "golden age," including the failure to use an "uncommon angle and perspective" for narrative story lines; insufficient encouragement to explore new, especially cinematographic, aspects; the lack of a marketing network; the blind adoption of foreign practices and themes, neglecting "unique local cultures" which express people's self-esteem, and wrongly assuming the public only wanted entertainment from comics, not "deeper meanings or social commentary."

Distribution problems were blamed by Karna (2007: 314), who said that in the 1970s, comics were widely distributed at street markets and *taman bacaan* (small public libraries), but they never made it to the big book stores. In the late 1980s, comics had almost totally vanished from the market. Among cartoonists, Masdiono (interview, 2008) was most strident, attacking comics companies of the 1980s–90s for not working as an industry and for producing cheaply-made comics sold at high prices. Masdiono said the quality was so low that some comics were "even printed on the backs of calendars." Other reasons he gave were that the masters had tired of working alone on all aspects of production of "boring" stories borrowed with minimum change from China, and the public considered comics to be "trash."

A *Jakarta Post* article of September 28, 1995 (reprinted in the Singapore *Straits Times*) summed up reasons why the comics industry was thought to be in "ruins," e.g., a lack of drawing skills, fresh ideas, and professionalism, and the deluge of foreign comics. Other causes given were that Indonesian artists were not in touch with "universal themes, concentrating on village life, the irrational and mystic, all dull and tedious" (*Jakarta Post*, 1995), and that they were abysmally paid[4] and denied royalties and legal contracts.

Berman (2001: 22), writing later, added another factor: it is less expensive for comics producers to buy the rights of foreign works, rather than pay local cartoonists who have a limited repertoire of stories. She came to the artists' defense, saying that they had to contend with a mentality (colonial?) that equated the indigenous as inferior to the foreign product, and with governmental and societal norms that did not allow them to deal with less-boring, "real, modern social issues and contemporary concerns" (Berman 2001: 22). What she could not fathom was why popular newspaper strips did not make it to comic book format. She showed how Javanese legends such as *Jaka Tingkir*, *Ramayana*, and *Imperium Majapahit* were very well-received in full color serialization, published in every Javanese-language magazine and newspaper, but, yet, they never appeared as comic books (Berman 2001: 21).

Efforts in the 1980s to revive comics and cartoons did not yield many results. Editorial cartoons and newspaper strips were nearly the only Indonesian comic art at the time, but, according to Berman (2001: 22), about two-thirds of these were translations of foreign strips. One market comics publishers tried to tap in the 1970s and especially 1980s was that of the Muslim community. Comics appeared about Quranic prophets, Islamic caliphs, Nasruddin Hoja, Ali Baba, Aladdin, pilgrimage to Mecca guides, etc. A publisher of Muslim comics over the years has been Mizan, which in 1996, revised its aims and contents to meet the needs of *dakwan* (struggle), rather than of an industry (Budiyanto 2006; also see Karna 2007: 314). However, these educational/instructional comics did not compete well with foreign titles; they also caused concern in the Muslim community, sections of which felt the comics brought in unwanted views and were a form of expensive, unappealing, verbal expression not favored by children (Budiyanto 2006; also see Karna 2007: 314). Realizing the popularity of manga in Indonesia, Mizan began converting manga icons to Islamic values, for example, having Japanese favorites Doraemon and Nobita doing a Ramadan fast. A more recent line-up of Mizan (now Dar! Mizan) series includes *Novel Comic*, *Teenage Novel Comic*, *Islamic Comic*, and *Devotion Comic*. The first two have mystery and detective-themed stories, while a title under *Islamic Comic* is "Prophet Ibrahim 5: The Little Ismail" and a couple *Devotion Comic* works are "The Unique World of Birds" and "A Friend from Outer Space."

Revival of Indonesian comics commenced in the early to mid–1990s, a result of determined efforts by Dr. Rahayu Hidayat, Edi Sedyawati, and Dwi Koendoro, and some high school and college students who gathered in comics-producing groups. Mrs. Hidayat formed and was chief organizer of Lembaga Pengkajian Komik Indonesia (Indonesian Comics Studies Committee), located in the Literature Faculty at the University of Indonesia. According to Koendoro (interview, 2007), Hidayat tried to "study comics in all dimensions from their earliest roots." Communities such as LPKI were started throughout the decade by young lecturers who aimed to hold a couple comics seminars before proceeding to launch regular Indonesian comics exhibitions (Karna 2007: 316).

Another booster of Indonesian comics in the mid–1990s was Edi Sedyawati, general director of cultural affairs in the Department of Education and Culture. With government support by virtue of her ministry-level office, Sedyawati organized a cultural congress which included comics and cartoonists. According to Koendoro (interview, 2007), she asked him to create a forum "to make comics nationwide and continuous." She also appointed Koendoro to head a comics contest jury. A

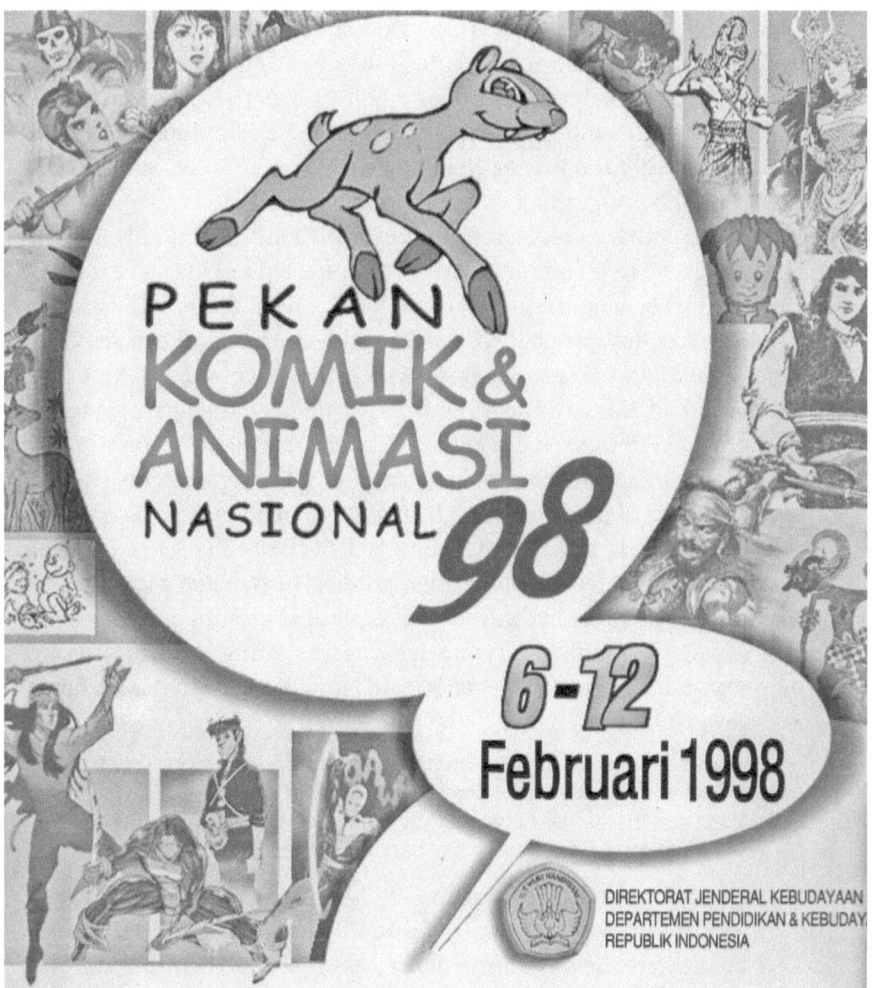

**PEKAN comics festival catalogue.**

21

result was the first Pekan Komik dan Animasi Nasional (Comics and Animation Week) in the National Gallery in 1998. The week featured competitions and exhibitions. Other comics contests, exhibitions, and activities followed in various cities, including comics discussions in cultural centers, bookshops, and private galleries, the culmination of which drove publishers to devote more of their production to local works (Karna 2007: 316).

One outgrowth of Pekan Komik dan Animasi was the formation of the comics community Masyarakat Komik Indonesia (MKI), with its slogan, "Support Your Local Comics Movement." MKI was started by Ardie of the comics studio Karpet Biru (Blue Carpet), located on a campus. MKI, though famous, was not the first of these communities. Others from the early 1990s onwards were based on campuses, or were associated with hobbyist, mailing list, and online groups.

Among active comics communities was Kamikazi, initially a small comic about the referendum in East Timor, started in 1999. A year later, it became a Website for Indonesian and local comics. Some of the groups and their activities were backed by the publishing houses Mizan, Gramedia Komik, and Grasindo, from which they received royalties and sometimes had the good fortune to have their characters registered (Putranto and Purwanti n.d.). Yet, some of the "strongest" communities died because of economic problems or internal disagreements (Koendoro, interview, 2007). Other problems these small groups faced were the new media luring away audiences; a lack of clarity about new cultural patterns in the country's economic and political turbulence; a "peripheral and unprofitable" position in the marketplace (Putranto and Purwanti n.d.); expensive publishing materials, necessitating the use of copy machines; and the invasion by manga and Hong Kong comics. Masdiono (interview, 2008) said,

> We worked as a team on these independent comics, not alone. We tried to move from independent to mainstream with my *Kaptan Bandung* and other titles, but the market was poisoned by manga and Hong Kong comics. We tried to get government money but that was not easy.

Independent comics during the 1990s tended to fall into categories of art school and NGO. Berman (2001: 28) wrote that the art school comic books were the most limited in accessibility and distribution. She said they had "little if any story," and leaned toward pornography. Actually, it was a drop-out named Athonk, from the Yogyakarta campus of

22

the Art Institute of Indonesia, who spearheaded a "new interest in comic book production," with his self-published *The Bad Times Story*. The small book's "playful mix of the idealism of youth with biting social and political commentary" (Berman 2001: 28) was deemed illegal, as evidenced by its confiscation by police in 1994.[5]

Other student-originated independent comics came to the fore in the 1990s, among them *Caroq*, produced by the group Qomik Nusantara, fourteen art students from the Bandung Institute of Technology in West Java. Though this book featured a West Javanese hero who wore Madurese clothing and fought with that ethnic group's swords, it was still heavily criticized as an import. On the other hand, other local comics such as *Patriot* and *Captain Bandung* were "harshly criticized for not being as slick and attractive as the import," showing, according to Berman (2001: 22), the "no-win" situation in which local comics have operated.

A comics community known for its innovative method of "distribution" was Apotik Komik in Yogyakarta, formed by thirteen Art Institute of Indonesia students on April 25, 1997. The group used a wide range of materials and modes of expression to do comics, with the aim of making art more accessible than just being on gallery walls. Apotik Komik's alternative comics included *Komik Seni* (Art Comic), *Komik Underground*, *Komik Ampyang* (Peanut Candy Comic), and *Komik Haram* (Forbidden Comic). The books employed metaphors and a playful style to discuss actual socio-political issues, giving a "broader, more disturbing view of some aspects of Indonesian society such as its reckless government, amoral bureaucrats, poverty, religious conflict and the rise and fall of its democratic life" (Putranto and Purwanti n.d.).

The other independent comic books of the 1990s were those produced by activists through funding from development groups. These tackled social issues and problems and stayed committed to the common people. However, most were merely translations of activist comics from abroad, with very little artistic relevance to the local scene. There were exceptions, such as *Outran-Outran ing Muria* (Chaos in Muria, 1993), written by Brotoseno and drawn by Marto Art (Art Institute in Yogyakarta students), and funded by an independent environmentalist group in North Central Java. Anti-nuclear in purpose, *Outran-Outran ing Muria* was started to give villagers of Muria district, proposed site of Indonesia's first nuclear plant, another side to the issue other than that of government (see Nugroho 2009a). Containing "good pictures and a great dialogue," as well as Javanese, rather than Indonesian-language-text, the comic book provided an alternative voice, but, to Berman (2001: 31), this could be worrisome, because it presents an "idealistic and unrealistic view of the righteous as victorious." Berman (2001: 32) had reservations more generally about the effectiveness of activist comics, because their student creators followed "aggressive western trends which are often inappropriate in Indonesian contexts" and, because they must contend not only with government interference, but also "dominant ideologies that train the population to dislike and distrust many of the poor their comics are attempting to defend."

Another example of activist comics provided by Berman (2001: 32) were those in *JeJAL*, a monthly newsletter funded by an NGO to empower and educate Indonesia's very oppressed and persecuted street children. *JeJAL* permitted children "so outside the mainstream society that they are mainly invisible" (Berman 2001: 33), to freely express themselves, usually through comic strips. Apparently a threat to authority, *JeJAL*'s office was raided and issues confiscated.

Unlike comic books, comic strips remained popular in several newspapers and magazines throughout the 1990s and 2000s. In 1992, each Indonesian city had newspaper and magazines with comic strips, nearly all of which were humorous. Badrudin (interview, 1992) said at least *Jawa Pos, Pos Kota, Wawasan, HumOr, Bisnis Indonesia, Suara Pembaruan*, and *Suara Merdeka* contained comic strips, but overall, only about fourteen of 240 daily and weekly newspapers carried strips (Sudarno, interview, 1992). A few newspapers, both in their daily and Sunday editions, outperformed western counterparts in space allotted to, and the variety and display of, strips. What I found in an informal survey on Sunday, July 26, 1992 attests to this. *Pos Kota* that day, in its four-page, color comics section called "Lembergar" (acronym of Lembaran Bergambar untuk Keluarga, or Funnies for the Family) had three full pages of comics and a total of twenty-two different titles. Most of the strips were humor-based; others used adventure, jungle setting, or old Indonesian tales themes. *Suara Pembaruan* devoted nearly a page to humor strips, drawn simplistically by fourteen cartoonists; "Ripley's Believe It or Not" was the only non–Indonesian strip. These observations can be partly explained by Berman's (2001: 19) statement that strips are "far more relevant" and humorous than comic books. However, she also said that by the 1980s and well into the 1990s, two-thirds of newspaper cartoons were translations of foreign ones (Berman 2001: 22).

Among the oldest comic strips are G. M. Sudarta's "Oom Pasikom," a political, social cartoon started in 1967; Johnny Hidajat's "Djon Domino" (1970), and Dwi Koendoro's "Pailul & Panji Koming" (1979).

"Oom Pasikom" attempts to make "funny news to decrease the possibility of being disturbed" (by criticism from the government or public) (Badrudin 1988: 36). Sudarta (interview, 1992) explained the philosophy behind his strip and editorial cartoons:

> I want to bring up situations and this will create a dialogue among us. With dialogue, I hope there is improvement. I do cartoons as early warning that something is wrong. I don't want to persuade my opinion on other people. This is only my opinion. In Indonesia, we have a way: we want to make those in government we criticize to smile, and make people smile to bring up their aspirations. We have to make ourselves smile or we can be jailed.

He added that as a result, he never breaches the policy of *Kompas*, the newspaper for which he works, and if the government or public is upset with his cartoons, he tries to appease them through dialogue. To do otherwise, he said, could jeopardize *Kompas*'s circulation or existence and destroy "our mission that there be dialogue between critics and those being criticized." In 1992, Oom Pasikom became the first Indonesian cartoon character made into a film. Called "Oom Pasikom Parodi Ibu Kota," it used both live action and animation techniques.

Hidajat's "Djon Domino" had no social message as Hidajat (interview, 1992) himself said: "I make him [Djon Domino] not to have a special message either as a bad or good guy. He changes regularly day to day. He can be a judge, lawyer, criminal, doctor, or bad guy." The strip appeared simultaneously in five newspapers and magazines in Jakarta and Medan, its character's name and persona changing in each: "Djon Domino" in *Pos Kota*, which pokes fun at Jakarta people and traditions; "Djon Tik" in *Waspada* of Medan; "Djon Kaget" in *Pos Film*, obviously about cinema; "Djon Taremolneok" (Indonesian word for conglomerate spelled backwards) in *HumOr*, about big firms' executives and businessmen; and "Si Djon" in *Terbit* (Hidajat, interview, 1992). As stated before, since 1970, Hidajat has put numbers in the strip that readers use to play the lottery. He said, "Many people buy the paper to get that national lottery (SDSB) number. Many of them visit me or phone me to get the number. If the person is lucky and wins, I get some money" (Hidajat, interview, 1992).

"Pailul & Panji Koming" was started after Koendoro was asked by the *Kompas* owner to join the staff as a cartoonist in 1976 and later to draw a strip about humor and politics. Koendoro (interview, 1992) said "'Pailul & Panji Koming' deals with anything of social, political significance," but because of such themes, sometimes the strip does not pass editorial review, despite discussions with the editor beforehand. He explained that "sometimes the bargaining weight of the editor changes" (Koendoro, interview, 1992). Particularly off limits during Suharto's regime were the monopolization of big business by the president's sons, elections, land business (the trend to turn agricultural land into real estate and golf courses), and clashes between government personnel (Koendoro, interview, 1992). While *HumOr* existed, Koendoro drew another comic strip, about the Dutch East Indies Company 300 years ago. The humor/adventure comic, which occupied five pages in *HumOr*, featured two warrior heroes who fought the Dutch company.

Notable strips in recent years have included "Mr. Bei," "I Brewok," "Lotif," "Doyok," and "Benny and Mice." The character Mr. Bei, known for getting it wrong despite good intentions, appeared during the 1990s

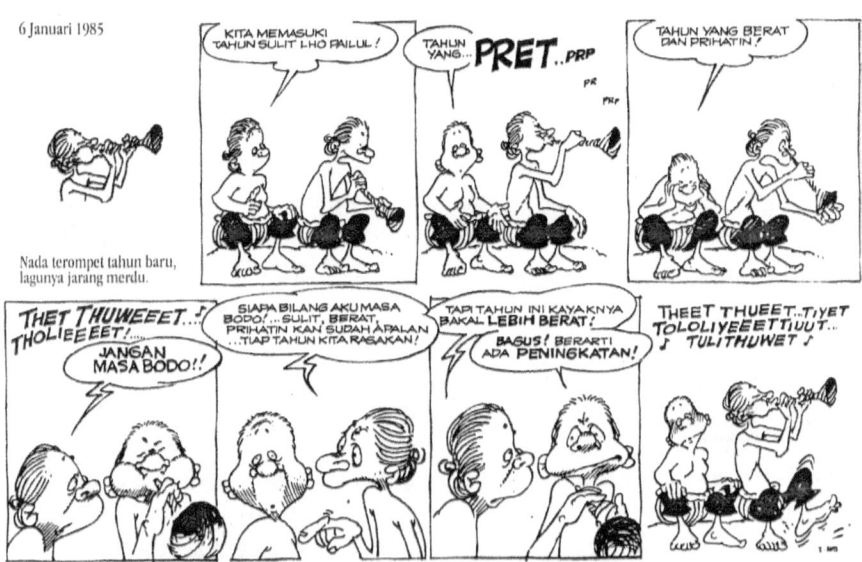

**"Pailul & Panji Koming" by Dwi Koendoro, a popular comic strip of the mid-1980s (courtesy Dwi Koendoro).**

in the Sunday, color comics section of Semarang's *Suara Merdeka*. "I Brewok" was the creation of I Wayan Gunasta (Gungun). The political strip was a regular feature of the Sunday edition of *Bali Post*. "Lotif" debuted in the newspaper *Tempo* in 2005, but later found a home in the *Jakarta Globe*. The character was created by freelance illustrator and animator Beng Rahadian. Lotif has been described as a "skinny, bug-eyed urbanite" with "naïve charm and socially conscious behavior" (Thee 2009). In the early days of the strip, concentration was on Lotif's misadventures while trying to impress women. Later, Rahadian added social layers to the stories, raising issues of which Lotif was also guilty.

Also a daily commentary on social or political issues was "Doyok,"[6] created by Keliek Siswoyo and carried by *Pos Kota* in its "Lembergar" section. A survey revealed "Doyok" was the most popular "Lembergar" strip. Doyok was a shrewd thinker, sarcastic but realistic, who provided insight into the mind of the populace (Ajidarma 2002). The strip was systematically organized. In the first panel, Doyok said a word (examples: cold, going abroad, bent) that served as the discussion topic; panels two and three delivered his comments, and the final panel yielded a question seeking a reaction "forever out of the frame," too complex to put into words (Ajidarma 2002).

"Benny and Mice" is a collaborative effort of Jakarta Institute of Arts friends Benny Rachmadi and Muhammad Misrad. Combining comic strip and scheduled book projects methods of presentation, "Benny and Mice" has existed in strip form since 2003 and as books since 1997. "Kartun Benny & Mice" appeared in the Sunday comics section of *Kompas*, where Rachmadi and Misrad themselves appear as comic characters. Rizal and Elsanti (2008) described the characters as

> Jakarta citizens with average looks and no attributes of a hero whatsoever. When they want to be somebody, something silly happens. Their skinny frames also make it easy for them to be portrayed in a variety of ridiculous situations.
>
> In terms of age, they are over thirty, more or less, or perhaps in their forties. Still, it appears that they act like, and have the characteristic of, teenagers, ever trying to be free from various norms and rules.

Though such behavior is frowned upon in Indonesia, it is the very reason "Benny and Mice" has been so successful in *Kompas*. Rizal and Elsanti (2008) saw this do-as-we-please behavior as "their protest against the

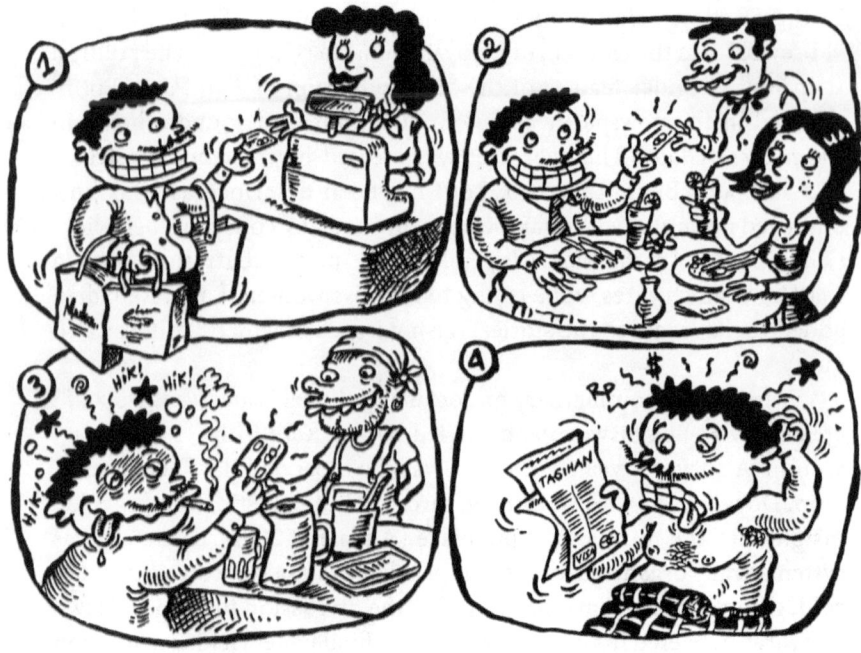

**"Benny & Mice" by Benny Rachmadi and Muhammad Misrad, a popular comic strip that was compiled into a book in 2008 (courtesy Benny Rachmadi).**

government and the rich elite that have left their ubiquitous mark too strongly on Jakarta. It is an act of resistance."

Humor magazines were important venues for comic strips during the 1980s and 1990s, with the publication of *Astaga, Idola* (Ideal), and *HumOr*. Two periodicals called *HumOr* existed; the first started in 1980, the second on October 10, 1990. The latter, part of Tempo, one of the ten largest media groups, took over the management of the first *HumOr*, which had "many problems" (Badrudin 1992). Editor of *HumOr* Kemala Atmojo (interview, 1992) emphasized, "We have a different style, quality, design, and performance from the old *HumOr*." A benefit of being part of Tempo was that the company had its own distribution network. *HumOr*, published fortnightly, had eighty-four pages, 40 percent of which were cartoons. In 1992, *HumOr* had forty thousand subscribers, far short of its seventy thousand to one hundred thousand target but above the break even figure of thirty thousand (Mahtum, interview, 1992). At that time, the magazine was the most important venue for both professional and amateur cartoonists. The staff consisted of fifteen cartoonists and writers and more than one hundred freelancers. Atmojo (interview, 1992) said at the rates paid, cartoonists could earn a living, if they lived in small cities with low living cost indexes and if they drew about ten cartoons per month. Goals of *HumOr* were to entertain readers with excellent drawings, funny ideas that were easily understood, provoked instant laughter, and stayed within government guidelines. Believing humor was normally associated with the middle and lower classes, *HumOr* sought to upgrade it to higher level Indonesians.[7] Because of economic difficulties and the closure of its parent company Tempo, *HumOr* quit publishing in 1996 (Koendoro, interview, 2004).

## Contemporary Scene

Publishing of comic books was revived in the twenty-first century when every major publishing house developed its own comic book production section and the comics groups continued to operate.

The largest producer of comics in Indonesia is m&c! Comics, which started in the 1980s as Komik Majalah, a publisher of foreign comic books, and after the late 1990s, mainly manga. An arm of the huge business corporation Kompas Gramedia Group, m&c! Comics also includes Indonesian comics under its Koloni titles, which it aims to distribute worldwide. Other comics also fall under Gramedia affiliates—for example, KPG (Kepustakaan Populer Gramedia) brings out the popular Benny & Mice collections. KPG editors nourished the careers of Benny (Benny Rachmadi) and Mice (Muhammad Misrad) when in 1977, they gave them the opportunity to publish their book series *Legak Jakarta* (Jakarta Exploits). The series has yielded titles such as *Trend dan Prilaku* (Trend and Attitude), *Tranportasi* (Transportation), *Profesi* (Profession), *Krisis...Oh Krisis* (Crisis, O, Crisis) and *Reformasi* (Reformation). *(Huru-Hara) Huru Huru Pemilu '99* ([Chaos] Carnival of '99 General Election), *Lost In Bali*, and *100 Tokoh yang Mewarnai Jakarta* (100 Figures That Color Jakarta) are other Benny & Mice books under the KPG imprint (see Rizal and Elsanti 2008). Papillon Studio of Semarang also has ties to Gramedia through Elex Media Komputindo, which publishes its books. With a staff of twelve, Papillon is a major producer of comics that are highly influenced by manga.

Mizan Press in Bandung, with its children's division Dar! (Divisi

Anak dan Remaja!) Mizan publishes textbooks in comics style, as well as local comics series, such as *Alakazam* by Donny, *Dua Warna* by Alfi Zachkyelle, and *Tomat* by Rachmat Riyadi. Mizan Publika started in 1983, responding, according to its own historical account, to the "demand for quality books for Indonesian Muslim readers." Dar! Mizan followed in 1992, officially becoming a business unit of Mizan Publika in 2003; its comics line was developed in 1997. More than twenty-five authors, twenty studios, and twenty illustrators work for or with Dar! Mizan. The Mizan Indonesian Comics line aims to resurrent Indonesian comics by local artists (Widyawanti 2003).

Also creating and publishing comics are Terrant Comic, Dahara Comic, Komunitas Nisita, Riko Amer Production, Gagas Media, Asy Syaamil, Jagoan Comic, Bajak Laoet, Mediacela, Kamikazi, Daging Tumbuh, Baskara, Caravan Studio, Creativ Media, Concept Media, and Curhat Anak Bangsa, among others.

Caravan Studio, founded in 2008, is a group of artists working on comics pages, graphic novels, illustration, toy and concept design commissioned by Marvel, Tokyopop, Hasbro, Mattel, and other foreign companies. An older comics publisher is Creativ Media; in 1998, it issued Toni Masdiono's short manual on techniques, *14 Jurus Membuat Komik* (Creating Comics in 14 Steps). Concept is a design company sponsored by an international advertising agency. Concept's title, *Alia*, is called "100% Komik Indonesia," although drawings, characters, and stories have little resemblance to the national culture. In 2008, Concept held a youth comicon called Bangkit (Wake up for Cergam). Some children's and youth comics were published in 2009–10 by Curhat Anak Bangsa, including two books created wholly or partly by Sheila Rooswitha, *Cerita Silala* and *Duo Hippo Dinam's Tersesat di Byzantium*.

Comics production in Indonesia often involves groups and studios of artists that publish independently or in conjunction with media and publishing houses. Independent works are the strength of Indonesian comics. Berman (2005) said they and their creators have "grown in numbers, with the largest number of independent komikus (comic artists) in South-East Asia. Indonesia is the envy of its neighbours in terms of quality of work, and the number and professionalism of its comics organisations and conventions." She explained that studios and the many groups allow artists to work independently while forming collectives with friends who support their individuality.

As a gauge of the prevalence of groups in creating Indonesian comics, when Cergambore, the Festival of Comics was held in Surabaya, March 2009, the nineteen comics producers that participated were predominantly such communities of artists and fans. They included Comics Gangster, Suicide, Sungsang, Imaji, National Child Work, False Comic, Neo Paradigm Neo, Outline Reborn, Syndicate, Virgin Is Suck, Wipe, Nasih Putih, Romance Surabaya Comic, and Wind Ryder. Nasih Putih of Jember is a group of youth from various educational backgrounds that initiates art community events. The group publishes comic books and a bulletin also called *Nasih Putih.* Romance Surabaya Comic Group, whose members are film, independent music, and comics practitioners or aficionados, set out to publish a host of original comic books in 2008 (see Nugroho 2006c). Another young people's community, Akademi Samali, founded by Beng Rahadian, published a series of comic books that mapped problems of Jakarta: *Jakarta Senggol Dikit* (A Tiny Bump into Jakarta), *Jakarta Senggol-Senggolan* (Bumping Around in Jakarta), and *Jakarta Senggal Senggol* (Jakarta Bumping). One writer (Shiddiq 2009) criticized the books for their poor technical mastery and their creators' lack of life experiences from which to draw on when shaping stories.

Some groups create mainstream in addition to independent comics. Wind Ryder Studio publishes *Wind Ryder,* but also the independent work *Komikugrafi* in black and white; Neo Paradigm Neo brings out the full color comics *Aquanus* and *Benuake Tujuh,* as well as black and white titles under the title *Defragment.* Nugroho (2009b) felt it necessary that groups move into the mainstream industry, because their independent titles had limited scope and impact.

Various other comic books have appeared in recent years. Dwi Koendoro and his Citra Audivistama Studio issued, in 2005, a Komik Laga Canda series that tell of legends, with his famous character Panji Koming involved. In 1999, Koendoro with *Kompas* and Mizan Komik Indonesia, compiled Panji Koming stories for 1985–86 and 1987–88 into two comic books. Notable also was *Sequen,* a comics magazine that appeared in four numbers in 2006. The product of Iwan Gunawan, the bi-monthly featured articles, profiles, news, and reviews, primarily concerning Indonesian comics and their creators from both historical and contemporary perspectives. Cartoonists profiled were Kosasih, Doank, Anto, and Taguan Hardjo.

Still popular in contemporary times are old Indonesian classic comics, reprinted and republished by small presses such as Pustaka Satria Sejati and Komikindonesia.com. Some of these are remade or redrawn by artists of an earlier generation, e.g., Hans Jaladara and Mansyur Daman (Man). Works of comics leaders Kosasih, Mintaraga, Ganes Th., Hasmi, and Gerdie W. K. have also been reprinted recently. Karna (2007: 318) felt this activity closes the generation gap, "allowing the young generation to learn from their predecessors." Remaking of Indonesian classic comics has come under fire at times, the fear being that the new versions could take away "the value or characteristics of the original works" (Karna 2007: 317) and that they could lose some of their creativity.

Most of the younger cartoonists adopt or adapt styles, stories, and ideas from foreign comics, mainly from Japan, and to lesser degrees, the U.S. and Europe. The most pervasive outside influence today is the manga, which still controls 90 percent of the country's comics market. Even legitimate publishing houses print pirated manga. Manga can be bought or rented nearly anywhere; many titles are national obsessions among the young. A manga graphic novel sells for Rp12,000 (U.S. $1.07) and rents for Rp2,000 (17 U.S. cents) (Abraham 2010: 47). An impact of this availability is that indigenous sequential art usually is done in manga style. Fueling this manga mania are art schools and many anime/manga conventions, e.g., Animonster Sound.

Of the manga, *yaoi* (boy's love) has much appeal in Indonesia, especially among women, a number of whom produce this comics genre. It is usually underground, online and at anime/manga conventions; the largest online forum for boy's love is Indonesian Yaoi Front. Although the Internet is mostly unrestricted, yaoi publishers must be careful under Indonesian governmental and moral law. There are vague, long-standing laws that stifle yaoi, one of which is Kitab Undang-undang Hukum Perdata (1945), which restricts "prurient materials," prohibits anything that arouses teenagers' sexual urges, or materials that violate "ethical norms" (Abraham 2010: 48). A new bill passed October 30, 2008, is more clearly defined and includes cartoons. Publishers of yaoi make sure that at conventions, their books are wrapped with a front cover warning.

At times, there is discourse in Indonesia concerning manga's effects on a national style, but some cartoonists, for instance, Dwi Koendoro and Toni Masdiono, are not disturbed by their presence. Koendoro (interview, 2007) thought manga can be models for effective marketing and communications; Masdiono (interview, 2008) said much can be learned from manga about the development of stories and drawings.

Graphic novels as a type of comic art have existed in Indonesia for nearly a half century, since 1962, when Taguan Hardjo created *Morina*, published by Firma Harris in Medan. On *Morina's* cover were the words "Nopel Bergambar," in the Sumatran dialect, meaning picture or graphic novel. During the 1970s, *komik bundels* (equivalent to the English word bundle) appeared as complete series of comics (cergam), consisting of about 200 pages (Masdiono 2010: 578). To stretch the claim further, if comics anthologies are graphic novels, as some scholars have contended, then, by the 1970s, collections of the works by cartoonists Pramono, Hidajat, Sudarta, Koendoro, and Priyanto S. constitute being graphic novels (Pramono, interview, 1992).

During the 2000s, more finitely-labeled graphic novels appeared, particularly from m&c! Comics publisher. With goals of producing local work, while instilling the Japanese work ethic in their creators, m&c! in April 2009 invited twenty Indonesian cartoonists to produce graphic novels under strict guidelines. Ten were signed by the company; each was given a three-month deadline to draw a graphic novel which m&c! would publish under its brand, Koloni. Eight artists rose to the challenge of making forty to sixty pages a month. The result was eight black and white titles in the genres of action, mystery, and romance. According to the founder of Komikindonesia.com, Surjorimba Suroto, two Koloni titles stood out: Azisa Noor's *Satu Atap* (One Roof), about the ups and downs of a teenager, and Yuniarto's *Garudayana*, concerning the Hindu mythical bird Garuda. Another Koloni title, *Ngabuburit*, is an anthology of five short comics on the theme of fighting temptation during Ramadan. Ngabuburit is a Sundanese term for whiling away time before breaking fast at dusk (Siahaan 2009). Generally, Koloni aims to publish stories to which teenagers can relate. A recent Koloni catalogue provided synopses of thirteen titles that fit categories of action, fantasy, adventure, school life, mystery, genki style action, sci fi/romance, shōjo, and shonen. Although only the latter two were labeled as Japanese genre, almost all books had manga-type characters. Two books consisted of 192 pages each, the rest 128 pages; only two were in full color.

An historical graphic novel, *Lebur Ring Klungkung* (Annihilated at Klungkung) came out in 2004, part of an effort by a group of Balinese animators, poets, and a publisher to boost youth interest in the island's history. Seven hundred copies of the graphic novel were distributed free to Klungkung schools. The story depicts efforts of the royal house of Klungkung to resist the invading Dutch on April 28, 1908. The publisher of the Lintang children's tabloid organized the project, as he had done earlier of the first comic book competition in Bali. Two poets wrote the story, and four winners of the Lintang contest drew it (Juniartha 2003). A second graphic novel on an historical event was also planned.

The graphic novel form is used for other educational and social consciousness-raising purposes in Indonesia. The group Lazuardi Birru launched *Ketika Nurani Bicara* (When Conscience Speaks) as a 130-page graphic novel in 2010 with the aim of showing young Indonesians that they are seen as potential targets for radicalization. Reviewing the 2002 terrorist bombing in Bali, the book is told from the viewpoints of one of the actual bombers, a rescuer, and a victim. Meticulously researched, *Ketika Nurani Bicara* was distributed in bulk, free to schools and mosques (Barley 2010).

Unlike some countries of Southeast Asia, Indonesia has had for a relatively long time, an abundance of cartoonists and humor associations, some ready to advance the profession. In fact, the major organization, PAKARTI (Persatuan Kartunis Indonesia, or Indonesian Cartoonists Association) was started December 13, 1989, to unite the many small groups that existed previously and to form something akin to a union. PAKARTI's first president, Pramono (interview, 1992), said, all cartoonists associations in Bali, West Java, East Java, and Sulawesi were put under the umbrella of PAKARTI.[8] A rundown of some of the groups Pramono mentioned indicates they were disparate in their memberships and purposes; some were designed for fans, others for professional, high school, or street cartoonists. PAKARTI held exhibitions, yearly conducted a couple of short training seminars for aspiring cartoonists, and aided the government in campaigns about HIV-AIDS education and other developmental topics.

Discussing training of cartoonists, Pramono (interview, 1992) lamented the lack of a school for that purpose, indicating that most cartoonists were self-taught or learned from veteran artists. He offered, "If a student is talented, come to me and I will help." In the few PAKARTI seminars held, students were encouraged to develop their own styles and characters, not those emanating from Japan and the West. Pramono (interview, 1992) said students were shown examples of western work, not to be influenced by their "ideas, but by their techniques."

Dwi Koendoro was heavily involved in educating and training cartoonists and animators during the late 1980s and early 1990s. Part of the staff at his studio, Citra Audivistama, consisted of interns from four universities and institutes of Jakarta and Solo. The internships lasted three to four months. Koendoro also taught at workshops he organized, particularly a monthly one for *HumOr* staff, in collaboration with Pramono. In his training schemes, he tried to enlarge students' scope by also providing knowledge on advertising and film.

More recently, training has moved from occasional workshops to more structured and extended courses at institutes and universities and on their periodicals—e.g., Petra University's *Comic and Animation Weekly* and similar comic art periodicals at institutes in Bandung and Bali (Koendoro, interview, 2004).

Comics workshops also are held in conjunction with growing numbers of comics and animation events throughout Indonesia. These festivals, exhibitions, and competitions existed earlier (e.g., Festival Kartun International in Semarang, February 1988; an international cartoon exhibition in early 1989 when twenty-nine countries participated; and the already-discussed PEKAN), but they became more frequent in the 2000s. A couple in 2004 were Komik-Komik-Komik Indonesia in Yogyakarta, an exhibition of comics of the past as a reminder of the prominence of comic strips then, and MKI's comic festival in West Jakarta, which featured a three-day comic making workshop, a talk on Indonesian comics, a book fare, and comic coloring competition. In 2009–10 alone, there were among others, Cergambore: the Festival of Comics and Surabaya Urban Art, "Awaken Indonesian Comics" exhibition, Indonesian Comics Festival, the week-long "Comic Days," and the third KOMIKASIA, first held in 2003.

## Problems and Issues

During interviews with Indonesian cartoonists in 1992, similar problems of the profession were repeated: excessive control by government and newspaper/magazine editors (Badrudin, Pramono, Sudarta, interviews, 1992), low compensation (Badrudin, Hidajat, Koendoro, Pramono, Setiawan, Sudarta, interviews, 1992), fewer opportunities and limited venues/space for cartoonists (Hidajat, Koendoro, interviews, 1992), insufficient training (Koendoro, Mahtum, Sudarta, interviews, 1992), stagnant, imitative ideas of cartoonists (Mahtum, Sudarno, interviews, 1992), and low appreciation of cartooning by media owners, editors, and the public (Koendoro, Mahtum, Setiawan, Sudarno, interviews, 1992).

On the training issue, Sudarta (interview, 1992) said cartoonists self study and that they actually start out as painters. Koendoro (interview, 1992), who was training cartoonists and animators at the time, said he tried to "innovate the cartoonists, not just in technique, but in ideas too. I tell them to read books, speak to a lot of people. I try to educate new cartoonists. Read, read, read. To learn, learn, learn. To speak, speak, speak. To work hard." He tied low pay with media owners' attitudes, stating, "According to media owners, cartooning is not a work of art, but just a frame. They pay us just little, by how many columns we fill. We get the same fee for the same size—whether the cartoonist is a beginner or old timer like me. They pay me the same as a beginner."

Cartooning continues to cope with some of these issues, particularly low payment, imitative storytelling and drawing techniques, and lack of respect and support by government, publishers, and the public. Nugroho (2009b) thought it was still difficult to make a living from cartooning, quoting a reason given by artist Gerdy WK, that society's and entertainment's values changed with the rise of new media outlets. Berman (2005) blamed the problem on limited distribution of cartoonists' works. On the other hand, Masdiono (interview, 2008) saw increased opportunities for cartoonists to publish comics, and thus, earn a living, through numerous publishers and comics groups, and institutions using comic books for educational and social consciousness purposes. In recent years, the United States and Japanese comics industries have tapped into the Indonesian comic art labor force, paying artists such as Admira Wijaya, Rizki, Chris Lie, Erufan, and Toni Masdiono, higher fees, and on time.

Also a change for the better since 2000 has been the breaking of the male domination of comics production. Karna (2007: 322) said that today "most young comics artists are female"; Elex Media Komputindo is their major publisher. Masdiono (interview, 2008) added that there also were "many" women writing the comics. Women have their own exclusive comics community, Kasa Komic, started so its female members can create stories pitched from women's perspectives. A few women komikus have been especially successful, exemplified by twenty-two-year-old (in 2010) Azisa Noor, with her debut series *Satu Atap*, a blend of humor and fantasy with ordinary daily situations.

The tendency for Indonesian cartoonists to imitate still applies; now, they copy the manga style. Manga are so popular that publishers have been known to instruct artists to draw in that style, or to change aspects of comic books to look Japanese. Publisher Edi Lim (interview, 2004), said he cannot sell Indonesian comics, but, "once we convert them to Japanese style and change the names," the books sell. He gave reasons other than popularity for using manga: "most of the time, it is cheaper to pay a license fee to Japan than it is to use Indonesian titles" and, because Indonesian cartoonists do not meet deadlines, manga provide a steadier supply of books (Lim, interview, 2004).

Complaints remain about publishers not doing justice to comics and cartoons, nor to their creators. Comic book publishing is relatively new; as a result, company owners do not have a "total marketing concept" relative to promotion (Koendoro, interview, 2004), merchandising, and international markets. Most publishers want to maximize profits quickly without expending much effort in developing local comics products or nourishing their creators.

Traces of the perception that comics are solely for children can still be found (Masdiono, interview, 2008). Adult comics, particularly manga, are readily available; however, they are publisher-censored because of the lack of a system to keep such fare out of children's view. Government censorship, so common and repressive before, does not exist to any noticeable degree.

## Conclusion

Though there are those like Nugroho (2009), who feel Indonesian comics are "drowning, yes, but not quite dead," generally, an upbeat mood pervades the profession. There are reasons for such optimism: 1. New publishers are emerging, not just in Jakarta and Bandung, but also in Solo, Yogyakarta, and Surabaya; 2. Some studios sustain themselves, and, therefore, make local comics, because of revenue from outsourcing work; 3. A spirit of creating Indonesian-style comics is prevalent, with big publishers adding other formats to that of manga (for example, the graphic novel), popularizing local characters (Panji Koming, Timun, Bung Sentil, Benny & Mice, Sukribo, Kompopilan, and others), and reprinting cergam of yesterday's masters (Masdiono, correspondence, 2010); 4. Artists are much freer than during the New Order regime. Perhaps also playing into this mix is the augmented interest taken in comic art worldwide because of its adaptability to cinema, television, and new media, and its potential for profit in the global market.

## Notes

1. As others claim for China, India, and Japan, Indonesian cartoonists and researchers point to temple art hundreds of years old as being similar to comics in their storytelling, sequencing, and formatting styles. Cartoonist and researcher Toni Masdiono pinpointed Prambana Temple, Jago Temple, and the ceiling of the Karta Gosa in Bali as examples (Masdiono, interview, 2008). The Middle Ages Borobudur Temple included 1,460 comics-like images on the manners of praying for mankind.

2. Sukarno's cartoon appeared in the opposition newspaper *Fikiran Rakyat* in 1935. According to Sudarta (interview, 1992), the drawing resembled a "poster, showing an Indonesian man pointing to the Dutch colonialist, saying to leave, to free our people."

3. Later these foreign strips were compiled into comic books by local publishers Gapura and Keng Po in Jakarta and Perfects in Malang.

4. At the time, if an artist's work appeared weekly, he/she was paid RP50,000 to RP200,000 (about U.S. $11 to $45) per month. By comparison, an unskilled construction worker was paid RP10,000 per day.

5. Others of Athonk's works were censored and confiscated, such as his comic illustrations on land rights issues and on military abuses of power.

6. In Indonesian folktales, Doyok is a punakawan, a unique figure in Javanese puppet theater, similar to Semar, Gareng, Petruk, and Bagong in wayang.

7. After *HumOr*'s discontinuance, the humor magazine *Bogbog* (Humor) was started in Bali by Jango Pramartha, head of the Indonesian Cartoonists Association.

8. Pramono (interview, 1992) identified the following cartoonist groups in 1992: PAKYO (Yogyakarta), SECAC (Semarang Cartoonist Club), PERTAMOR (Semarang fans of humor club), Kokkang (Semarang), TERKATUNG (cartoonist/humor club in a city near Semarang), PAKARSO (Cartoonists Association of Solo), PECAHBAN (Humor Fans from Bandung), SENJA (Seniman Jalanan, street artists, a Jakarta cartoonists association), KALEM (Kelompok 86 High School Cartoonists Association), PERKARA (a district of East Jakarta cartoonists association), LHI (Lembaga Humor Indonesia, located in Jakarta), Ikan Asin (Salty Fish, West Kalimantan).

# 2

# Philippine Komiks

## 1928 to the Present

### JOHN A. LENT

As in many countries, the Philippine comic book (*komik*) was a result of an evolutionary process, growing from, first, humor magazines and political cartoons, and then, comic strips. Although Dr. Jose Rizal, the nationalist later proclaimed national hero, is often called the first cartoonist in the Philippines, cartoons probably appeared before he drew the fable, "The Monkey and the Tortoise," in 1885 (see D. Redondo 1979). Before and at the time of Rizal's drawing, Manila magazines *La Semana Elegante* (1884), *La Puya* (1885), and *Manila Alegre* (1885) are likely to have carried cartoons. Others of a satirical nature, such as *Te Con Leche, El Tio Verdades, Biro-Biro*, and *Miau*, appeared between 1898 and 1901 mainly to lampoon both Spaniards and Americans (Lent 2004: 74; also see McCoy and Roces 1985: 7–18).

During the early American occupation, other magazines, some satirical containing two-toned cartoons and caricatures, were published in Manila. Four dominated—*Lipang Kalabaw, Philippine Free Press, Telembang*, and *The Independent*. Other illustrated weeklies –*Liwayway, Monday Mail*, and *Graphic*—came onto the scene by the 1930s, providing a growing body of cartoonists with outlets for their works. *Liwayway* (see Villegas 2007) and *Graphic* were launched in 1923 and 1927, respectively, by Ramon Roces, who played very significant roles in the development of vernacular-languages magazines, and with Tony Velasquez, comic strips and the komiks. In fact, the first Philippine comic strip, "Kenkoy," created by Tony Velasquez in December 1928, was at the encouragement of Roces. A translator in *Liwayway*'s advertising department, Romualdo Ramos, had a vision of bringing out illustrated funnies

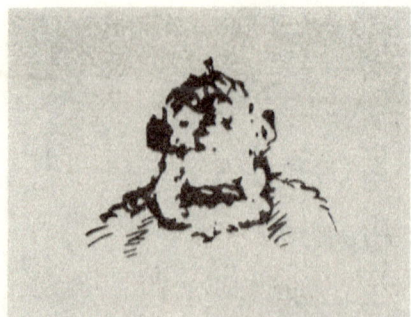

BUT AS I AM VERY GENEROUS

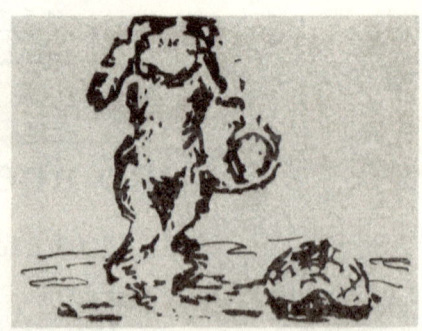

I WILL LEAVE TO YOU THE CHOICE OF YOUR DEATH.

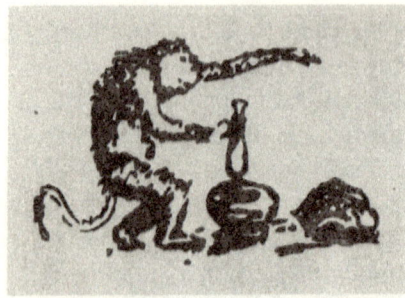

"SHALL I POUND YOU IN A MORTAR OR SHALL I THROW YOU INTO THE WATER? WHICH DO YOU PREFER?"

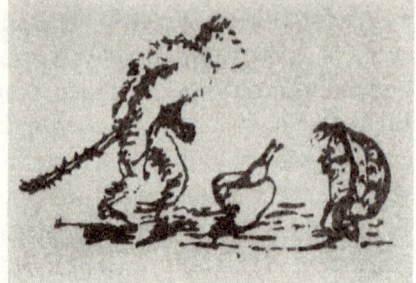

"THE MORTAR, THE MORTAR," ANSWERED THE TORTOISE, "I AM SO AFRAID OF GETTING DROWNED."

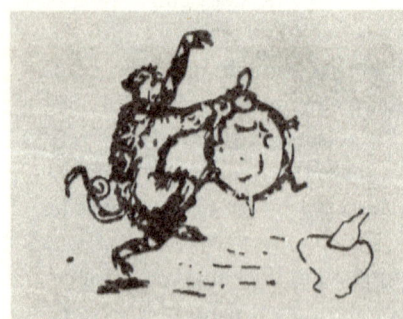

"O HO!" LAUGHED THE MONKEY. "INDEED! YOU ARE AFRAID OF GETTING DROWNED! NOW I WILL DROWN YOU."

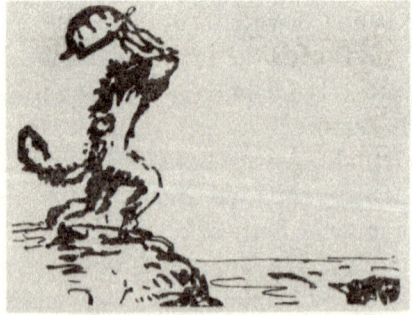

AND GOING TO THE SHORE, HE SLUNG THE TORTOISE AND THREW IT IN THE WATER.

BUT SOON THE TORTOISE REAPPEARED SWIMMING AND LAUGHING AT THE DECEIVED, ARTFUL MONKEY.

**A segment of José Rizal's "The Monkey and the Tortoise," 1885, the first cartoon drawn by a Filipino.**

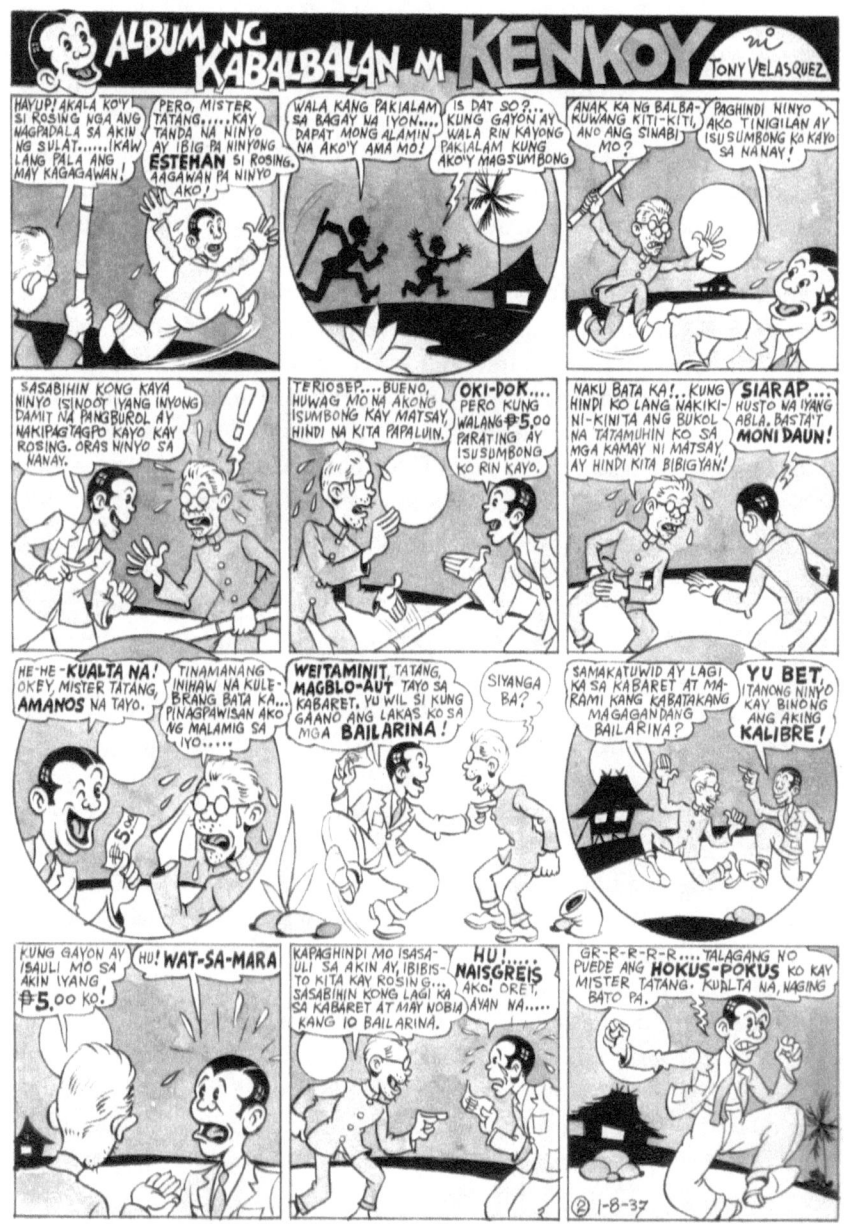

*Kenkoy* in *Album ng Kabalbalan ni Kenkoy*, by Tony Velasquez, January 8, 1937, the first comic strip reprinted in an album (courtesy Tony Velasquez).

as a supplement to the magazine. The artwork for the strip was assigned to a senior artist, but, according to Velasquez (interview, 1988; also see Lent 1993a), when the artist "for so many weeks, was not able to do it, Don Ramon told me, 'Tony, can you do it?' I told him I'd try." Ramos supplied jokes and storyline and Velasquez drew the strip, which debuted as four panels in the January 11, 1929 *Liwayway*. "Mga Kabalbalan ni Kenkoy," as the Tagalog-language strip was called, expanded to six panels ten issues later and to a full page in color within a year. When Ramos died in 1932, Velasquez did the strip alone.

"Kenkoy" was enthusiastically received by a large readership, as it eventually was translated into four other vernacular languages for use in Roces' magazines *Bannawag*, *Bisaya*, *Hiligaynon*, and *Bikolnon* and was made the subject of a song, a poem, movies, and komiks. Velasquez (interview, 1988) said a plan to animate Kenkoy failed when the producer thought the proposed budget was too high; Velasquez said he did not return the P5,000 advance he was paid.

In some ways, Kenkoy was a satire on the 1920s' trend to rapidly Americanize the Philippines. Carrying a ukelele, sporting a Valentino hairdo and bell bottoms, and mouthing English slang with a Filipino twist, Kenkoy was, in the words of noted komiks creator Nonoy Marcelo (1980), "a ludicrous portrait of the Filipino ... pathetically trying but barely succeeding in keeping up with his American mentors." To Velasquez's way of thinking, however, the character was Filipino, con-ceived in the Philippines without outside influences. When I relayed one writer's feeling that Mickey Mouse was the inspiration for Kenkoy because of some similarities in appearances, Velasquez (interview, 1988) reacted strongly: "It's not patterned after anyone. In fact, I had not seen his [Walt Disney's] Mickey Mouse when I created my Kenkoy. He was in the United States; I was in the Philippines. I beat him [Disney]; he went abroad [died], I'm still alive" (see Lent 1993a).

In the 1930s, Velasquez was an extremely busy man. As chief adver-tising artist for Roces' six magazines, he pioneered in the use of cartoons in advertising with a cast of characters, and also conceived another strip, "Ponyang Halobaybay," and introduced new characters to "Kenkoy," some of which soon became separate strips.

Strips proliferated in the 1930s, most published in magazines and some modeling themselves after prominent American funnies, such as Francisco Reyes' "Kulafu," which owed much to "Tarzan," and Procopio

Borromeo's "Goyo at Kikay," which imitated "Bringing Up Father." In the mid–1930s, Jose Zabala Santos introduced four characters to *Sampaguita* magazine—"Titina," the "Popeye"–like "Lukas Malakas," "Sianong Sano," and "Popoy," and two years later, fifteen-year-old Francisco V. Coching created "Bing Bigotilyo" in *Silahis Magazine*. J. M. Perez contributed two popular strips to *Liwayway* in the early 1930s—"Abilitat sa Akong" and "Si Pamboy at si Osang."

"Kenkoy" alone among the funnies survived throughout the Japanese occupation, continuing to appear in *Liwayway* but published by the Japan Information Bureau. Velasquez (interview, 1988) said the Japanese used the character in their health campaign; he claimed "Kenkoy did not get involved in politics or war, just sanitation." The Japanese also commissioned Velasquez to do a daily strip for *Tribune*. Called the "Kalibapi Family," it showed life of Filipinos under the new Japanese social order. Velasquez said there was no public reaction after the war concerning Kenkoy working for the Japanese. Some of these strips continued after World War II, either as parts of the general interest magazines or the newly born komiks. Also, most pre-war strip cartoonists, such as Velasquez, Reyes, Coching, Borromeo, and Jose Zabala Santos, in addition to a host of newcomers, lent their services to the birthing of komiks.

American comic books brought in by U.S. soldiers during World War II were the impetus for the development of *komiks*, the first of which was *Halakhak* (word that sounds like and denotes laughter).[1] Universal Bookstore owner Attorney Jaime Lucas started *Halakhak* at the urging of former editorial cartoonist and wartime guerrilla propagandist, Isaac Tolentino, who became editor (S. P. Redondo 1979). Besides humor, love, and mystery stories, the forty-two-page komik carried an adventure series, "Bernardo Carpio," about a Philippine mythical hero. *Halakhak* closed after ten issues, because, according to Velasquez (interview, 1988), of lack of facilities: "no press, only a bookstore owner and publisher and no finances."

Roces and Velasquez teamed again in 1947, starting Ace Publications with the sole intent to publish komiks. Velasquez was appointed editor of Ace's first magazine, *Pilipino Komiks*, a fortnightly with an initial print run of 10,000, a 25 centavo price tag, and an operating budget of ₱10,000 (see Villegas 2007). Velasquez said Roces asked him if he would start a new business, the komiks. "I was flattered," Velasquez (interview, 1988) said, elaborating,

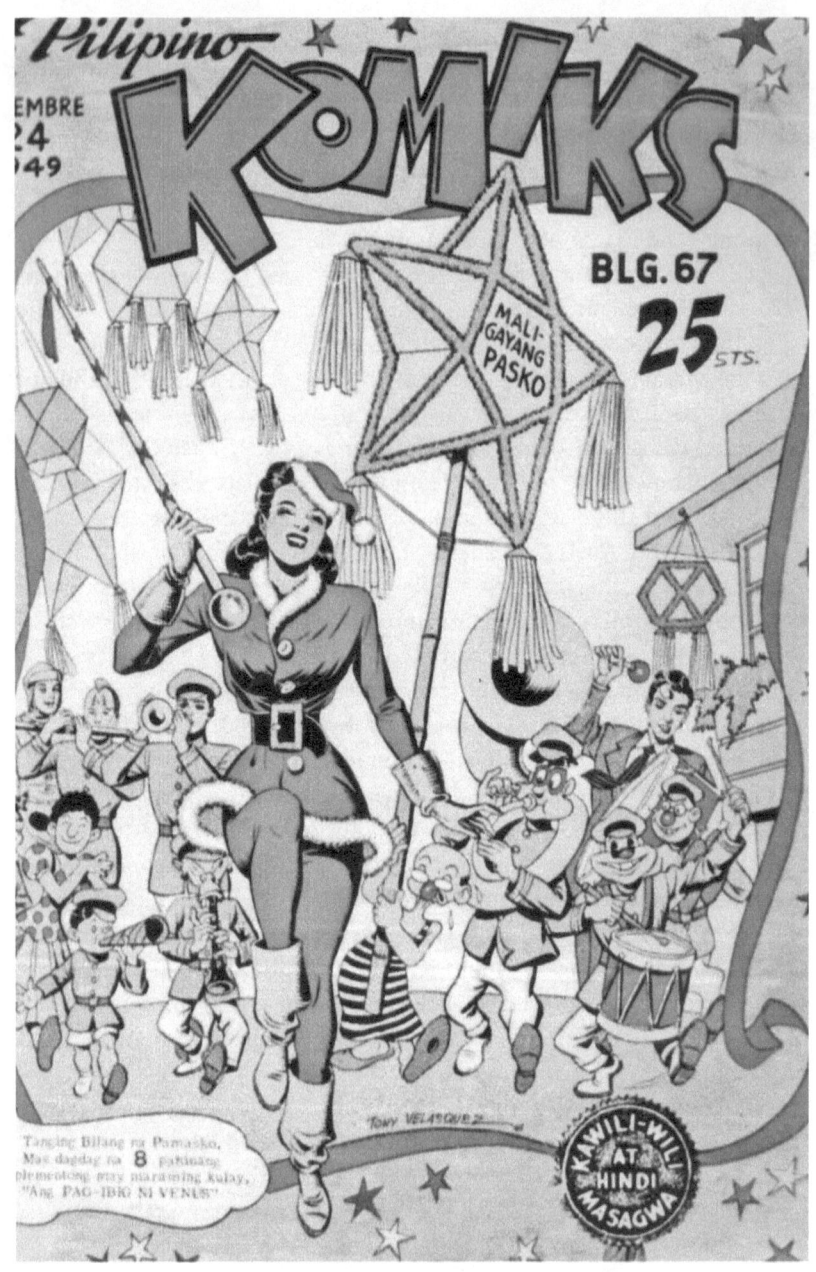

*Pilipino Komiks*, **December 24, 1949.**

Don Ramon said he'd give me a month to do it. Then, artists were not very busy so I could meet his deadline. Don Ramon told me, "I don't think this [komik] will last; just do what you can about it." I kept insisting, "This will last, Don Ramon." I had already a plan to do my own comics magazine when Don Ramon called.

For the first two years, Velasquez handled *Pilipino Komiks* alone, but the staff grew, as did the komik's popularity, prompting Ace to start *Tagalog Klasiks* (1949), *Hiwaga Komiks* (1950), *Espesyal Komiks* and pocket-sized *Kenkoy Komiks* (both 1952).

By 1950, other titles entered the komiks field: *Extra Komiks* by Eriberto A. Tablan; *Silangan Komiks* by Ben Cabailo, Jr., and *Bituin Komiks* by Felix J. Quiogue. Additionally, by 1950, comics supplements appeared in *Liwayway, Bulaklak, Ilang-ilang, Tiktik,* and *Sinagtala*. Some publishers also issued U.S. comic books as verified by Chronicle Publishing Company publisher Oscar Lopez (interview, 1964), who said his company quit publishing American comics with the proliferation of Tagalog komiks. He added, "so many of the U.S. books we reproduced were brought in by U.S. servicemen anyway."

## Golden Age of Komiks

Komiks' golden era of the 1950s churned out increasing numbers of works in various genres[2] and nurtured some of the great names of cartooning. One of them, Larry Alcala (interview, 1988), who started his career in 1946 with the help of Tony Velasquez, said in the 1950s, "Cartoonists had love for their work. It was not as commercialized then as now." The good times unraveled, according to Alcala, when a 1963 strike of the printing industry closed Ace: "When that happened, a lot of contributors [to Ace komiks] put up their own books. With the proliferation of books, quality went down." Nevertheless, the 1960s saw the revitalization of the komiks when new types and genres appeared, komiks became a prime vehicle to promote Tagalog, the careers of some of the Philippines' most famous cartoonists took off, and the industry reorganized with new companies and titles that survived until contemporary times.

Two types/genres singled out as products of the 1960s are *bomba* and developmental. Existing side-by-side with bomba films, pornographic bomba komiks were published by fly-by-night operators and carried titles such as *Bikini, Sex-see,* and *Toro*; they thrived from 1967 to 1972, until the crackdown on mass media during the martial law era. By the 1980s, they resurfaced, published by Sagalongos Publications (*Playmate, Sakdal Sexy, Sakdal Bold, Sakdal Erotik, Macho,* and *Tiktik*) and R. G. Publication (*For Gents Only*). Others, such as *For Adults Only* and *He and She,* did not contain publication information. A court ruling in 1985 gave the more established outfits the right to publish as long as they used staff boxes. Some publishers, such as Amador E. Sagalongos, ran installments of the earlier obscenity court ruling or political messages along with photos and drawings, some of which showed sexual penetration (see David 1990: 156).

Ironically, bomba culture flourished in a country where the Roman Catholic Church is politically powerful and societally censorious and, at a time, when the komiks industry was guided by a strict, self-imposed code. In January 1955, just after establishment of the U.S. Comics Code, Ace Publications drew up rules to guide its editors and quickly pushed for industry-wide acceptance of their code. With other publishers' approval, the Association of Publishers and Editors of Philippine Comics-Magazines (APEPCOM) was created to oversee the self-censorship process, with Velasquez presiding (see Lent 1999c: 180–90; Roxas and Arevalo 1985: 58). APEPCOM merged with the Catholic Laymen's Committee for Decency with the joint mission to "strip comics of lavish sex, horror, gangsterism and other filth harmful to morals." A few months after martial law, APEPCOM was revived as Kapisanan ng mga Publisista at mga Patnugot ng mga Komiks-magasin sa Pilipino (KPPKP), broadening the APEPCOM code to more closely align the komiks industry with the government's national development goals. Later, Graphic Arts Services instituted its own code. At best, the effectiveness of these codes was modest.

The other komiks birthed and nourished in the 1960s were developmental, used in campaigns to bring about social change (see Jones 1987: 1, 8). At the time, no country emphasized developmental komiks as the Philippines did, which was fitting, for the concepts "development journalism" and "development communication" were coined and framed there. While the Population Center and governmental National Media Production Center published developmental komiks, built mainly around family planning themes, researchers at the University of the

Philippines Institute of Mass Communications (and to a lesser extent, University of the Philippines at Los Baños Department of Development Communication) tested ways to use them and ascertain their effectiveness (*AMCB* 1978: 12–13). The studies usually showed that developmental komiks did have an effect (for more on developmental komiks, see Maglalang 1976; Chen 1989; Bundoc-Ocampo 1983).[3]

Also of significance in the 1960s was the ascendancy of the national language. Most other print media were split between use of English and Tagalog, but all komiks, except one or two, were in the national language.

In the 1950s and 1960s, the careers of cartoonists and writers who had important impacts on Philippine [and in some cases, American] comics were set. Among them were Alfredo Alcala, Larry Alcala (see Matawaran 1987; Paulino 1995, 1998); Clodualdo del Mundo, Nestor Redondo, Mars Ravelo (see Matienzo 1979), Francisco Coching, Fred Carrillo, Alex Niño, Pablo S. Gomez, Federico C. Javinal, Jesse F. Santos, Menny Martin, and Tenny Henson.

With an abundance of talent, and some cartoonists' eagerness to strike out on their own, more publishing companies joined Ace Publications and Extra Komiks Publications in bringing out komiks between the 1950s and 1970s. Among them were G. Miranda and Sons Publishing Corporation/Mapalad Publishing Corporation, which together issued *Lagim Komiks* (later *L'Amour Komiks*), *Diamante Komiks*, *Sweethearts Komiks*, *Short Stories Komiks*, *Wakasan Komiks*, *Heart-Throbs Komiks*, *Sampaguita Komiks*, and others; Bulaklak Publications with *Manila Klasiks* and *Bulaklak Express*; Soller Press, *Wow Komiks*, *Romantic Klasiks*, and others, and Gold Star Publishing House. Five years after Ace folded in 1963, Ramon R. Marcelino, recently resigned from GASI, organized a new Ace Publications as a sister of Graphic Arts Services (GASI). Its first magazine was *Bondying Komeex*, followed by *Kiss Komeex*, *Pogi Magasin*, and *Hapi-Hapi Komeex* (later *Happy Komiks*).

In 1963,[4] komiks novelist Pablo S. Gomez established PSG Publishing House and published *United Komiks*. Gomez (interview, 2008) said he was motivated to start PSG when Ace folded after a devastating strike and "I had to think of how to help people who lost their jobs." He was head of the komiks union at the time of the strike. Gomez moved quickly and added four more titles, (*Planet Komiks*, *Universal Komiks*, *Continental Komiks*, *Kidlat Komiks*). Because of a subsequent national economic downturn, Gomez sold the rights to *United* and *Universal* in 1973 to Affiliated Publications, Inc., organized in 1970 by Tony Tenorio after he left PSG where he had been editor (Gomez, interview, 2008). Gomez (interview, 2008) placed much of the blame for his and other komiks downturn to bomba. Affiliated designed komiks to appeal to movie fans, many of whom were avid komiks readers. Its initial publication was *Nora Aunor Entertainment Magazine* in October 1970, named after the most popular film star at the time. Three months later, *Pip Entertainment Magazine* debuted, taking the pet name of the top male star, Tirso Cruz III. Both komiks were instant successes. Other Affiliated komiks soon followed, including *Movie Idol Entertainment Magazine* and *Pilipino Reporter*.

Mars Ravelo also joined the ranks of komiks publishers, setting up RAR Publishing House in 1970. Initially, RAR had four titles—*Ravelo Komiks, Kampeon Komiks, Teenworld,* and *18 Magazine*—different in that they were slightly larger in format than other komiks. Naturally, they featured many of Ravelo's stories, but they also carried a considerable number of articles about films and entertainment personalities. Because of another economic crunch and Ravelo's illness, RAR closed in 1983.

Another Velasquez venture got off the ground in July 1971, when Tony's brother Damian opened Adventures Illustrated Magazines, Inc. and within a few days, published *Adventure Komiks* and *Voodoo Komiks*, followed by *Love Story Illustrated Magazine* named after the American movie hit by that title. *Adventure Komiks* and *Voodoo Komiks* soon folded but *Love Story Illustrated Magazine* continued as one of the top komiks in the Philippines. In an effort to use their presses to the fullest all year, textbook publisher Rex Printing Co., Inc. moved into komiks in 1978, first with *Rex Komiks* and *Astro Komiks,* and then eight other titles. Of the Rex Group of Komiks, *Tapusan* featured only short stories; the other books used serialized novels.

Children's komiks had existed in the Philippines only as translated versions of Disney and other characters until, in 1978, Islas Filipinas Publishing Co., Inc. was set up and issued *Pilipino Funny Komiks for Children.* Its full color pages printed on coated paper and its staff of top cartoonists made *Funny Komiks* a hit. *Funny Komiks* differed from other books as it featured non-illustrated materials to help children morally and scholastically; encouraged children to send in their own drawings and photographs to be published, and used short humorous anecdotes about children submitted by parents. When a survey revealed adults also read *Funny Komiks*, strips for their enjoyment, such as Roni Santiago's "Mr. & Mrs.," were added, as well as a joke column.

Amidst the closings of publishing firms because of economic problems, the enticing-away of key creators in the 1970s by DC and others in the U.S., and complaints leveled at komiks by an authoritarian government and Roman Catholic society, the industry was stabilized with the establishment of Graphic Arts Services and Atlas Publishing Co. (GASI), both in the 1960s and published by Ramon Roces,[5] who had decided he wanted to recapture this lucrative business from the small competitors that had sprung up.

GASI was started in 1962 with Damian Velasquez as publisher and his brother Tony and Ramon Marcelino in other key positions. By the end of 1963, they issued *Kislap Komiks*, *Pioneer Komiks*, *Aliwan Komiks*, *Pinoy Komiks*, *Pinoy Klasiks*, and *Holiday Komiks*. With their vast knowledge of the field and acquaintances with all top artists and writers, the threesome prospered. GASI circulations mushroomed (*Pinoy Komiks*, 120,000 weekly sales) because of the gifted talent pool they recruited and their use of interesting genres. Roces' bid to dominate komiks again led to a re-organization in 1968, during which, two of his daughters were put in publisher roles at GASI and a new Ace Publications. In the 1970s, GASI added more titles and upgraded its equipment, resulting in a four-fold increase in total circulation and profitability between 1975 and 1978. In February 1978, the company merged with Affiliated Publications, adding another five komiks titles.

Tony Velasquez also had his hand in another publishing venture— the revival of *Pilipino Komiks* in 1964, while a consultant of Pilipino Komiks, Inc. (PKI). As PKI grew (under Ramon Roces), other titles of old were given a new life, such as *Espesyal Komiks* (action-adventure), *Hiwaga Komiks* (fantasy and the mysterious), and *Tagalog Klasiks* (classical stories). Later, *TSS* (*Teenagers Songs & Shows*), *Darna Komiks*, *King Komiks*, *Love-Drama Komiks*, *B'wisheart Komiks*, and *Kasaysayan Komiks*, were started by the company. Roces and other incorporators of PKI handled increasing marketing and distribution requirements by establishing Circulation Service, Inc., and eventually renamed PKI the Atlas Publishing Co., Inc. Atlas became known for its popular love-drama-action novels, the inclusion of movie gossip columns in all of its komiks, and the impressive number of its komiks novels converted to movie box office hits. The company also established the Atlas Scholars to help readers attain goals through learning.

## Martial Law and Komiks

Almost all media were closed when martial law was declared in September 1972, and when some were permitted to resume, they did so usually under new names, owners, and conditions that favored the authorities. In the case of komiks, most remained under their old names and publishers. But, some of the conditions under which komiks operated changed, such as those stipulated in the resuscitated comics code. Whereas the 1950s' code emphasized a need to play down crime in its preamble, that of November 1972, used its first five guidelines to protect the government and the president and to paint a beautiful picture of the Philippines; thus, stories dealing with poverty and social unrest disappeared. Furthermore, the Marcos regime created its own komiks to support pet projects or the image of Marcos. For example, in 1977, the Metro Manila Commission lavishly launched *Superaide*, a comic book about a metro aide who battles street litterers (see *Philippine Daily Express*, September 12, 1977: 28) and, for his 1986 re-election bid, Marcos published comic books that depicted his administration's accomplishments and his self-proclaimed heroism during World War II (Sacerdoti 1986: 31).

Among cartoonists on the Marcos blacklist was Nonoy Marcelo, well known for his comic strip "Tisoy," which was started in the *Manila Times* in 1963. Marcelo's role relative to the Marcos forces is difficult to discern, for he both worked for and attacked the regime. He was the editor of the aforementioned anti-littering komik and worked for the governmental National Media Production Center, but he also created the mouse character Ikabod to act as a "balance to the big fat cats" (Marcelo, interview, 1988). Marcelo (interview, 1988) said the "cat has three mice under him—fisherman, politician, and business mouse. Ikabod was created to counter the opposition." Marcelo was a kind of cartoonist double agent, working for the oppressive government at times, but also carrying on a subtle mission to bring it down (Marcelo, interviews, 1988, 1992). Rafael (1995) wrote, "Marcelo's use of Taglish [mixture of Tagalog and English] permitted him to double-code the dialogue of the characters in ways that deflected even as it acknowledged the regime's power to regulate discourse."

Marcelo explained how he was able to be paid by the government, at the same time he took potshots at it. He had moved to Hong Kong in 1969, and then New York City the following year. There, he worked in publishing until 1977, simultaneously, contributing political and other cartoons to an overseas Philippine periodical and magazines in Manila. Because of the political cartoons, he was placed on the Marcos blacklist, until a former editor informed him it was safe to return to Manila as long as he worked at National Media Production Center and did not get arrested. At NMPC, Marcelo produced three full-length and twelve five-minute animated works. He called his two years at NMPC his "security blanket," explaining that when he returned in 1977, he also resumed doing cartoons: "The security blanket that NMPC promised me was saving my strips from being censored or abolished. No matter what I put in my cartoons, they did not censor. I put in a lot of political. The authorities did not hit me, because they thought it was coming from NMPC" (Marcelo, interview, 1992). Marcelo continued punching at the government even after "People Power" dethroned Marcos in February 1986, explaining, "Marcos left but the establishment is still intact, still corrupt, so I keep hitting it. The things in the establishment that don't work were there in the 1960s too, when I started" (Marcelo, interview, 1992). Ikabod appeared in various forms—newspaper strip, komik, pocket komik, and jumbo book compilations.

In the early 1970s, a number of Philippine cartoonists began working for American comics; some moved to the United States, while others stayed in the Philippines but contributed their work directly or through brokers to American publishers. One of the first Filipino cartoonists to arrive in the U.S., Tony De Zuniga, called DC Comics' attention to the pool of Philippine talent, after which DC editors/officials went to Manila to convince Nestor Redondo and some of his CRAF artists/writers to work for DC under a broker system. Marcelo (interview, 1988) said the brokers were Filipinos already in the U.S. who skimmed off for themselves much of the payment to the artists. Marcelo (interview, 1988) explained:

> Illustrators in the Philippines received ₱75 per page. Those Filipinos who went to the U.S. subcontracted illustrators in the Philippines. The U.S. comics paid them the equivalent of ₱800 per page and they gave the subcontracted

51

illustrators in the Philippines ₱100 per page, still better than ₱75 they got here. Then those back in the Philippines decided they'd also go to the U.S. and get the full 800.

Because this arrangement allowed for minimal editorial control, DC stopped sending work to the Filipino artists in 1978. The outsourcing may have stopped because many Filipino illustrators (a couple dozen) had already moved to the U.S., sparking Marcelo (interview, 1992) to quip:

> All good cartoonists of the vernacular are hiding in the U.S.—from immigration—drawing for Marvel and making big money. Years ago, Francisco Reyes did an imitation of "Tarzan" in his Philippine strip "Kulafu"; now his son Frank is in the U.S. doing the original Tarzan.

Although the Philippine invasion brought international attention to Filipino cartoonists and raised the bar of American comics, it also depleted the talent pool of the komiks.[6]

## Types of Komiks

Also characteristic of 1970s komiks were the supernovels, started in 1975. Novel and short story writing had declined in the Philippines with virtually no periodical carrying serious literature; in this void, the komiks assigned itself the task of providing Filipinos with literary fare through the *wakasan* (short story) and *nobela* (novel). A typical komik contained three segments of nobelas and four or five wakasan stories. Some books were devoted to one or the other of these types, e.g., *Wakasan Komiks*, *Tapusan Komiks*, or *Lovelife Komiks*, for wakasan; *Nobela*, strictly for novels. Because of the popularity of serialized novels, beginning in 1975, editorial houses made sure that each of their titles included at least one established or potential supernovel as its hallmark (Bejo 1986: 161). *Anak ni Zuma* in *Aliwan* was the biggest komiks bestseller, lasting week after week, for at least a decade. The story, based on Aztec mythology, was written by Jim Fernandez, who penned a long list of best-selling novels. Almost as long-lived and successful was *The Hands* in *Pioneer Komiks*, adapted from Egyptian mythology and narrating the story of a pair of chopped-off, one-eyed, living hands with super strength and telekinetic powers. With *The Hands*, Hal Santiago joined the ranks of supernovel writers such as Fernandez, Pablo S.

Gomez, Elena Patron, and Carlo J. Caparas. Another supernovel lasting years was Patron's *Sleeping Beauty*, about a sick woman who sleeps for eighteen years, watched over by a young doctor who falls in love with her and continues to love her when she wakes up acting like a baby in a woman's body. Through works like these, the writers turned the last part of the 1970s into the golden era of fantasy stories.

Fantasy stories typically feature victims of "life's cruel jokes" who gain magic powers (a magic stick or golden gun, or a magic piggy bank) and seek societal acceptance. Soledad Reyes (1980: 20) wrote that fantasy titles try to "rectify nature's neglect and contemporary society's lack of concern by endowing the crippled, the ugly, the sickly, and the poverty-stricken with marvelous gifts ranging from a magical typewriter, ballpoint pen, or winnowing basket, to the more standard folk amulet." A survey she quoted (Reyes 1985: 51), showed that of 200 stories studied, 70 percent revolved around a character with magical powers. Freaks gracing komiks pages included Phantomanok (part phantom, part rooster), Darko (a satyr), Petra (a girl with the body of a horse), women with snakes or rats as their twins, a three-headed girl, talking dolphins, and others, some of which (such as *Lastikman, Kapteyn Barbell, Bulko,* etc.) were copies of American comics figures. Fantasy stories such as these encompassed aspects that could be classified as separate genres, including the macabre and magic. Macabre stories featured evil in its most sinister forms—Satanic possession, hypnosis, levitation, and mind reading—all with horrible consequences. Mixing of modes in stories was common. For example, *Espesyal Komiks* had action-adventure-fantasy stories, *Love Story Illustrated Magazine*, love-drama-action, and *Nobela*, love-drama. Equally, Filipino komiks storytellers were fond of blending mythologies and heroes, as Marcelo (interview, 1988) explained:

> When komiks started in the late 1940s, artists and writers mixed up Roman, Greek, and Philippine mythology. The people in barrios had no idea where this is coming from originally. They were thinking it was all created by Filipinos, not Greeks or Romans.... Basically the way komiks creators approach the medium is to jumble up all types of heroes.... The public laps that up.

Love and romance was a favorite type among women readers, and the mushier the story, the better. Usually these books pitted forces of good against evil with a requisite happy ending. Stories abounded of the long-suffering mother, the eternal triangle, the daughter who gave up personal happiness to serve the family, the woman victimized by her lover, the kind-hearted prostitute, and the orphan persecuted by her stepmother. According to Reyes (1980: 22; also interview, 1986), extraordinary powers were attributed to love; "[O]veraged babies, thumb sucking men and women, ugly ducklings, and effeminate men are transformed overnight into men and women of pride and self-confidence, deeply conscious of their sexuality." Many love-romance stories were set in Manila's slums, thus tieing them to social and economic factors and turning the love to bitterness and disillusion.

Epic hero komiks appeared as early as the 1930s in the Philippines. In all epics, the hero towered above common folk, protecting or saving the community from crooked landlords, wild beasts, or foreign forces, be they the Spanish *guardia civil* or Japanese soldiers of the 1940s. The 1970s also popularized sports and Bondesque spy komiks (popular during the James Bond craze, 1960s–70s). Sports stories, whether about cycling, bullfighting, jai alai, or basketball, produced Filipino athletes who were world champions. Real people were often placed in the stories, and readers were asked to send in their life experiences, which writers and artists then proceeded to make "unreal." The top sports komik story for years was *Magic 5*, which followed a Filipino basketball team that dominated league play through the help of a fairy godmother who loved one of the players.

Humor komiks, spinning off from TV shows or imitating *Mad Magazine*, have not been Filipinos' first choice. Marcelo's spoofs were within this genre, as were take-offs on Bruce Lee (*Brute Lee*), Rocky (*Roque II*), and Muhammad Ali (*Muhimud Ali*), all by Luis Calixto, and on the exclusive section of Manila called Forbes Park (*Tipin of Pobres Park*, or Tipin of Poor Park). Humor was a mainstay also of the already-discussed children's komiks.

Pseudo-science komiks were popular by the 1980s, honing in on futuristic and space adventures, as well as phenomena such as heart and limb transplants, cloning, and test-tube babies. Writers such as Elena Patron, Luis Calixto, and Ed Plaza often plucked an item from the news and developed it into a mixture of fact and fancy that might carry on in a komik for a year or more. Patron pioneered in opening the male-dominated komiks field to women, with her work in pseudo-science and other genres. Other women prominent in the komiks were Nerissa Cabral, Gilda Olvidado, Pat V. Reyes, and Helen Meriz. By the 1990s, Patron, Cabral, and Olvidado were the most prolific komiks writers in the Philippines, each cranking out fourteen episodes of continuing novels weekly. Cabral alone wrote an astronomical 350+ illustrated short stories, more than ninety prose short stories, and 120 komiks novels in her first twenty years of komiks.

As the 1980s dawned, melodrama, with an emphasis on sex, violence, class divisions, and familial turmoil, was favored in komiks and movies. Readers seemed to prefer tearjerkers that reminded them of their own plight. Also popular were pocket komiks, which had been around for some time, but took off in the 1980s. The industry also produced new titles in the standard 7 × 10¾-inch format. Artmark Publishing Company debuted in December 1985 with *Pilya Komiks* and *K'wela Komiks Magasin*, and the already-established companies, such as Atlas, Rex, and GASI, beefed up their lists as komiks continued to be the favorite reading fare of Filipinos into the 1990s. Forty-seven komiks (not counting at least twenty-four bomba, as well as religious and educational titles) existed in the mid–1980s, with an estimated weekly[7] total circulation of 2.5 to 3 million and a readership six times that figure. A 1989 survey claimed komiks had the highest readership (54 percent) of print media, towering over newspapers (37 percent) and magazines (33 percent).

Exposure to komiks stories was expanded many times through their adoption by the film industry. During the heyday of Philippine filmdom, when the industry reeled out upwards of 160 feature-length films yearly, komiks were a major content provider. The komiks made good scripts because they related to the so-called *bakya* public (clog-wearing common people) and their problems and fantasies, thus ensuring box-office success. Melodrama, romantic comedy or comedy, and adventure fantasy (encompassing action, action drama) particularly suited the screen. Certain komiks, writers, and movie studios were identified by their use of a particular type. Melodrama komiks appealed to movie audiences because the structure of the narrative is often a dichotomous situation (rich-poor, good-bad, etc.), women are the central figures in stories, and the sources of conflict are clearly delineated (between rich and poor, men and women, etc.) (Reyes 1989: 73).

In 1986, an estimated 30–40 percent of the big studios' scripts emanated from the komiks. Philippines' most noted director, Lino Brocka (interview, 1986) explained, "It is understandable to use komiks as it is a presold audience." The nearly incestuous relationship between movies and komiks mutually benefited both, according to Brocka, providing cinema a ready-made audience, directors the money to finance better quality, festival-bound films, and komiks a continued readership. Brocka (interview, 1986) said most komiks-movies had convoluted stories, a mixture of "*Dallas, Dynasty,* rapes, abortions, accidents, catastrophes all rolled into one like a soap opera." To survive as a director, Brocka made one komiks-based movie with box-office appeal for every artistic one. Director Romy Suzara (interview, 1986) of Viva Productions emphatically stated, "If you want a box office hit, you have to get the story from komiks or radio." He told how Viva "monitored" the komiks to see which ones sold well. "We don't wait til serialization is done. As long as it has a good sell, we get the komiks story," he explained. Other directors such as Manuel "Fyke" Cinco (interview, 1986) and Peque Gallaga (interview, 1986) concurred, the latter saying, "Most movies are from the comic books. You have an idea, sell it to the komiks, they do the books, and in the last few weeks of the serialization, you bring out the movie version." Actor Jimmy Fabregas (interview, 1986) elaborated on ways conversions took place: movie personnel developed scripts from plots they read in komiks, or planted stories in komiks that were made into films before the serialization ended. "Some producers will do a story from scratch—make the character in the komiks look like a movie star and then commission the star to play the movie role," Fabregas (interview, 1986) said. Prominent cartoonist Nonoy Marcelo (interview, 1988) looked askance at the latter method, because the komiks writer and movie personnel share the profits, leaving out the artists.[8]

Producers sometimes bought komiks serials and paid scriptwriters to provide the endings, often giving the komiks and film versions different conclusions. But scriptwriter José "Pete" Lacaba (interview, 1986) said such practices hurt scriptwriting. "Some writers specialize in adapting komiks, and their presence limits scriptwriters who are forced to compete; they have to use this same formula adapted from komiks that the audience has grown used to," he said. Another veteran scriptwriter, Ricky Lee (interview, 1986), said he does not like komiks but realizes their prevalence must be acknowledged. In recent years, the komiks have lost much of this profitable connection with cinema as the prevalence of larger numbers of U.S. movies has squeezed local production (maybe as low as one-eighth/one-ninth of peak years).

Throughout their entire history, a large segment of komiks remained in the hands of Ramon Roces. In 1992, of seventy-one komiks published in the Philippines, sixty-two came from komiks companies owned by Roces–GASI, thirty-seven; Atlas, twenty; Affiliated, five. Roces products included the country's four largest books (*Love Life, Aliwan, Pinoy Klasiks,* and *Pinoy Komiks*), each published twice weekly with a circulation between 200,000–250,000. Atlas' *Pilipino Komiks* also published twice weekly in 1992; nearly all other sixty-six komiks were weeklies.

As the komiks approached contemporary times, they had settled into a pattern concerning size, contents, and names. The average book was thirty-two to forty-eight pages, typically containing several wakasans and nobelas, as well as an assortment of other features (crosswords, drawing lessons, gag cartoons, etc.). The latter differed according to whims of editors (Martinez, interview, 1992). Over the years, the extras varied widely, from movie gossip columns or pen pal sections, to biographical sketches or views on current events, to items providing tips on household maintenance, health and cleanliness, and spiritual advice.

Komiks story names often were intriguing but were kept simple and relevant for bakya readers. Some were one word, such as Caparas' *Pieta* and *Mong* or Patron's *Leukemia*; some were adapted from generic terms (e.g., Caparas took his title *Bakekang* from *bakekong*, a fishing contraption; Helen Meriz used bubonic plague as the source of her *Bubonika*, about a girl with the face of a mouse); others were coined words, such as Ed Plaza's novel *Dabiana* about an extremely fat woman, and still others created names associated with already popular figures (Caparas' *Supermanugang* after *Superman*, Rod Santiago's *Badman* from *Batman*, or *Dolsky*, named for popular Filipino comedian Dolphy). *Simplicio Sampera*, a novel about a simple man who found a purse that provided him money whenever he wanted it, represented the common practice of Filipinos attaching to their first names their most outstanding characteristic or calling. English was occasionally used, such as *Sleeping Beauty, No Left Turn*, or Caparas' *Somewhere*. Many komiks titles were in English or Spanish—*Superstar, Topstar, Universal, United, Movie Specials, Espesyal, Diamante,* or *Kampeon* (Marcelo 1980: 38–39).

## Changing Nature of Komiks

There were important changes in readers' preferences by the early 1990s. Love stories had become number one, a survey (Pontenila 1992) reporting that of 122 nobelas and wakasans in the top ten komiks, love and romance accounted for 53 percent of the stories, followed by macabre, 8.2 percent, opinion molding, 7.4 percent, fantasy and social realism (social drama), 6.6 percent each, action-adventure, 4.9, humor, 4.1, epic hero and science fiction, 3.3 each; mystery, 1.6, and sports, 0.8.

Martinez (interview, 1992) said that to study komiks, one had to look at the Philippine economy, for "life is simple here; the standard of living is basically barely enough. All these komiks stories reflected the Filipino family...Filipino life." GASI research indicating the importance of the Philippine family in komiks was affirmed by a 1992-reported survey by Roberto J. Pontenila (1992), who examined the ten top-selling books in relationship to twenty-three societal values identified by Philippine sociologists. Familism was the value most seen in the books, followed closely by personalism, hero, and godly.

By the 1990s, the supernovel had lost some of its appeal, again because of economic reasons; audiences could not afford to wait weeks or years to get their endings of serialized novels. Martinez (interview, 1992) said more than half of GASI titles were in short story format, but, the novels were not completely abandoned as fifty running stories were in seventeen GASI books. Four pages were allotted for each short story and novel serial, except for novels by Jim Fernandez, which by agreement with the author, were given five pages.

A third change noted by the late 1980s and the 1990s was a deterioration in the quality of the komiks. Scriptwriter/scholar Clodualdo del Mundo, Jr. (1986: 183), the son of the famous komiks writer of post World War II, explained the lowering of standards: the passion of earlier komiks creators was gone, economies of scale by the industry had saturated the market with writers and illustrators speeding up production at the expense of quality, and the Roces monopoly had shut out other companies not capable of following its formula of producing komiks cheaply and quickly. del Mundo (1986: 183) said,

> Today's komiks would look like carbon copies of yesterday's komiks. The problem is that the carbon paper which produces today's komiks seems to have been used many times before. What cannot be recreated today is the fact that in the late forties and early fifties, the pioneers were excited by a new medium. Komiks then was an unexplored field. There was that passion for developing a new medium. Today, all that is lost. The excitement is no longer there; the passion has been replaced by a more practical need to survive.

He went on to say, "To earn a living on komiks … one has to produce a lot…. Unfortunately, good writing and good illustrations cannot be produced like hot *pandesal* [a favorite Philippine rounded bread]—without sacrificing quality."

Writers and illustrators were indeed prolific, as well as hard-working and underpaid; it is claimed that Carlo Caparas regularly wrote 36 weekly series (Roxas and Arevalo 1985: 99), but by the late 1980s, "slowed down" to nine continuing nobelas (two twice weekly). Illustrators drew five to eight weekly series. One, Mar T. Santana, managed seventeen series (nineteen episodes) each week. Like other "master artists" in Asia (such as in Japan, Korea, or Hong Kong), Santana oversaw a production assembly line, sketching and outlining faces and leaving dialogue, ink details, and background to others. Low pay and payment on a per piece basis (Martinez [interview, 1992] said, "The more stories you do, the more money you make.") forced such volume on creators.

In 1992, twenty-five writers and illustrators (called contributors) worked for GASI as regular freelancers, with an option to contribute to other komiks. On and off, about 150 illustrators (five women) submitted work. Martinez (interview, 1992) said few contributed to other komiks, because, "We try to keep them with us by giving them a higher rate, providing them with ideas, etc. They are after sureness of jobs—we give them that."[9]

Komiks production steadily decreased as the twentieth century ended. Many reasons were given, one of which pertained to lower quality work in favor of speed and quantity. Marcelo (interview, 1988) said komiks creation had become a "slapdash thing," explaining that "if you're doing three stories a week (twelve pages), you tend to rush the work." But, he found other deficiencies in development of plots and characters:

> Love and horror are the most popular genres. In a so-called developing country, you should harness reading materials for something more basic—food, shelter, etc., without depriving them of love and horror. Komiks are now a never-never land. In my work, I try to be funny first, and if I can get a message across, all the better. My thinking is that not everyone is given that space in papers and komiks, as newsprint is expensive here, so use it wisely. Not many komiks have characters looking like Filipinos. They have models who look like Westerners [Marcelo, interview, 1988].

Tony Velasquez (interview, 1988) highlighted the changes he had seen in komiks, as rushed work and less dialogue. Previously, when comics magazines appeared twice monthly, illustrators had more time to make a detailed illustration, Velasquez said; "Now, it's rush, rush." The shorter dialogue is demanded by the novels converted to komiks, Velasquez (interview, 1988) said. Velasquez (interview, 1988) also noted positive changes over his 60-year career, such as an increase in genres and a much more accepting public mood.

Other factors have seriously affected the komiks industry since the 1990s. Sporadically, economic and political turmoil, as well as disruptive natural disasters, drained Filipinos' finances and impeded their purchases of komiks, particularly the long, drawn-out nobelas. Martinez (interview, 1992) added augmented levels of commercialism and cut-throat competition to the list of trends. He reiterated what others said, that some publishers were strictly into komiks for commercial reasons, cranking out work speedily, without any regard for quality of workmanship. The seventy-one titles under five companies in 1992 made for a keen competitiveness that was not always good for the industry, according to Martinez. Philippine komiks also lost some of their huge readership to other diversions, such as television, video, gaming, Internet, and foreign comic books.

Certainly, komiks as they had been known since 1946 were losing their appeal in the late 1980s and 1990s, and with the demise of Atlas in 2005, the great tradition of masa komiks ended. Gone were some of the longest lived titles in comics history anywhere—e.g., *Pilipino*, *Tagalog*, *Espesyal*, and *Hiwaga* together had issued about 11,500 consecutive issues (Alanguilan 2007a).

Besides being affected by the already-mentioned depressed economy and the popularity of new media, the industry had other severe problems: 1. *bangketa* (newsstand) dealers rented, rather than sold, komiks, depriving publishers of income; 2. when the best creators were not paid well (also see Tiu 2001), they drifted to more lucrative jobs or went abroad, leaving the field to mediocre and untalented writers and artists; and 3. the industry did not mature, continuing to print on cheap paper and using archaic color separation processes (Mijares 2007: 52; also see Valiente and Salvador 2007). Reacting to comments of the general manager of Atlas, who blamed the collapse of komiks on everything from the eruption of Mt. Pinatubo to insurrection in Mindanao, Alanguilan (Website September 2005) said the most important reason was omitted—the "poorly made and substandard comic books they published in the last few years." Tony Velasquez saw komiks' death coming in the closing decades of the century; as the rise of consumerism led to affordability of TV sets, computers, etc. and as the quality of komiks worsened, readers sought their entertainment through these new media (Villegas 2007: 61). Mijares (2007: 53), however, felt the real reason for the komiks' downfall was the "coercive monopoly of one single komiks publisher/distributor," the Ramon Roces family. By the early 1990s, Atlas and GASI were the only komiks companies remaining, both owned by Roces daughters. Mijares said all 85 titles enjoyed preferential treatment of the Roces' nationwide distribution system, in the process, keeping komiks competitors from penetrating the market. With this "overwhelming coercive monology" also controlling content, new ideas languished while old concepts were mercilessly rehashed. Islip (2007: 5) summed up the situation, saying, "When the Roces comics monopoly fell in the late 1990s, it took everything with it."

## Resurgence of Komiks

From the ashes of the komiks grew new sprouts in the form of independent fanzines and comic books, what became known as Pinoy manga, and graphic novels.

Alanguilan (2006) related how, in the early 1990s, he and other budding comics artists published their books at local photocopy centers, usually paying for the limited number of copies (about 100) they could afford "out of their own pockets." Often, these drawers/writers gathered in small groups to compare work and share ideas; their comics, mostly superhero type, were sold at university fairs (Fondevilla 2007: 445). A group of La Salle College students, in 1993, published *FLASHPOINT*, an English-language comic book on glossy paper and in full color, featuring Spandex characters in Philippine settings.

Alamat Comics grew out of such groups when, in October 1994, a comics shop sponsored a convention for anyone with a comic book to show. Seven groups participated, taking turns occupying the only two exhibition tables provided. The following month, Whilce Portacio, who had found success working abroad for U.S. comics companies, returned to the Philippines and met with representatives of a dozen groups in his condominium. He admonished them not to compete against one another and to cooperate (Tan 2007: 48). After that, the groups met, organized themselves as Alamat (Legend) Comics, held an exhibition in February 2005, and published the first number of *Alamat 101 Comics* in December 1995. *Alamat 101 Comics* in English and Tagalog, featured three stories—"The Flying Phantom" (Budjette Tan and Bow Guerrero), "Anino" (Aris Lim and Rommel Tamayo), and "Timawa" (Gerry Alanguilan and David Hontiveros). The latter told the story of a mayor who raped and murdered seventeen teenagers, was brought to justice, and then was left in a room with survivors of the victims. Among other Alamat works was the three-issue series, *Batch 72*, released in 2001–02.

On occasion, the photocopied mini-comics were republished by bigger presses, such as with works by Budjette Tan, Arnold Arre, and Carlo Vergara. For example, Tan's *Trese: Murder on Balete Drive* first circulated as a photocopied mini comic sold at local comics conventions until Visual Print Enterprises eventually published the seven stories in two volumes (Lim 2008). Gerry Alanguilan's *Wasted* was done as an underground, photocopied comic book series of eight issues before being published by Alamat Comics in 1998, and then serialized in *Pulp Magazine* in 2002 (see Liquete 2007; Olivares 1996; Chan 2005). Initially, Alanguilan gave away fifteen copies of the mini-comic to friends for their reactions and was reluctant to have it published in *Comics 101* because it was so personal.

One of the spearheads of the new wave of comic books has been Gerry Alanguilan, an architect who became interested in doing comics in 1992, working, like so many other Filipinos, for the U.S. companies. His early story, "Wasted," resulted when "I had a breakup with a girl friend, and instead of going out drinking and maybe hurting someone, I did this comic book" (Alanguilan, interview, 2008). Alanguilan has worked feverishly to revive the country's rich komiks tradition, trying to unify and encourage young creators and make them aware of Philippine komiks classics through his online museum, Komikero group, and Website, and keeping up his own prodigious production locally through his own company, while continuing to work for U.S. comics firms.

Also responsible for the renewed interest in comic art have been Japanese manga and anime. Anime had a formidable audience in the Philippines before President Ferdinand Marcos banned the shows, especially "Voltes V," in the 1970s.[10] By the late 1990s, anime was back (even in primetime television slots), simultaneously when manga began to be commercially produced in the Philippines. Among the latter were *Culture Crash*, started by Elmer Damaso, Jerard Felix Beltran, and Melvin Calingo (publisher, Jescie J. Palabay), and *Questor*, both launched in 2000. Like komiks of old, these titles catered to Filipinos' penchant for diversity with articles on music, video games, and reviews, and, of course, comics with a very Japanese feel. *Culture Crash* folded for economic reasons in 2004 (after sixteen issues), as did *Questor*, soon after.

Nevertheless, the influence of manga continued as comic book companies/groups brought out titles in the highly imitative style of the Japanese. Among these were *Mango Jam*, a bi-monthly comic book for, about, and by girls in *shōjo* style, published by Mango Comics, which itself is part of Yonzon Entertainment Syndicate (YES!); the Mangaholix series of five titles, based on Philippine folklore and set in Manila, but in manga style (Garcia 2008); and books by Stephen Redondo (*Redondo Komix*), NEO, Nautilus Comics (*Cast*), and others. One group of twelve young writers and artists, calling themselves Groundbreakers, Inc., started producing English-language comics in manga style (*Mangaholix*) in 2007, shortly before they established the Mangaholix Manga Mania convention (Garcia 2008).

Most Pinoy manga are published in color, using both English and Pilipino and a wide range of themes. Philippine manga consumers are usually female, in the eight to twenty-five-year age bracket; they purchase the books at specialty comics stores and bookstores (Fondevilla 2007: 446).

Much controversy surrounds the Filipinos' adoption of the manga-style. Alanguilan (2007b: 99) found it inappropriate to use a style that is so uniquely a product of Japanese history and culture (or any other country) and then call it "Philippine-made comics." He added that in ten years of observing Philippine artists who started out with manga, he did not find any who evolved into a style of his/her own. Manga have a "strong and recognizable group style" not found in American comics drawn by artists hailing from many parts of the world, Alanguilan (2007b: 101) said. Further, he explained:

> Our culture is defined more by what we create, than by what we consume. We are no less Filipino when we eat Japanese food, and although we are no less Filipino citizens when we use Japanese art to create Filipino comics, it does put into spotlight that we no longer have a voice of our own (2007b: 105).

On the other hand, Calingo (2007) thought it "strange and utterly unfounded" that by accepting manga, Filipinos were accepting and promoting foreign culture. Claiming the major difference between Japanese and Philippine manga was the audience, Calingo, who had created a

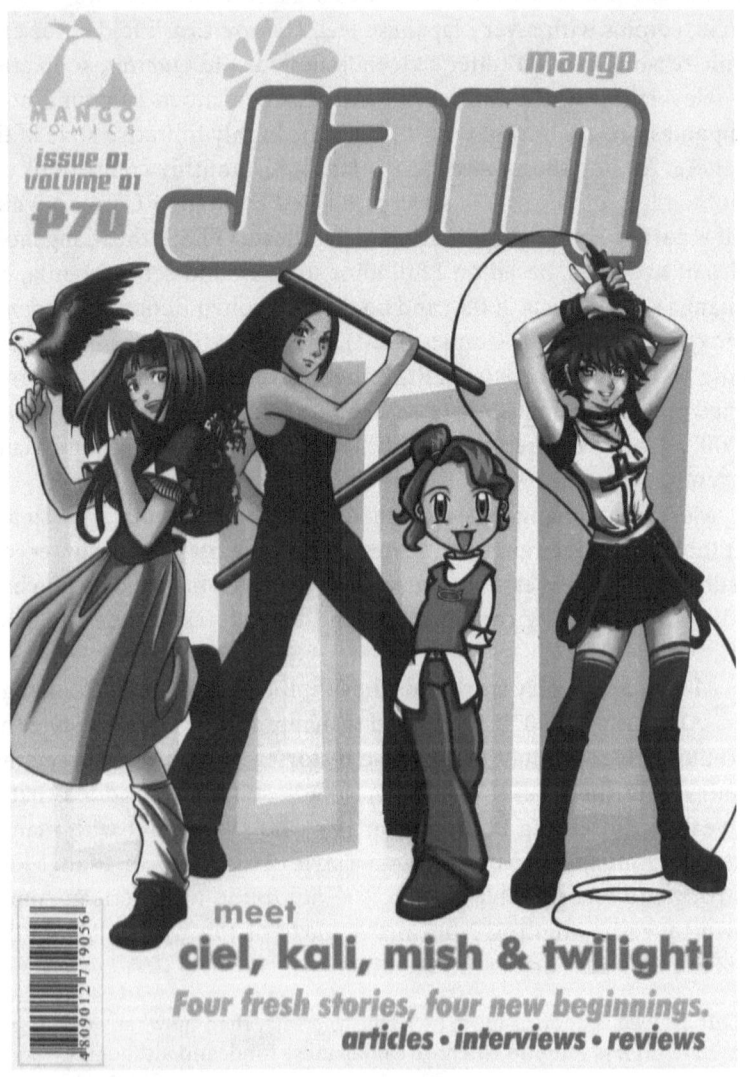

*Mango Jam*, inaugural issue, January 2005, Mango Comics (courtesy Boboy and Guia Yonzon).

fifteen-part manga series earlier for *Culture Crash*, then pointed to unique qualities of Pinoy manga as, having Philippine cultural and linguistic nuances and local settings, being oriented to the youth subculture compared to the mainstream in Japan, and using Philippine humor, drama, and cultural values even in fantasy stories. He felt manga had been appropriated and transformed into something "quite unlike itself back in Japan" (Fondevilla 2007: 449) and that Pinoy manga "suggest an intermarriage of influence between Filipino ingenuity and the usage of Japanese and American aesthetic conventions in creating comics" (451). Another writer said the Filipinos' decision to imitate manga was pragmatic, because more work opportunities opened up for those working in that style (Chua 2007). As it has elsewhere, the Japanese government has promoted manga in the Philippines as a valuable cultural and financial export. Filipino artists have been encouraged to enter international and other manga competitions sponsored by the Japanese Foreign Ministry (Caber 2007).

One savior of the Philippine komiks has been the graphic novel, ironic in that previously, the long-running romance novel komiks (nobelas) had damaged the industry, all folding when a weakened economy did not permit poor readers to buy them week after week to find a story's climax (De Vera 2008). In recent years, a number of graphic novels have appeared, from creators such as Arnold Arre (*The Mythology Class, After Eden,* and *Trip to Tagaytay*), Carlo Vergara (*One Night in Purgatory* and *Ang Kagila-gilalas na Pakikipagsapalaran ni Zsa Zsa Zaturnnah* [The Amazing Adventures of Zsa Zsa Zaturnnah]), and Budjette Tan (*Trese: Murder on Balete Drive*). Nautilus Comics published several award-winning graphic anthologies—*Siglo-Freedom* (a 2003 collection of ten comics stories about the Philippines' freedom experience over a century, published by Mango) and *Siglo: Passion,* a full-color anthology of stories about different kinds of passion and how they affect individual lives.

Similar to the diversity of graphic novel formats and contents elsewhere, those in the Philippines sometimes were anthologies (*Siglo*), collections of works in a miniseries (*The Mythology Class*), or individual titles. Topic matter varied from the fictional crime cases that made up *Trese* ... to the real life tribute to Sen. Benigno S. Aquino. The latter is a 105-page illustrated portrayal of highlights in the slain politician's life, collected by his grandson, Jiggy Aquino-Cruz (De Vera 2008).

One highly-touted project meant to revive the industry was that of Mango Comics and Sterling Paper Products (a notebook maker and conglomerate of diversified business interests) which, in 2007, tried to bring back the inexpensive, Tagalog masa komiks. Sterling issued *MNK*, a series of life stories it licensed from ABS-CBN television network, *Joe d' Mango's Lovenotes*, consisting of two fifteen-page love stories with quotes on love by famous people at the bottom of odd-numbered pages, and the following komiks titles in traditional Filipino style—*Tagalog Komiks, Estudyante Komiks, Gwapo Komiks, Klasik Komiks, Super Funny Komiks, Pilipino Komiks*, and *OKW Super Stories*, the latter for homesick Filipinos abroad. Each komik published 75,000 to 100,000 copies weekly (Alanguilan, interview, 2008), with release dates staggered so that a new title appeared daily. The Sterling-Mango relationship lasted only months, after which, Sterling quit publishing komiks. Alanguilan (interview, 2008) said, "We were excited about the revival of the industry. The chance was there but the stories were old-fashioned when Mango was no longer involved."

Veteran komiks writer and film director Carlo J. Caparas was involved in the Sterling project, his name preceding each of the titles. Caparas and his actress wife Donna Villa made headlines in early 2007 when they put up ₱300,000 in prizes for the most promising comics creators. Through them, a National Komiks Congress was initiated in February, followed a month later with the Komiks Caravan, both sponsored by the governmental National Commission for Culture and the Arts (NCCA). The idea of the caravan was for Caparas and Villa to lead a script writing seminar tour around the Philippines (Pulumbirit 2007; see Maragay 2007). The Congress sponsored an exhibition at NCCA, which then traveled around Manila and the country.

Caparas, who dubbed himself "King of Pinoy Komiks," said he was reviving the komiks of old, but critics such as Alanguilan thought that through the Congress and Caravan, he was spreading awareness, not resuscitating komiks. Writing on his Website (September 2005), Alanguilan said, "A comics industry cannot be revived by promotion, grandstanding, contests, and by other well meaning activities that seek only to relive the good old days." He thought comics creators cannot wait for the Congress or publishing houses to "magically" provide jobs, but they must be self-reliant, even publishing their own books, as was done by Arre, Tan, Vergara, Gilbert Monsanto, Rene Maniquis, and Alanguilan himself. Caparas ended the decade amid much controversy. In 2009, then–President Gloria Macapagal-Arroyo bestowed upon Caparas the title of National Artist; however, because of petitions from artists and others, the Supreme Court blocked the conferment of the award, questioning the president's process of choosing a national artist. The following year, Caparas faced a ₱540 million tax evasion case.

Self publishing of comics was the norm throughout the 2000s. Individual creators set up companies to publish their own works, as well as others, and to commission projects from foreign and local publishers. Gilbert Monsanto established Sacred Mountain (a translation of his surname), which issued his *Rambol* and *Tropa* comic books (both 2006). *Rambol* was in a flipbook format, with two covers and two stories— "Metropolitan" featuring all of the characters he had created for other comics, but now grown up, and "Alagad" (with Kriss Sison); *Tropa* is a story of childhood friends endowed with superpowers. Monsanto admitted the stories had a "tinge" of Western influence but contended that "their personalities, everything about them is Filipino" (Salazar 2008).

Alanguilan has Komikero Publishing, which has published his four *Elmer* comic books, about a chicken family that he has endowed with emotions, human consciousness, and awareness, and Carlo Vergara and Arnold Arre write, draw, and publish their own books. Rising Star brought out *Filipino Komiks* #1, which sold well nationally at ₱100, until Atlas threatened legal action with a cease and desist order prohibiting the use of that name. By 2006, other companies existed, such as Summit, a publisher of licensed foreign comics reprints; PSI-Com Publishing, doing mostly foreign reprints and a few Filipino anthologies; Nautilus, with fewer than a handful of original titles in English for the AB market, and Mango Comics (Islip 2007: 65).

Other independent comic books of different styles, shapes, and sizes, appeared in the mid–2000s; some, such as *Marco Dimaano's K. I. A.*, *Abono Digest*, and *Istrong Republik*, were strongly influenced by manga. *Marco Dimaano's K. I. A.*, about Kai, an indomitable assassin, was the creation of Team K. I. A. of about twenty-two writers and artists; it sold at the exorbitant price of U.S. $5.95 per copy. Oftentimes, comic books were done specifically for university and comics (mostly manga) fairs, some examples being *Kubori Kikiam* by Melvin Calingo and Michael David, about a band of Kikiam (a popular elongated fried snack

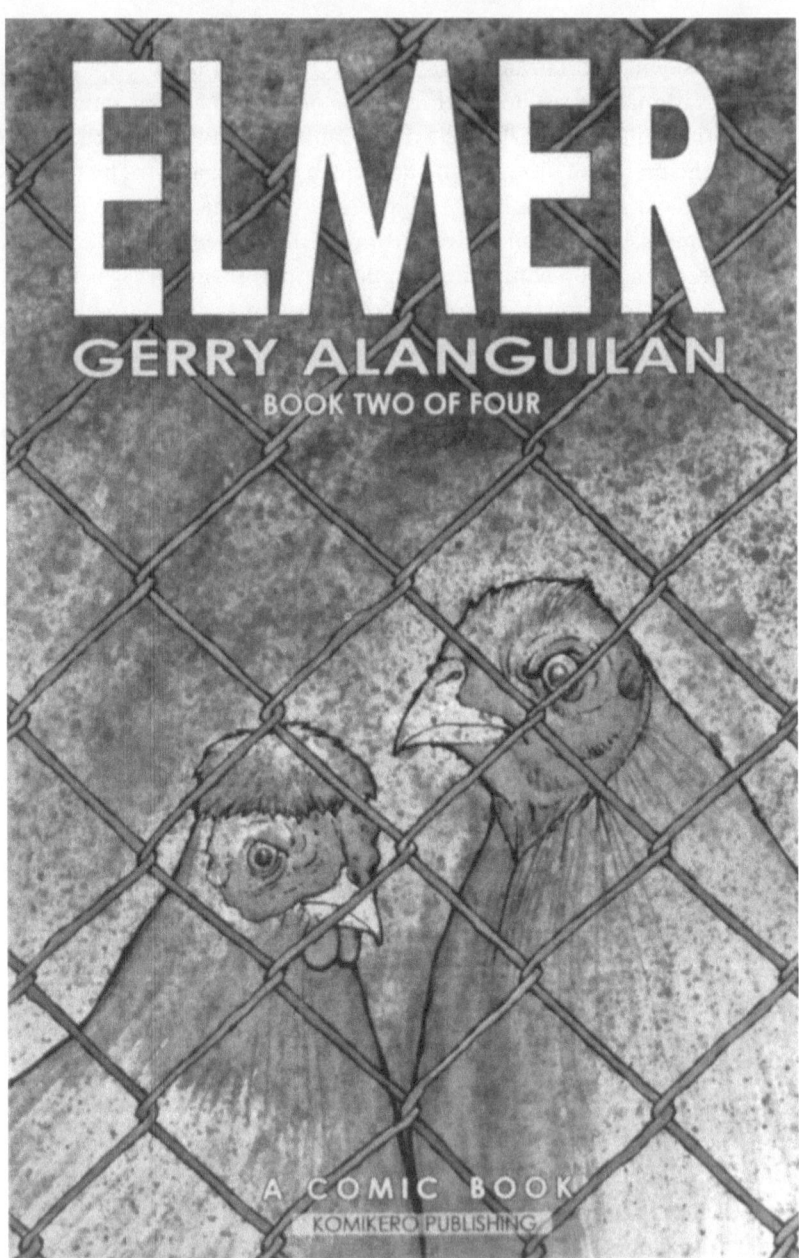

*Elmer* by Gerry Alanguilan, 2006 (courtesy Gerry Alanguilan).

on a stick) pitted against fish and squid balls; *D-Koi Junkie* by Joanah Tinio; *Minsan* by Jon Zumar, or *Prismatic Orb* by Ringo Bautista.

Some comics creators have also found an outlet for their stories in popular magazines. Gerry Alanguilan's *The Marvelous Adventures of the Amazing Dr. Rizal* and *Humans Rex* were serialized in the pop culture magazine *Fudge* (Callueng 2007); in fact, Alanguilan proposed a comic section for *Fudge*. His *Wasted: Final Edition* and "Tales of the Big City" were published in *Pulp Magazine* and his adventure graphic novel *Timawa* in the show business gossip *Buzz Magasin*. Alanguilan is on the staff of *Buzz*. He and other comics creators draw comics stories for ABS/CBN Publishing's *Sindak. Horror-Thriller Magazine*, which in its April-May 2008 issue, filled nineteen of its fifty-two pages with comics.

Besides the numerous new titles since the 1990s, some classic stories and characters have been re-popularized, published by Mango Comics, and briefly Sterling, and adapted to film and television formats. The Yonzons (Boboy and wife Guia), owners of Mango Comics (established 2001), published comics for the AB audience, selling them in specialty stores, as opposed to newsstand and street sales which is normal for CD market publishers. But in 2007, Mango teamed with Sterling Paper Products to publish Tagalog-language romance novels in komiks format, sold at one-tenth (₱10) of the price of other Philippine comic books. Guia Yonzon (interview, 2007), general manager of Mango Comics, told how they proceeded:

> We wanted the old style drawers. I went to find them. Many were down and out. One was actually living in a squatter area. Most were very poor. We told Sterling Paper Products that if you want to reach the mass market, you have to sell on the street, at newsstands.

Despite much optimism, as reported above, the collaboration with Sterling did not work out. In 2008, Mango Comics had a five-year contract with the Department of Science and Technology to publish four numbers yearly of *Tron*, a comic book for children (Yonzon and Yonzon, interview, 2008).

Shortly after Mango was started, the Yonzons were able to obtain the rights to reprint *Mars Ravelo's Darna* in 2003 and a year later, *Lastikman*, classic superhero komiks from about fifty years before. Darna is a poor, frail, coy, provincial lass who, in times of danger, swallows a magic stone and turns into a "brawny bra-and-bikini-clad superhuman defender of the oppressed" (Capino 2005: 45). She has also been described as the country's most popular hero, symbolizing the "strong Filipina without the Western feminist baggage" (Flores 2004: 5). Lastikman, who in a previous komiks life was a second-tier superhero, was elevated to the top level alongside Darna and Captain Barbell by Mango's

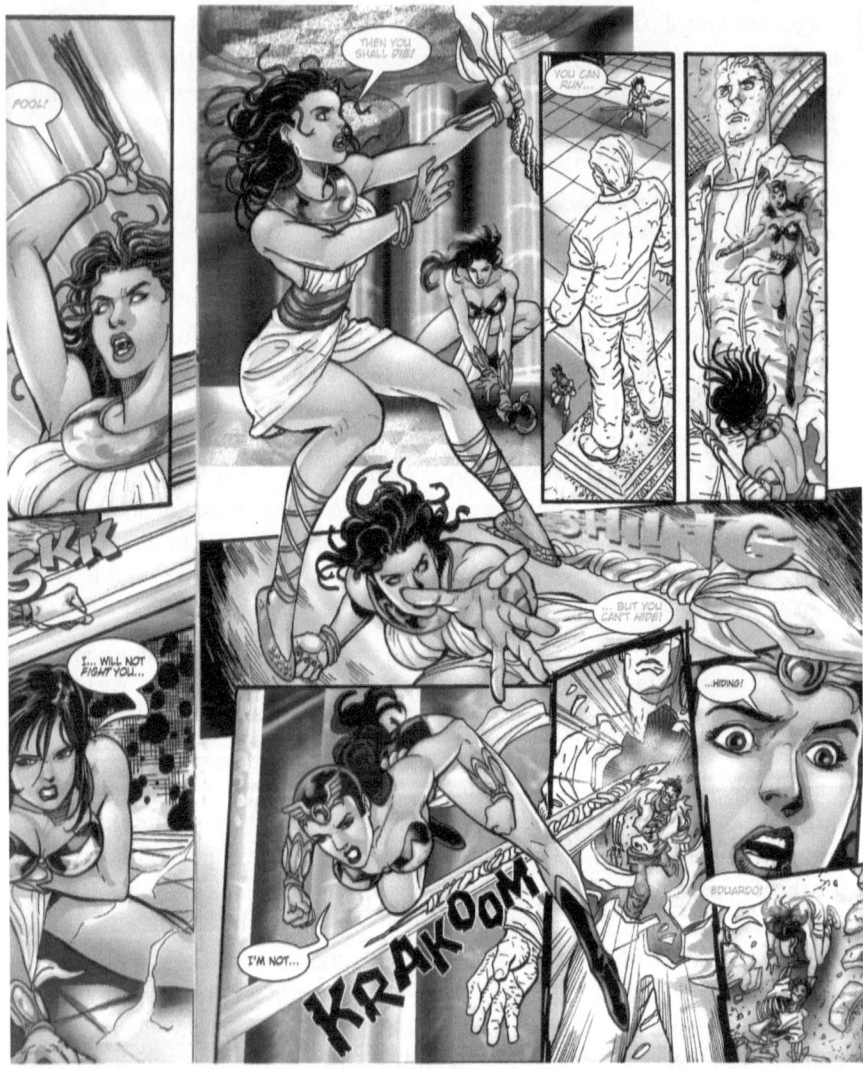

**A page from *Mars Ravelo's Darna*, 2003, reprint, Mango Comics (courtesy Boboy Yonzon).**

reincarnation. Gerry Alanguilan (2006), who was asked to rewrite the story, said his team, consisting of Arre as penciler/inker and Edgar Tadeo as colorist, and Mango tried to keep to the true characters and stories. He said, however, that some new touches were added, such as a less serious, tragic series than Ravelo's original version and a new female character, "Atomika." One writer (Ong 2005) liked the way *Lastikman* was set in local places ("Warts-and-all Manila") with local "things."

As discussed earlier, the Philippines has a long history of komiks' crossovers to other media, particularly to film and television. The twenty-first century has seen a number of classic komiks stories, as well as some new ones, translated into television series and films, most with high ratings. Some komik characters have long histories in film and television. Darna, whose license Hugo Yonzon obtained and signed for a series on GMA-TV in 2005, had featured in at least ten films[11] over four decades, as well as previous TV series, commercials, a ballet production, much merchandise, and a pop song "Hindi Ako Si Darna" (I Am Not Darna) (Flores 2004: 5). The 2005 television series was a mix of the old Mars Ravelo and new GMA characters and plotlines (Brillon 2007: 108). *Dyesebel*, the story of a mermaid who falls in love with a man and later is transformed by a sea hag into a human being, was also scheduled for television; the character had been the subject of at least five remakes and one spin-off since 1953 (Capino 2006: 38).

Other classics have been reworked for television since the mid– 2000s, including Ravelo's *Lastikman* and *Captain Barbell*, *Bakekang*, Francisco Coching's[12] *Pedro Penduko*, Pablo S. Gomez's[13] *Kampanerang Kuba*, among others. Recent original fantasies, such as *Mulawin*, *Encantadia*, and *Atlantika*, also made it to the TV screen; in 2007, Arre's graphic novel *Ang Mundo ni Andong Agimat* was being considered for film and/or television adaptation (San Diego 2007).

Because both komiks and film/television melodrama are hybrids of varied genres, they lend themselves to interchangeability. Capino (2005: 46) explained that the Philippines has a predilection for such hybridity because it is a nation of racial impurity and cultural schizophrenia brought about by centuries of colonialization. David (1995: 16), discussing Philippine film melodrama, wrote:

> Most local melodramas are komiks adaptations, but even the original ones are infused with certain elements carried over from the printed medium, notably the episodic developments and changeability of character traits.

71

## Towards Comics' Preservation and Professionalism

To predict that Philippine comics will advance to a plateau of greatness similar to that of the golden era of a half century ago is premature, if not inconsequential. The environment in which comics function in the twenty-first century is very different in terms of artistry, technology, outside influences, types of stories and formats, and audience.

What is more meaningful is to pay attention to current trends, such as publication of Pinoy manga, graphic novels, and old komiks in new settings and styles; the adaptation of comics/komiks to other media; the inspiration comics provide for advertising, film/TV production, and animation companies; the rise of interest in popular culture, commercially and academically, and the increased recognition (and in some cases, respect) afforded the art form.

The latter achievement is particularly noteworthy. In a short few years, Alanguilan's Komikero, the Yonzons' Mango Comics, the much older Samahang Kartunista ng Pilipinas, Groundbreakers' Mangaholix, and others have done much to rejuvenate what a decade ago seemed to be a moribund art and industry.

Today, the country has a number of comics, anime, and gaming conventions, including KOMIKON, first organized in 2005 by The Artists' Den and University of the Philippines Graphic Arts in Literature (GRAIL); Websites and blogs, the most important being Komikero, which also hosts an online comics museum; events such as Nat Gertler's annual twenty-four-hour comics day, where young creators in one day produce comics "to help shape the Filipino collective consciousness into one that celebrates local culture"[14]; exhibitions, such as retrospectives of Ravelo and Coching's komiks and "unprecedented exposure" in 2008 (in seven of Metro Manila's largest museums) to National Artist Fernando C. Amorsolo, who drew also magazine illustrations and a comic strip; and awards, such as those sponsored by KOMIKON and other conventions. In 2009, PICCA, the first annual international comics and animation festival was held, complete with a forum, exhibitions, award ceremony, trade fair, workshops, and a drawing session by Filipino cartoonists. Mostly responsible for the event were Hugo Yonzon III and his wife, Guia. An effort to preserve old komiks and introduce them and their masters to young artists has been made by Gerry Alanguilan, who, using his own savings, has purchased original art and vintage comic books to make available on his online gallery.

Perhaps a crowning achievement in comics' drive for recognition occurred in March 2007, when President Gloria Macapagal-Arroyo conferred the Presidential Medal of Merit on six comics-related individuals (four posthumously): Antonio Velasquez, Mars Ravelo, Larry Alcala, Francisco V. Coching, Carlo J. Caparas, and *Bulletin* publisher Emilio Yap, the latter for continuing to carry on Ramon Roces' tradition of using komiks in the five vernacular magazines now owned by Yap (Sy 2007).

## NOTES

1. Actually, Tony Velasquez had published a ninety-five-page album book in 1934, *Album ng Kabalbalan ni Kenkoy*.

2. During this heyday, one hundred komiks titles with a total circulation of three million (readership, 18 million) appeared weekly. They were popular because of their mass folk appeal in content, illustrated in full color format, and inexpensive price (equivalent to one soft drink [Maslog 2007: 190–91]).

3. Comic books used for development, education, and social consciousness raising still exist. Since 1980, the Communication Foundation of the Philippines has issued Tagalog and English editions of a bi-monthly, *Gospel Comics*. More recently, in 2008, The Commission on Filipinos Overseas—Task Force Against Human Trafficking sponsored a comics scriptwriting contest on migration, and Adolescent Health Issues and Perspectives comics tackled issues of teen pregnancy, puberty, and adolescent sexuality (Buban 2008).

4. Pablo S. Gomez (2008) said PSG was started in 1962.

5. Tony Velasquez (1988) took credit for establishing both GASI and Atlas and many of their magazines, stating,

> I started all of these books—*Pilipino Komiks, Tagalog Klasiks, Hiwaga Komiks,* and *Espesyal Komiks,* all leaders of Atlas. We started Graphic Arts Services also, with its leaders, *Pinoy Komiks, Pinoy Klasiks, Holiday Komiks,* and *Pioneer Komiks.* A circulation of two hundred thousand is good enough for a magazine to be a leader.

6. Filipino comics artists/writers are working with American companies again; some live in the U.S. (such as Rod Espinosa, Leinil Francis Yu, and Jay Anacleto) while others submit work for top U.S. comics from their Philippines homes (Gerry Alanguilan, Wilson Tortosa, Carlo Pagulan, etc.). Whilce Portacio, who was raised in the U.S., is co-owner of California-based Avalon Studios, from which both American and Philippine titles are produced (see *Manila Times* 1998).

7. Some komiks published twice a week (*Wakasan, Pilipino, Aliwan, Hiwaga,* and *Extra*).

8. Artists normally were subordinate to writers in the komiks, notable exceptions being the teams of Clodualdo del Mundo/Fred Carrillo and Francisco V. Coching/Federico Javinal (Alanguilan's Website; Cabling 1972).

9. Martinez (1992) discussed his editorial procedures at GASI:

The writer comes up with ideas for stories. We editors also sometimes come up with ideas, and we have the right to reject writers' ideas. My standard is if there is an obvious love plot (an expected ending; May-December romance, a shallow presentation, poor ideas or plot, ordinary story), then I reject. I like serious thought, on humans as strong beings, on positive values, positive characters. If it depicts Philippine tradition, yes, I like it. Conservatism, realism, real life story I like; integrity of story and character, which all ages can relate to. We have guidelines on sex and violence; if a story glorifies either, we immediately reject. If it depicts crime does not pay, we will use it.

Writers submit to us a detailed script. Just like a movie script, they describe the scene for the illustrator, with caption and dialogue. Komiks are frame by frame like the movies; usually a komiks story is finished in nineteen frames. A three to four page script is provided for a four-page, nineteen frame komik story. Then the script is approved by the editor. I can give comments to the writer, I can change dialogue, etc. I edit. Then, I give the script to an illustrator who will determine what the character will look like according to the writer's script. The illustrator is given a deadline, told to finish the art in three days (maximum of a week), and submit it to me for approval. The artist gives me a finished product in black and white, except for lettering. We have a regular letterer, typist here who puts in the lettering and a coloring department that puts in coloring according to the number of colors the editor assigns.

10. Fondevilla (2007: 445) attributed the banning to; 1. rising politics between government and private television companies; 2. Marcos' attempt to suppress a revolution as activists could use anime as a means to communicate; and 3. protection of children from accidents as they tried to imitate anime action.

11. Brillon (2007: 98) gave the number of Darna films as fifteen. She said an animated GMA-TV series was aired in 1989.

12. Over the years, fifty of Coching's fifty-six komiks novels became movies (Pulumbirit 2007).

13. Gomez had many of his komiks adapted to film and television, including, *Pitong Gatang, Kurdapya, Mga Ligaw na Bulaklak, Nobody's Child, Tatlong Magadlena*, etc.

14. Each participant was expected to produce a twenty-four-page story. Later, these works were compiled into a 144-page anthology, *The 1st Philippine 24-Hour Comic Book Challenge*, published by Mango.

**3**

# The Uphill Climb to Reach a Plateau

## Historical Analysis of the Development of Thai Cartooning

### Warat Karuchit

In his article "The Uphill Climb of Thai Cartooning," John A. Lent (1997) pertinently summarizes that

> cartooning in Thailand has been an uphill climb, set back occasionally by "falls" caused by repressive regimes, inattentive audience and impingement from foreign comics and cartoons. Nevertheless, as the cartoonists inched their way upward, they continued to get their message across, using a combination of guile and guts... Despite even practising [*sic*] a certain measure of self-censorship, they even managed to establish one of the most liberal cartoon situations in all of Southeast Asia [108].

In writing his article, Lent had used data gathered in 1993 when he was in Thailand. This essay aims to find support for Lent's argument by focusing primarily on the history of Thai cartooning and biographies of some of Thailand's most prominent cartoonists. Looking through the historical timeline, one can see that the development of Thai cartooning has not only been an uphill climb as Lent argues, but also an intermittent climb, caused either by oppressive political climate or lack of interest from Thai readers, which oftentimes drove the cartoonists to quit their profession before they could reach a plateau, where they could settle down and create their works without having to constantly worry about their welfare. This essay also intends to update the situation of Thai cartooning that has changed in many aspects since 1993.

## Early History of Thai Cartooning

The earliest evidence of any artwork that resembled cartoons in Thailand is said to be the temple murals drawn by Krua In Khong, the legendary royal artist who had worked during the reign of King Rama III (1824–51) and Rama IV (1851–68). Even though the drawings looked realistic in the style of fine arts, some of them could be seen as poking fun at the people in that era. However, Thai historians generally do not regard these murals as cartoons (Sitthiporn and Chanansiri 2000).

The earliest cartoon in Thailand, according to an article by the Cartoon Association of Thailand, was made during the reign of King Rama V (1868–1910). Media historian Anek Navikamoon claims that the oldest cartoon in Thailand appeared in the magazine *Samran Wittaya* (Enjoyable Knowledge), published by British-educated Kru Liam (Teacher Liam), or Luang Wilas Pariwat in January 1907. The cartoon was a simple engraving depicting a Chinese pork seller sitting on a chair. On the right was a riddle in a form of a poem: "What is it? Two-legged sitting on three-legged. Four-legged came and snatches one leg away. Two-legged is angry, wielding three-legged. Throwing away four-legged, getting one leg back. What is it?"[1] (Sitthiporn and Chanansiri 2000). The cartoon basically tells a story about the Chinese pork seller (two-legged), a dog (four-legged), a chair (three-legged), and a pork leg (one-legged).

Cartooning in Thailand received a huge boost during the reign of King Rama VI (1910–25), also British-educated. The King had so much interest in drawing that in 1917, he designated a Thai word "Paap Lor" (parodic image) for the word "cartoon" (Chulasak 1999a). The King was particularly interested in political cartoons and often drew caricatures of people close to him to be published in three royal newspapers—*Dusit Samit, Dusit Samai*, and *Dusit Sakkee*. Even though the King's drawings were hardly at the same level artistically as those of the royal artists, they were brilliantly creative and meaningful (Chulasak 1999a). Not only did the King use his cartoons as a satire to embarrass corrupted officials who worked in various departments, but he also incorporated some characteristics of those departments in the drawings—for example, an illustration of the director of royal locomotives sitting on top of a train— so the readers would readily identify to whom the caricatures referred (Sitthiporn and Chanansiri 2000).

In 1920, the King held a second, internal, amateur[2] drawing competition among state officials (the first one was held in Bangpa-in Palace in Ayutthaya), which also turned out to be a public fair showing the works of participants (Chulasak 1999a). There were three categories in the competition: "Paap Lor" (cartoons), creative drawings, and realistic drawings. These categories clearly indicate that cartoons had been distinguished from other styles of art.

In 1923, Pleng Tri-Pin won the royally-endorsed competition, and later was hired as Thailand's first political cartoonist by *Krungthep Daily Mail*, and then, *Kroh Lek* (Karnjariya 2000; Sitthiporn and Chanansiri 2000). Pleng was able to use his Western-style drawing—which was new to Thailand at the time—to impress readers and the King. Moreover, Pleng, who earlier had run away on a commercial vessel to study art in Europe, returned to Thailand with the knowledge of using metal blocks for the press. This new technology helped speed up the process of publishing cartoons in the newspapers, therefore, encouraging cartoonists to produce more works. Pleng's contributions to the fledgling Thai cartooning ultimately earned him the title "Khun Patipak Pimlikit" (the nobleman who prints like writing) from the King (Chulasak 1999a).

The economic lull during the reign of Rama VII also slowed down the growth of Thai cartooning. After Kana Rat (People's Party) ended absolute monarchy in a bloodless coup, and formed a semi-democratic government in 1932, cartoonists gained much more popularity, to the extent that the government had to issue a law to control their political comic strips. Among the famous cartoonists at that time were Than Utthakanon (pen name, Thanya), who drew anti–Chinese cartoons for the Japanese *Yamato*, and later *Kroh Lek*; Chalerm Wuttikosit (pen name, Chalermwut), who worked for *Lak Muang*, and, later, also drew a cartoon that reflected social issues for the *Monday Daily Mail*, with poems from Juangjan Jankana (pen name, Pran Boon) (Chulasak 1999b; Karnjariya 2000; Sitthiporn and Chanansiri 2000).[3]

Cartooning in Thailand also evolved from political strips to other popular genres, especially traditional literatures and well-known fables such as "Pra Apai-Manee"—a classic by poet Soonthornpu, "Sri Thanon Chai," "Pla Boo Thong," and many more. These comic strips were published daily in popular series, and, later, separately as a comic book. The first artist who did this type of long-story cartoon was Sawas Jutharop, with a series of "Sang Thong" (The Golden Conch), a fable about a boy who lives in a conch, in *Siam Rath* from 1932 to 1933 (Sitthiporn and

Chanansiri 2000). Sawas later drew many more series, chiefly based on Thai fables, and, in the process, developed a main character, whom he named "Khun Muen," that would eventually appear in every series. This Popeye-like character, whose role was always that of a joker, was so memorable and popular that he appeared as a logo on young people's clothing (Lent 1997a).

Other popular serial cartoonists included Fuen Rod-Ari (pen name, Dej Na Bang Klo), who worked for the monthly magazine *Krung Thep*; Jamnong Rod-Ari, who drew fable cartoons "Raden Landai" in *Sri Krung*, and "Prayanoi Chom Talad" (Little Noble Visits the Market) in *Thai Rath*; Witt Sutthasatien (pen name, "Wittamin"), who was the first Thai cartoonist to draw a strip comic, "Nai Dang" (Mr. Dang), with English captions, in the *Siam Chronicle*; and Chant Suwannaboon, credited as the pioneer of the children's cartoon in Thailand with his innovative "Pong & Priew," a series published in the *Daily Mail* which used

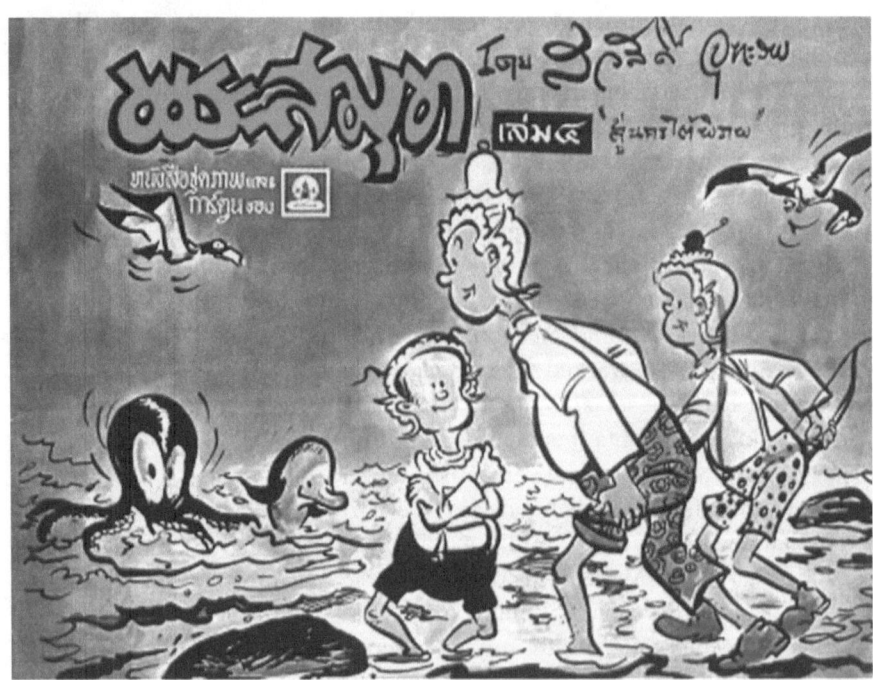

Sawas Jutharop's cartoon *Phra Samut*, the cover of a textbook published by the Ministry of Education after the end of World War II.

"Klong Lok Niti" (world proverbial tales in verse form) to narrate the story (Chulasak 1998b; Lent 1997; Sitthiporn and Chanansiri 2000). However, World War II in Thailand and the Pacific temporarily froze the newspaper industry, as well as the comic strips and series.

## The Golden Age of Thai Cartoon (1953–62)

After World War II, Thai cartooning resumed. The period from 1953 to 1962 was called "the golden age of Thai cartoons" (Sitthiporn and Chanansiri 2000). Several publishers—such as Bangkok, Padung Suksa, Pramuansarn, and Banlue Sarn—started the comic book business; several talented cartoonists burst onto the scene, who have since become famous and very influential to Thailand's cartooning. Among them were Adirek Ariyamontri, whose popular characters "Nu Lek Loong Krong" (Little Baby and Uncle Krong) were based on Disney's Mickey Mouse and Goofy, respectively; Mongkol Wong-Udom (pen name, Mongkol), who drew political cartoons for *Monday Daily Mail*, and children's cartoons for Thai Wattana Panich company; Weerakul Thongnoi (pen name, Por Bangplee), who was well-known for "Asawin Sai Fa" (The Thunder Knight), a story of a crippled boy who became a superhero; Pimon Kalasee (pen name, Tookkata), who, in 1952, published Thailand's first comic book for children *Tookkata* (his daughter's nickname, meaning "doll"), whose four main characters later became the basis for a television program; and Sa-Ngob Jampat (main pen name, Jaew Waew), whose character "Sibgree Jam" (Lance Corporal Jam) became a representative of Thai policemen for many readers (Chulasak 1997; Chulasak 1998a).

Perhaps the most celebrated cartoonist in the early period of Thai cartooning was Prayoon Chanyawongs (pen name, Suklek and Chan), whose cartoon "The Last Nuclear Test" made him the first Asian to win the Cartoons for Peace contest in New York in 1960, and in 1971, became the only cartoonist to win Asia's prestigious Magsaysay Award, "for use of pictorial satire and humor for over three decades in unswerving defense of the public interest" (Lent 1997a; Magsaysay Awardees 2003).

Honorably called the "King of Thai Cartoon," Prayoon first became interested in cartooning when he was in high school, so much so that he put aside his lunch allowance and walked to school in order to save enough money to buy some old newspapers in order to read the cartoons (*Lok Wannee,* December 28, 2001). His first professional work "Lang Baan" (Backdoor) appeared in *Dao Nakorn,* parodying officials taking bribes from businessmen through the backdoor of their houses (*Lok Wannee,* December 28, 2001). Prayoon became well-known in 1939, from his long series "Chanta Korop," in *Supaap Burut,* the work he was apparently so proud of that he later named his son after the series' main character "Suk Lek," which was also one of Prayoon's pen names (*Matichon,* August 29, 1999).

In 1946, Prayoon started drawing political and social cartoons, and, like other political cartoonists, had to struggle against the people in power. In 1968, Field Marshal Thanom Kittikachorn ordered Prayoon to stop his political cartoon. Prayoon responded by drawing Suk Lek with his lips sewn together, symbolizing the restraint. The government then issued another warning to Prayoon, after which he changed the subject of his cartoon to nature. Nevertheless, Suk Lek's sewn lips were replaced by a big mustache (and no mouth). After Thanom was ousted in 1973 by the democratic movement, Suk Lek got his mouth back, and Prayoon introduced his new illustrated column about agriculture and other self-employed professions; called "Kabuan Karn Gae Jon" (The Project to Rid Poorness), it was a very popular column for many years (Kong Tun 1997). Prayoon died in 1992.

Another noteworthy figure who lived during this period was Hem Vejakorn. Often called "Kru Hem" (Teacher Hem) by many top cartoonists who once were his apprentices, including Witt Sutthasatien and Payut Ngaokrachang, Hem Vejakorn is considered one of the most respected and influential artists in the modern history of Thailand. Struggling in his childhood, with no proper education or professional training, but innate artistic talent, Hem began his artistic career in 1932 by drawing novel covers for Ploenjit, a publishing company he helped found. The novel enterprise was a big success, and many young and aspiring artists came to study with Hem, who taught for free. Hem's unique style was his innovative use of angles and shadows to create a three-dimensional and realistic look, without having to draw spectacular detail (which was the traditional technique). Hem's later works also included drawings for the daily *Pramuanwan* and weekly *Pramuansarn,* an illustrated biography of Buddha, and the haunting covers of ghost novels. Hem died in 1969, but before he drifted into unconsciousness,

Hem held up his hand and started drawing in the air, muttering, "It must be drawn like this" (Saran 2000).

## The Coming of Foreign Cartoons

Another trend that developed after the war was the presence of Western cartoons. International trade expanded quickly from Western countries to Asia, and many Westerners brought their cartoons with them to Thailand. Also, Thai soldiers who fought with the allies returned with comic books they collected during the war. Some soldiers had the cartoons, most of them superhero themed, translated and sold them. In 1957, the *Weeratham* (Courageous Righteousness) comic book was published, a compilation of translated Western comics such as "Flash Gordon" and "The Adventure of Tintin." Consequently, some Thai cartoonists began drawing their own superhero stories (instead of traditional fables), including "Jom Apinihan" (Master of Marvel) by Lang Chak; "Jao Chai Pom Thong" (The Blond Prince) by Chulasak Amornwej (pen name, Juk Biewsakul); "Asawin Sai Fa" (The Thunder Knight) by Weerakul Thongnoi (pen name, Por Bangplee); and "Singh Dam" (Black Lion) by Niwat Tarapan (pen name, Raj Lersuang). Although these superhero cartoons were modeled after Western comics, the authors did not forget to include mysterious attributes, such as magic and miracles, common in traditional fables (Sitthiporn and Chanansiri 2000).

In 1955, Thailand became the first country in Asia to start regular television broadcasting. The number of television sets nationwide increased from 2,556 in 1957 to 187,460 in 1965 (Ubonrat 2001); correspondingly, the period after 1962 saw a sharp decline of books and cartoons in Thailand, because of the fascination of television animation. Meanwhile, Japanese cartoons emerged as a dominant force for both children's comic books and television programs. The legendary Japanese animation "Astro Boy" by Osamu Tezuka made its first appearance in Thailand in 1961. After that, the live-action series "Karmen Raiders" (known in Thailand as "Ai Mod Dang" or The Red Ants) became a children's favorite, as did other Japanese comic books (Sitthiporn and Chanansiri 2000).

## Banlue Sarn and Humor Comics

Amid the Japanese domination of the teen and young adult market with action and romance genre comics series, one Thai publisher, Banlue Sarn, has impressively expanded. Banlue Sarn's niche has been family-oriented humor comics. After two years of selling second-hand goods, Banlue Usahajit started Banlue Sarn in 1956, to sell old comic books that he bought from other publishers. The first title Banlue Sarn produced itself was *Sing Shirt Dam* (Black Shirt Hero); its four thousand copies were successfully sold at one baht, while others comics sold at 2.50 baht (Rana 1997).

In 1957, the publisher launched a children's comic book, *Nuja* (Little Children), under supervision and drawing of Jamnoon Leksomtis (pen name, Jum Jim). To compete with Pimon's *Tookkata*, the only other children's cartoon at the time, characters in *Nuja* were designed to be more frivolous (Rana 1997). Two years later, Banlue Sarn published its second comic book, *Baby*, under the direction of Wattana Petchsuwan (pen name, Ar-Wat, meaning Uncle Wat). Today, *Nuja* and *Baby* are the longest-running comics of their genre after the demise of *Tookkata* in 1989.

The person most responsible for the success of Banlue Sarn is Vithit Usahajit, Banlue's oldest son of nine children. Since youth, Vithit was always active in Banlue Sarn. When the company tried investing in the movie business as a producer, Vithit went to England to study film, after which his future in the film industry seemed to look very promising. He was a staff member for the film *The Deer Hunter*, whose photographer invited Vithit to work with him in the United States. When Banlue disapproved, Vithit directed his first film for Banlue Sarn, "Pee Hua Kad" (The Decapitated Ghost), a horror movie starring Sorapong Chatri, Thailand's number one actor at the time (Rana 1997).

Nevertheless, Vithit found his family's comic book business more fitting to his personality. He turned the focus to *Kai Hua Roh* (Selling Laughter), a comic book he created himself in 1973, when he was still in school. His idea was that since all comic books in the market were the works of individual artists (i.e., *Tookkata* by Pimon, *Nuja* by Jumjim, and *Baby* by Ar-Wat), there should be a title that was a compilation of several different cartoonists. *Kai Hua Roh* was made up mostly of one-frame and three-frame cartoons with a gag or unusual twist at the end. Vithit said that he borrowed the name "Kai Hua Roh" from the name of a popular television comedy show, featuring the master of comedy in Thailand—Sawong Subsamruay (stage name, "Lotok") (Rana 1997).

In 1975, Vithit published another comic book, *Maha Sanook* (Super Fun), made up mostly of short illustrated series from some of the regular staff artists for *Kai Hua Roh*. Many of the series later became so popular that they were published separately, such as *Ai Tua Lek* (Little One—which recently became an animation called "Pang Pond") by Tai (Pakdee Santaweesuk), one of the most popular children's cartoonists today; *Sao Dok Mai Kub Nai Kluay Kai* (The Flower Girl and the Banana Boy) by Fane; and *Nu Hin Inter* (Little Hin Goes International) by Oah. Banlue Sarn also publishes several other family-oriented books. Other businesses include a printing company, a graphic design company, and a 3-D animation company (with a ten-million baht project of "Pang Pond, the Animation") (Rana 1997).

Despite the popularity of other publications, *Kai Hua Roh* has always been the cornerstone of Banlue Sarn. According to Vithit, a survey revealed that *Maha Sanook*'s readers were mostly children who love to read cartoons, while *Kai Hua Roh* appealed to both children and adults, the latter who read it to relax, especially during long waits in Bangkok's infamous traffic gridlocks (Rana 1997). *Kai Hua Roh* is one of the best-selling comic books in Thai history (sales estimated at two hundred thousand copies per week), especially after it changed to pocket size format (Sitthiporn and Chanansiri 2000). The success of *Kai Hua Roh* created several imitators with similar format and names, such as *Sue Hua Roh* (Buying Laughter) or *Fah Hua Roh* (Laughing Sky). Banlue Sarn also planned to produce *Kai Hua Roh* in other languages, including Chinese, Indonesian, and Japanese, for overseas distribution (Lent 1999a).

## Children's Cartoons in the 1970–80s

The success of *Tookata, Nuja,* and *Baby* prompted Thai Wattana-panich, a major publisher of school textbooks, to launch a children's comic magazine, *Chaiyapruk Cartoon*, in 1971. The popular characters in this magazine are Tarzan and his monkey Joon, created by the magazine's editor Narong Prapasanobol (pen name, Rong). Other regular artists include Thamrong Sirichu, Panut Lertsomboon, and Kosin Chitamorn. *Chaiyapruk Cartoon* received considerable praise, perceived as a fun and wholesome alternative to the prevalent violently and sexually-explicit Japanese manga and Thai one-baht comics. The magazine survived until the late 1990s (Chaiyapruk Cartoon 2008).

During the early 1980s, five cartoonists created a group called Benjarong (five colors). The original members were Triam Chachumporn, Ohm Rajawej, Somchai Panpracha, Surapol Pittayasakul, and Chalerm Akapu. In 1981, the Benjarong Group launched its monthly children's cartoon book, *Puen Cartoon* (Friends of Cartoon), but it did not last long. However, Triam Chachumporn himself became one of the most successful and acclaimed Thai cartoonists of this period. Besides his magazine, he also worked for *Chaiyapruk Cartoon* and drew covers for one-baht comic books. His famous individual work is a graphic novel, *Puen* (Friend), about the meeting of a city girl and a country boy. With his specialty of drawing Thai country landscapes, Triam was selected to do illustrations for several official government textbooks used in schools nationwide. Triam also won several awards, including the Prime Minister's Award for Best Graphic Novel for *Jon's Recollection* in 1981. Four of his graphic novels, all about social problems and left-out citizens, are included in the Ministry of Education's "100 Best Books for Youngsters" (Cartoon Thai 2008; Sitthiporn and Chanansiri 2000).

Triam Chachumporn died after being hit by a bus in 1990. However, the Benjarong Group continues until today, with Surapol Pittayasakul, who went on to become a political cartoonist (Pol Kaosod), as the leader. Ohm Rajawej has also become an elite cartoonist with several publications using Buddhist and Thai culture themes.

## One-Baht Cartoon

During the late 1970s, a trend in Thai cartooning emerged with the publishing of thin, sixteen-page graphic novels, generally known as "cartoon lem aa baht" (one-baht cartoon; one baht roughly converts to U.S. three cents), first published by Sakol Publishing. Because of its inexpensive price and simple, moralistic, and traditional values story plots, the one-baht cartoon was initially well received by both children and adults, and thus attracted several talented cartoonists. Some of the prominent artists of that period were Chaichol Chewin, Rung Chaokao, Nukrob Rungkaew, and Maewmeow. At its peak, the one-baht cartoon exceeded a total one million circulation, with almost one hundred artists and more than ten publishers—a phenomenon never seen before in Thailand. One publisher—Bangkok Sarn—became the leader in the market when it offered readers twenty-four pages per issue, instead of sixteen pages, and hired veteran cartoonists Juk Biewsakul and Triam Chachumporn to draw covers. In 1978–79, Bangkok Sarn increased its comics pages to thirty-two per issue, before rising paper costs and cartoonist's wages forced it to go back to twenty-four, and eventually sixteen pages (Cartoon Thai 2008; Chulasak 2001b: 607–23).

However, the economic recession in 1982 forced many publishers to lower creators' payment to about 400–800 baht (about U.S. $16–32) per story, driving out a number of veteran artists. As a result, the one-baht comics became a practice ground for amateurs who mostly used formulaic, human-interest themes such as prince and princess, ghosts, and sex (Sitthiporn and Chanansiri 2000). With lower wages and longer work hours, quality undoubtedly suffered. Some cartoonists started drawing without having a plot, which usually led to a situation whereby, to end the story, the artists just wrote the description on the entire final page, instead of drawing the pictures. Copying other artists' work also became an issue. These negative factors led to growing criticism and dismay on the part of Thai readers toward one-baht comics, and ultimately, the sharp decline in the number of these books and their publishers, including Bangkok Sarn.

Today, the one-baht comics cost five baht and consist of thirty-two to forty-eight pages and two or three stories per issue (normally sixteen pages per story). Because of the simple plots revolving around three themes—ghosts, violence, and sex—they are generally regarded as targeting readers with lower socio-economic status. Some of the publishers today are Cartoon Thai, Samdow, Sri-Udomkij-Sermmit, Pandee Sarn, and Sakol. Unlike publishers of Japanese manga or upscale Thai comics, there is usually no information available regarding the publishers of one-baht comics.

## Political Cartoons

While humor comics (and the sensational style for newspapers) have been popular in Thailand since the 1950s, political cartoons, as well as press freedom, were heavily suppressed after Field Marshal Sarit took total control after a coup in 1957. The tense political climate peaked during the mid–1970s. On October 14, 1973, a students' uprising successfully ousted Field Marshal Thanom Kittikachorn and revived the fate of the newspaper industry and political cartoonists. The suddenly-loosened press controls led to the birth of several of today's influential newspapers and the popularity of political cartoonists. Some of today's prominent political cartoonists are Sakda Sae Eow (pen name, Sia) for *Thai Rath* (replacing Prayoon Chanyawongs after his death in 1992); Palungkorn Suradej (pen name, Palungkorn) and Narong Jarungthammachote (pen name, Kuad) for *Daily News*; Sol and Tin (pen names, real names unknown) for *Matichon Daily*; Wallop Manyam (pen name, Wallop) for *Matichon Weekly*; Surapol Pittayasakul (pen name, Pol) and Jae (pen name, real name unknown) for *Khao Sod*; Arun Watcharasawat (pen name, Arun) and Tewat Patarakulwanij (pen name, Mor) for *Krungthep Thurakij*. But the most famous among them is undoubtedly Somchai Katanyutanant (pen name, Chai Rachawat), who draws the oldest and longest-running political strip "Pu Yai Ma Kab Tung Ma Mern" (Headman Ma and the Village of Tung Ma Mern) for the largest newspaper, *Thai Rath*.

Chai[4] had an unusual path that led him to political cartoons. As a boy, he seemed like a perfect prospect to become a political cartoonist, because he had an interest in both politics and drawing cartoons. Every day, he went to a local public library, ripped off the page of Prayoon Chanyawongs' cartoon in *Siam Rath Weekly*, and took it home to copy Prayoon's drawing style (Sukree 2006). However, because his parents did not encourage him to draw—as most artists in those days struggled financially—Chai ended up studying accounting, and became a banker, despite his desires to draw and natural artistic talent. After nine years as a banker, as fate had it, a series of incidents led him to draw a political strip for the newly published, pro-democracy *Maharad* (Great People), while he was still working at the bank. Chai did his strip for free, just to have a drink with his friends after work. After *Maharad* was closed, Chai began drawing a strip titled "Ngew Karn Moeng" (Political Chinese Opera) for *Daily News*, the second biggest daily, which offered him an attractive pay (Chai Rachawat 1997).

At that point, press freedom flourished after the October 14, 1973, incident that forced out Thanom. Like most cartoonists, Chai used this loose political climate as an opportunity to boldly criticize politicians. Unexpectedly, Thanom's return to Thailand culminated in one of the bloodiest coups in modern Thai history on October 6, 1976. Suspected to be a communist sympathizer and, thus, immediately blacklisted from drawing his political strip, Chai opted to draw an illustrated story of *Song Kung*, a Chinese novel about a group of commoners who went into the hills to organize a guerrilla movement against the corrupted government. Even though Chai said he did not intend to convey any underlying implication, the story was too close for comfort for the government, who banned the cartoon, claiming it encouraged people to "go to the jungle" and join the Communist Party. Chai then drew another strip, which he copied from a Western cartoon, showing an animal paw giving directions to the zoo. Incredibly, the government banned his cartoon again, this time charging that he tried to send an encoded message, telling the left-wing activists to meet at the zoo (Chai Rachawat 1997).

Fearing for his safety, Chai quit his bank job, sold his car and belongings, and fled to Los Angeles in 1977, while many of his friends "went to the jungle." Not able to draw cartoons, Chai moved from one job to another, including an artist at a card company, a darkroom worker, a bartender, and an editor at a Thai newspaper in Los Angeles. When General Kriengsak Chamanan successfully toppled the government, many cartoonists were allowed to resume their works. Soon after his seniors at *Daily News* assured him that the situation was safe enough, Chai returned to Thailand after two years in the United States (Chai Rachawat 1997).

This was when he came up with the idea to draw his famous strip "Pu Yai Ma Kub Tung Ma Mern." Inspired by an anti-government piece by the respected Puay Ungpakorn, former president of Thammasat University, Chai created Pu Yai Ma (headman Ma) to represent the inept leaders; Ai Joi to portray poor citizens with not much to wear and skinny from being taken advantage of, and Tao Yoi (Old Yoi) to represent local intellectuals who love political debates (Lent 1997). The village of Tung Ma Mern, which literally means "the field that dogs disdain," symbolizes an abandoned and hopeless area in which even street dogs do not want to live. However, only two months after he rejoined *Daily News*, just when the new strip was receiving favorable attention, an internal problem led to the resignation of many of its staff members, a number of whom were Chai's close friends. During a drink with his senior friend one night, Chai made a pact that "who goes back to work there is a coward,"[5] to show spirit to his colleagues (Chai Rachawat 1999: 141).

Chai was recruited almost immediately by *Thai Rath*, the largest and most powerful daily, where he has continued his famous strip until today. During his twenty-five years working at *Thai Rath*, there was another case of political unrest that stopped him from drawing. Following the bloody incident known as "Black May" in 1992, many newspapers, including *Thai Rath*, practiced self-censorship to avoid being closed down by the authorities, at least until the situation cleared up. Disgusted and knowing that he could not be neutral, Chai decided to discontinue his strip so that it would not affect the well-being of other *Thai Rath* employees. In his May 18, 1992 strip, one day after the shooting began, Chai drew the village of Tung Ma Mern as a wasteland, occupied only by vultures and carcasses, with a description, "One day, there was a severe outbreak in the Village of Tung Ma Mern that came together with a drought. The laughter from the group of Pu Yai Ma and Ai Joi disappeared, along with all the characters"[6] (Chai quoted in Lent 1997: 102). Chai resumed the strip eight days later when the situation returned to normal (Parinya 1994).

Chai is perhaps the cartoonist with the most accolades in Thai history. In 1996, Chai, along with Payut Ngaokrachang, was awarded for his "outstanding cultural work" by the National Culture Committee. In 2000, he received the "Highness Ayumonkol" award for cartoonist, and a few months later, he became the first cartoonist to receive the prestigious "Sri Burapa" award for best writer. However, Chai received perhaps the highest honor a Thai cartoonist can have, when, in 1999, he was selected as the head artist to draw the cartoon version of His Majesty the King Bhumibol (Rama IX)'s novel *Pra Mahajanaka* (The Great Father). Although Chai admitted that it was exhausting, he proudly called it his best work and reward: "I do not need any award after this, because no award could be as prestigious as this one" (Chai Rachawat 1999: 146). In 2004, Chai was selected again as the head artist to draw the cartoon version of another of the King's novels, *Rueng Tongdaeng* (The Story of Tongdaeng).

Chai is still one of the most popular and influential cartoonists in Thailand. His strip, internationally compared to the American "Doonesbury," has been developed into commercials, a live-action film, and a short animated series shown nightly after the news; it has also been a topic of many scholarly research articles and dissertations (Lent 1999b). He is frequently interviewed in the media, invited to judge many cartooning competitions, and teaches the first cartooning course in Thailand at Silpakorn University (Lent 1999b). Nonetheless, he has expressed his weariness of having to do the perilous work of mocking powerful people: "I tried to make heavy political issues lighter for readers so they will not be so depressed. But it turned out that I have made more and more enemies ... many of them called and threatened me"[7] (Prieng 2000: 21). Once asked what he wanted to be if he were to be born again, Chai answered that he would still want to be a cartoonist, but he would want to be born in the U.S. (Thammakiat 2000). Chai dreams that one day he can retire and drive away without a preplanned destination, with one bag of clothes, one bag of golf clubs, and one bag of drawing tools, so that he can stop and make a color painting wherever he sees a beautiful scenery: "No more black and white drawing. I am tired of 'Pu Yai Ma' and 'Ai Joi.' I am so tired of political cartooning that forces me to wake up every morning thinking who I am going to mock today. I just want to throw it all away and finally be myself"[8] (Chai Rachawat 1997: 147).

Just when the political cartoon in Thailand in the early 2000s seemed to be losing its edge and popularity, the political unrest after 2006 provided much fodder for political cartoonists. As with a large number of Thai people, many political cartoonists are divided by those who support former Prime Minister Thaksin Shinnawatra, ousted by a military coup in September 2006 and now living in self-exile in England, and Thaksin's current, allegedly "proxy" prime minister and government, and those in the "anti-Thaksin" camp, who believe Thaksin had been involved with corruption on an enormous scale, and is still controlling the current government to whitewash his wrongdoings. The newspaper that exemplifies this contrast is *Thai Rath*, where two of the most famous political cartoonists, Chai and Sia (Sakda Sae-Eow), work. With a page buffering between their strips, their political views are at polar opposites; Sia belongs in the first group, Chai the second. When asked if this political difference has had any effect on their relationship, since both are co-workers and prominent and active members of the Thai Cartoon Institute, Sia said, "Not at all. But we don't talk about politics" (Chai and Sia, interview, 2008).

This political rift also gave rise to "Kamin and the Gang," whom Chai and Sia both see as a promising core of new generation political cartoonists (Chai and Sia, interview, 2008). For more than twenty years, Kamin and the Gang drew for several publications of the Manager Group, the main force behind the anti–Thaksin rally in 2006 and 2008. The openly impartial stand of their publications gave the cartoonists an excellent opportunity to express their sharp and caustic views almost boundlessly.

Kamin and the Gang started as a duo Bancha-Kamin before their increased popularity and workload required them to expand the team. The leader of the team is Kamin (pen name), an advertising executive who does not reveal his real name publicly (even the secretary at his office does not know about this pen name). Each day, Kamin thinks of the gags before calling the rest of his team to visually translate his ideas, be they strips or the popular sarcastic pictorial article called "Pu Jad Kuan." The current "Gang" is composed of the team's head artist, Bancha Sangtanchai, and Bancha Orndee, "Bug Lam," "Pui," and "Ngao" (Ploen-pit 2006).

## The 1990s: The Beginning of the "Modern" Thai Cartoon Era

During the 1990s, Japanese comics publishers in Thailand faced fierce competition from small publishers that had mushroomed in a few years. To distinguish itself, in 1992, Vibulkij, one of the oldest and biggest Japanese comics publishers, launched *Thai Comics*, the first Thai produced non-humor comic book. Several other Thai comics magazines tried to follow suit, such as *Katch*, *Manga Katch*, *Comic Quest*, *CX*, and *Fusion Comics*, but only *Thai Comics* has lasted. With the high license fees of Japan-originated manga, many publishers of Japanese comics magazines tried to develop their own series, at least one in each issue. Even though the drawings of many younger generation cartoonists were obviously influenced by the Japanese style, many have incorporated Thai culture into their stories (Chulasak 2001a). Examples of Thai series in Japanese comics are "Han Su Pi Narok" (Duel with the Devil) by Chaiyan Suyawej in *A-Comic* and "Meed Tee Sib Sam" (The 13th Dagger) by Nop Witoontong (pen name, Whitecrow) and Booncherd Champrasert (pen name, Ice Hornet) in *Boom Comics*. It is noteworthy that "The 13th Dagger"—a story of the never-ending revenge of a martial arts fighter—has been a huge success, running continuously for more than ten years, almost forty-seven issues, and remaining in print in *Boom Comics* til now. It is not an exaggeration to say that "The 13th Dagger" is one of the most widely-known Thai fantasy cartoons, with more than nine million hits when searched with google.com. The creators are planning to make an animation of the series soon (Meed Tee 13, 2008).

A big break for Thai comics came in 1999, when His Majesty the King Bhumibol (Rama IX) proposed making his long novel *Pra Mahajanaka* (The Great Father) into an inexpensive and easy-to-understand cartoon book. Drawn by a team of veteran cartoonists, led by Chai Rachawat and Ittipol Rajjawej (pen name, Ohm Rajjawej), not only is the King's project the best-selling cartoon book in Thai history with more than two million copies sold, it has also become the 1999 best comic book for children (*Matichon*, December 12, 1999; *Baan Moeng*, December 12, 1999). In 2004, these same artists were asked to convert the King's non-fiction book about his pet dog *The Story of Tongdaeng* into cartoons, which again was hugely popular with estimated sales of more than a million copies.

Another promising movement for Thai cartoonists is the founding of two cartoon organizations. In 1997, the Cartoon Association of Thailand was established with many respectable cartoonists from different genres serving on the board of directors, including Chai Rachawat, Juk Biewsakul (veteran novel illustrator), and Worawut Worawittayanant (editor of *Thai Comics*). One of the official objectives of the association is "To study and research, so that Thai cartooning can make progress" [9] (Kor Moon, n.d.). To help expand the pool of research in cartooning, the association issues a journal once every three months, and created a project that encourages more research and dissertations about Thai cartooning.

In 2003, the Foundation For Children (FFC) established the Cartoonthai Institute to help create constructive cartoons for children, and develop Thai cartooning to become sustainable enough to serve the public (Sataban Cartoon Thai, n.d.). Many members of the Cartoon Association of Thailand also serve as the institute's committee members. The Cartoonthai Institute has since published several cartoon books that are successful both critically and financially.

## The 2000s: Enter the New Generation of Thai Cartoons

Because of the popularity of the cartoon versions of His Majesty the King's novels, *Pra Mahajanaka* and *The Story of Tongdaeng*, Thai cartooning in the 2000s seems to be revived from the doldrums. The Cartoon Association of Thailand and Cartoonthai Institute have held several activities to promote awareness and interest in Thai cartoons, and to encourage new Thai cartoonists. More non-cartoon publishers and media companies are willing to enter the cartoon business and try something new. Thai cartoon publications (excluding political cartoons) can be categorized into two general groups—entertainment-oriented and knowledge. A breakdown of the comics publishing industry follows. (Also see Appendix I.)

### ENTERTAINMENT-ORIENTED CARTOONS

**General Entertainment Comic:** These are comics sold in bookstores to the general public, especially middle-upper class teenagers and young adults, in the forms of periodical magazines or pocket books. The content ranges from action to romantic to fantasy, to name a few. An emerging trend of Thai entertainment cartoons is the publishing of "alternative" comics which have an unrefined, but unique, style of drawing and somewhat philosophical stories. Some are in the form of what publishers call "graphic fiction," books composed of narration and illustrations on each page. Some of the current Thai entertainment cartoon magazines are:

*Thai Comics:* A monthly magazine published since 1993 by Vibulkij Publishing, a major publisher of Japanese comics. It was the first magazine that consisted only of cartoons drawn by Thai cartoonists.

*Let's:* A monthly magazine published since 2004 by Star Pics Publishing, publisher of a movie magazine of the same name, under the supervision of "Let's Gang."

*Mud:* Thailand's latest cartoon magazine published once every three months by Typhoon Books (first issue published in 2008). By positioning itself as a channel for "out of this world" cartoons, *Mud* is a distinct example of Thailand's alternative cartoons.

*I H.A.T.E Cartoon Book:* This "unscheduled" comics magazine was first published in 2008 by Green-Panyayan. It features six comics from the new wave of Thai cartoonists.

In addition to these, some Japanese comics magazines include at least one series of Thai cartoonists. Among them are *Neoz* and *Viva Friday* from Vibulkij Publishing; *C-Kids* from Siam Inter Comics Publishing; and *Boom Comics* from NED (Nation Edutainment, an affiliate of Nation Multimedia Group).

The publishers of Thai entertainment cartoon magazines:

**A Book:** Publisher of magazines and pocket books for middle-upper class teenagers and office workers, A Book's comics are not known for their delicate drawings, but for sophisticated and unique storytelling. Songseen Tewsomboon, a former illustrator for A Book's non-comic magazine, emerged as one of the top Thai cartoonists, after the huge success of his graphic fiction *Beansprout and Firehead: In the Infinite Madness* which has recently been published for the seventh time. Cartoonthai Institute calls Songseen "the idol of the new generation of Thai cartoonists" (Cartoonthai Institute 2008).

**Cartoonthai Institute:** An affiliate of Foundation for Children, the Cartoonthai Institute initially published cartoons for young children, and has won several national awards. Recently, it has published more cartoons that attract adolescents, many of which also won national awards. As a result, many artists, such as Ittitwat Suriyamart and Weerachai Duangpala (pen name, The Duang), have become wider-known to readers and received job offers from other publishers.

**Vibulkij Publishing:** The publisher of *Thai Comics*, Vibulkij has spun off several popular series from *Thai Comics* as pocket books. Among many Thai professional cartoonists whose works first appeared in *Thai Comics*, and later became well-known for their series, are Chaiyan Suyawej (pen name, Tapone) and Eakasit Thairat.

**Typhoon Books:** Established in 2005 by Prabda Yoon, the son of Suttichai Yoon, top executive officer of The Nation Group, which publishes the English daily newspaper *The Nation*, and the Thai daily *Kom Chud Luek*, plus several other publishing-related enterprises. Typhoon Books is the pioneer in publication of "alternative" content aimed toward middle-upper class, educated, and art-loving readers. Its most popular artist, Wisut Pornnimitr, is exemplary of the alternative style of Thai cartooning with his series *hesheit* (he-she-it), incorporating untidy, childlike drawing style and unstructured, little or no dialog storytelling. In 2004, Wisut went to Japan to study Japanese and expand his cartooning skills, and within a year, his work *everybodyeverything* was released by a Japanese publisher. Wisut still lives and works in Kobe, Japan, where he has plenty of job opportunities, including several books already published, animation work for commercials and mobile phone, illustrations for CD covers and novels, and a long series of his own in the monthly comics magazine *Ikki*. He has also been named by *Elle Japan* as one of the world's 250 most interesting people to watch (Wisut Pornnimitr, n.d.).

**Bongkoch Publishing:** A major publisher of Japanese comics for female readers, Bongkoch, in 2003, started to publish the monthly *Comic Club*, a magazine with both Japanese and Thai cartoons. By August 2008, it was already in its fifty-seventh issue. About ten *Comic Club* series have been turned into pocket books. In 2008, Bongkoch launched two comic books—*Comic Club Fantasy Red* and *Comic Club Fantasy Blue*—each of which consists of short cartoon stories, all created by Thai female cartoonists. Some of *Comic Club* regular artists include Kanda Wangdee, Kanitha Boonyathasaneekul, Thanikarn Khemakongkanont, and Neeracha Sinchai.

**Burapat Comics Publications:** An affiliate of the Manager Group, which publishes *Manager Daily* and operates the highly influential Manager.co.th Website, which along with the cable television ASTV, are the main mass media for the anti–Thaksin camp. Burapat's main comics publications are cartoons from Hong Kong and China, but since 2000, the company has published eight Thai long series. In the last three years, only one such series appeared.

**Humor Comics** (e.g., *Kai Hua Roh* and other publications from Banlue Sarn): Sold to mass readers, mainly lower to middle class of various age ranges, from high school students to office workers, depending on the theme of each comic.

**Graphic Novels (Five-Baht Cartoon):** Sold at newsstands in markets, bus or train stations, with lower class readers as main target. Some of the publishers today are Cartoon Thai, Samdow, Sri-Udomkij-Sermmit, Pandee Sarn, and Sakol.

## KNOWLEDGE CARTOONS

This type of cartoon aims to provide information to young readers in areas such as history, general knowledge, and Thai culture. Three main publishers of this category are:

**E.Q. Plus Publishing**: Established in 2004, E.Q. Plus has become the major publisher of cartoon version biographies of Thai and international historical figures. E.Q. Plus has recently expanded to include cartoons based loosely on historical figures, which are published by its affiliate Cleanative.

**Sky Books Publishing**: Publisher of several comic books that are adapted from Thai classical novels such as *Pra Apaimanee, Krai Tong*, and cartoons with a Buddhist theme, such as Buddhist fables and the life of Buddha.

**Action Frame Kids:** An affiliate of Burapat Comics Publications, it has been publishing cartoon versions of the lives of Thai and Asian historical figures, including several prominent respected Buddhist monks, since 2006.

## The Future of Thai Cartooning: In the Hands of Readers or Cartoonists?

Thai cartooning has great potential to grow, and actually has been doing well since the 2000s, evidenced by the increasing number of publishers and comics publications. Importantly, the increase is not limited to only one genre; types of Thai comics have expanded slowly but steadily since the late 1990s. In the past, Thai cartooning had always been the "me-too" industry, where publishers followed suit after the success of a genre: one-baht in the 1970s, superhero in the late 1950s, and children's comics in the 1970s–80s. Thai cartooning in the 2000s is more diverse regarding the genres than at any other period, as the categories and sub-categories of Thai comics listed in the above section suggest. Also, the increased number of comics publishers should provide sufficient job opportunities for cartoonists, and this is before considering a rapidly expanding animation industry in Thailand.

On the question of which side—the readers or the cartoonists—is more responsible for ensuring that the potential of Thai cartooning is realized, opinions differ.

Sakda Sae Eow (Sia Thai Rath), current chairman of the Thai Cartoon Association, estimated in 2007, that of the one billion baht (about U.S. $29 million) comic book market in Thailand, less than 10 percent belongs to Thai comics. He attributed this to a lack of industry-like production from both the publishers and the cartoonists. Thus, publishers need to do better marketing to ensure artists continued job opportunities, and thus expanding the pool of new cartoonists. More importantly, Thai readers must improve their attitude toward Thai cartoons (*Manager Online*, April 4, 2007). This opinion is reflected by Wirat Teekaputtisakul, editor of Siam Inter Multimedia, publisher of *C-Kids* magazine, who said Thai comics are not sufficiently appreciated by Thai audiences, although the situation has improved somewhat from the past (*Business Thai*, April 15, 2004).

Suranit Jumsai na Ayutthaya, managing director of E.Q. Plus, the publisher of knowledge cartoons, said Thai people "adore heroes, but don't like to invest in making them," meaning that Thai people lavish adulation on successful individuals only after their achievements, whether they are athletes or cartoonists, but are not very interested in supporting or encouraging those individuals while they struggle along the way to fame. On the other hand, Suranit also mentioned that it is important for cartoonists, especially young ones, to be level-headed and keep their egos in check. He ensured that cartoonists on his payroll can make rather steady income at a desirable rate if they keep producing their works. However, he said some of his cartoonists have been unhappy, feeling that drawing knowledge cartoons was not as admirable as developing their own entertainment series (Suranit, interview, 2008).

Other key people in the comics business see the bigger obstacle to be the cartoonists. Worawut Worawitayanont, executive editor of Vibulkij Publishing, said that both the acceptance and fan base of Thai comics has improved from sixteen years ago when the first issue of *Thai Comics* was launched. However, he sees the big hindrance for Thai cartoonists to be their lack of discipline to manage their income and their lack of understanding of the business and marketing sides of their jobs (Worawut, interview, 2008).

Similarly, Poomchai Boonsinsook, editor-in-chief of A Book, calls this present era of Thai cartooning "lively" and believes that the cartoonists who have "made it" in the business (having their work published or having become professional cartoonists) earn enough to not have to hold other jobs. Poomchai sees that the market has continued to expand, as have the channels for new cartoonists to have their work showcased. The obstacle in his view is not the readers, but the cartoonists themselves, many of whom fail to practice and improve, not only their drawing skills, but more importantly, those of storytelling. Poomchai explained that his most famous artist, Songseen Tewsomboon, became successful because he understood three things better than most cartoonists: the market, the target, and himself (Poomchai, interview, 2008). Sudjai Promkerd, general manager of the Cartoonthai Institute, who helped develop and polish several Thai cartoonists, agreed with this opinion—that the main shortcoming of Thai cartoonists is their storytelling technique (Sudjai, interview, 2008).

## Conclusion

Thai cartooning was off to a flying start that seemed to have a very promising future with the royal support of King Rama VI, who had a special interest in cartoons. This positive trend continued even after absolute monarchy ended in 1932, with the emergence of several influential artists, including Hem Vejakorn. However, the situation had become an "uphill climb" for Thai cartoonists, as Lent (1997) argues, when authoritarian governments under military regimes took control of the country. Oppressive politics in Thailand also led cartoonists to avoid being critical and to focus more on non-political humor. Banlue Sarn's success is a prime example of benefiting from the humor-oriented direction of Thai cartooning. But, for others, especially political cartoonists, life has been a constant struggle. As influential and successful as he is, Chai has faced (and still faces) several kinds of pressures that bar him from expressing his opinion and that make him tired of his profession. Other cartoonists, mostly part-timers or freelancers, did not have many options either. Even with the despotic government no longer in control, Thai cartooning already had been ignored so long that most Thai readers, especially the younger generations, had lost interest. With Japanese manga owning the market, leaving low demand for Thai comics, and consequently, awfully poor wages for Thai artists, the "uphill climb" for Thai cartooning after the 1970s seemed to be a journey too steep for many cartoonists. Even though *Thai Comics* withstood the difficulties and lasted, many seemingly promising Thai comics publications, such as *Katch, Manga Katch, Comic Quest, CX*, and *Fusion Comics*, folded.

Fortunately, the situation began to turn around after the late 1990s. The cartoon version of the King's novel *Pra Mahajanaka* has had a positive trickle-down effect on the fate of Thai cartooning, leading to the rebirth of locally produced comic books, and especially animation. This has brought renewed hope to many veteran cartoonists who see Thai cartooning finally reach a plateau after a long "uphill climb."

Because there are more publishers and channels for their works, the new generation of Thai cartoonists has been able to find jobs that pay sufficiently to qualify as full-time employment. A few young Thai cartoonists have risen to be prominent authors in a relatively short time, with their own comics in bookstores nationwide, handsome compensation plus proportional payment from sales volume, and possibly possession of copyrights to their works. All of this had been unprecedented in Thailand. However, as some of the publishers have said, it is unwise for Thai cartoonists to be content with their good fortune, or to think that this is the final destination, as Thai cartooning apparently has not reached the summit. The fact that only 10 percent of the comics market in Thailand is Thai, reflects the virtually limitless potential of the Thai cartooning industry to grow. On the other hand, it indicates that the plateau Thai cartooning has reached is, in fact, not very high above the ground, and a long way to the summit.

The major sources of difficulty in the expansion of Thai cartooning seem to come from the readers and cartoonists. The lack of reader interest in Thai comics is not insurmountable, or even unexpected. The unwillingness of the mass audience to support unfamiliar (or substandard by their judgment) Thai comics is only natural in the age of global media, with many choices from which to pick. A majority of Thai readers of this generation grew up reading Japanese manga; as a result, they compare what Thai comics lack with what Japanese manga have. This negative perception of Thai comics will continue to lessen as they gradually catch up with manga, and as the new generation of readers becomes accustomed to Thai comics. The perception of Thai comics will ultimately not be a factor once readers no longer think whether they are reading a Thai or Japanese comic book, but rather, whether it is a well-written or poorly written story.

Therefore, it is of the utmost importance that Thai cartoonists continue to improve their skills, especially those of storytelling. Several key people in Thai cartooning expressed their concerns about the lack of compelling or coherent plots, which they considered the main reason, not the unimpressive drawing, that makes readers shy away from Thai comics. All interviewees for this chapter also agreed that a good Thai comic book does not need to include Thai traditional art, nor does it have to be based on Thai folktales, history, or classical novels. Not one interviewee could define the "Thai cartoon drawing style," as there is not a single style that represents Thai cartoons or comics. The consensus points toward defining a Thai cartoon as simply "a cartoon that is created by a Thai artist." Therefore, Thai cartoonists need to unbind themselves from the cultural factors and start with an attractive, attention-capturing storyline, whether it be a love story or Thai history.

Finally, Thai cartoonists need to realize that the future of Thai cartooning lies heavily on their works. The market and publishers have opened up as they never have previously, a hard-earned achievement of Thai cartoonists of previous generations. By describing how the pioneers of Thai cartooning have struggled to create their works, despite the grave difficulty they had to confront, the author hopes to have shown, that the toil of Thai readers and cartoonists has not been wasted, but helped blaze the trail for artists of later generations. Now that Thai cartooning seems to have reached a plateau, it is up to today's cartoonists to decide whether Thai cartooning is to stay idle here, or continue to the summit.

# Appendix I: Profiles of Thai Cartoon Publications and Publishers

## A BOOK

A Book is a Thai up-and-coming publishing company. After being successful with books and magazines geared toward middle-upper class high school and college students, A Book started to expand its market share with graphic fiction. One of its first publications, and apparently its most successful, is *Beansprout & Firehead: In the Infinite Madness* by Songseen Tewsomboon, first published in 2005 and, by June 2008, already reprinted for the seventh time. This work has made a star out of Songseen, who used to draw for other A Book's non-comics magazines. Since then, A Book has slowly, but steadily, continued to produce a few other graphic fiction works, including *Nine Lives* and *Improvise* by Songseen, *Kwam Suk Kong Mali* (The Happiness of Mali) and *Going Places* by "Tong Karn" (pen name), and *Roop Roop Kum Kum* (Pictures, Pictures, Words, Words) by Pang (illustration) and Buarai (story). In March 2008, A Book launched *ABC Comic Volume 1: Seven Deadly Sins*, which is a collection of seven graphic fiction works written by its artists. With a circulation of ten thousand—relatively high for Thai cartoons— Poomchai Boonsinsook, A Book's editor-in-chief, confirmed that it was "very well-received" (Poomchai, interview, 2008).

## CARTOONTHAI INSTITUTE: FOUNDATION FOR CHILDREN

Cartoonthai Institute was founded in 2003 as part of the Foundation for Children (FFC) that is responsible for the promotion of Thai cartoons in creative and constructive ways to serve Thai society. Its stated three missions are Academic: To collect, study, research, promote, disseminate, and develop the body of knowledge related to comic arts through various activities; Network: To create a network of cartoonists and cartoon organizations; Production: To promote, disseminate, and produce quality cartoons; to advocate for cartoonists' copyright; and to provide opportunities to the new generation of cartoonists (Sataban Cartoon Thai, n.d.).

The key person behind the birth of the institute is Ms. Sudjai Promkerd, who has been serving as the manager since its beginning. Sudjai had been working for the Foundation for Children and, in 2001, was responsible for producing the cartoon version of the biography of the respected statesman Pridi Banomyong on the one hundredth anniversary of his death. When that cartoon won a top government award, Sudjai pushed the Foundation for Children to develop a unit exclusively about cartoons. That plea became a reality in 2003 with the cooperation of several Thai prominent cartoonists serving as committee members, including Somchai Katanyutanan (Chai Rachawat), Surapol Pitayasakul (Pol Kaosod), Om Rajawej, and Sakda Sae Eow (Sia Thairath). Its first publication in 2003—the cartoon version of the October 14, 1973 incident (in which mass demonstration of university students led to the ousting of the military authoritarian government), won an honorable mention from the national "Book of the Year" award. The institute's publications won several awards since then, including four honorable mentions and two first prizes in the "cartoon or picture novel" category from the national "Book of the Year" award.

While Cartoonthai Institute has produced a number of cartoons for children, it has recently been publishing more cartoons for teenagers and young adults, with their content still void of violence or sex. Most of these cartoons are sold in chain bookstores nationwide under the novel categories, and many of them have won awards and/or been republished. This gives excellent opportunities for the new generation of cartoonists to hone their skills and get their names noticed by other publishers. Some of the cartoonists who got their first publication with Cartoonthai have now published with other publishers. Among them are Ittiwat Suriyamart, Weerachai Duangpala (pen name, "The Duang"), and Tripuck Supawattana (pen name, Puck).

Sudjai, herself a writer of several Cartoonthai books, believes the future of Thai cartoon will be brighter, as the companies get bigger, the production system gradually changes into one of teamwork, and as more adults longing for their past turn to reading cartoons. She said two of the biggest obstacles of Thai cartoonists are their storytelling technique and work discipline. There is enough work, Sudjai believes, for Thai cartoonists to make a good and steady income if they keep producing. She said the institute is pushing to set the 10 percent share of sales revenue a standard copyright practice in Thailand. On a bigger scale, the institute plans to have a workshop for cartoonists from ASEAN (Southeast Asia) nations (Sudjai, interview, 2008).

## E.Q. Plus

E.Q. Plus Publishing, a major publisher of Thai knowledge cartoons, was founded in 2004 under the leadership of Suranit Jumsai na Ayutthaya, the company's managing director. After having to fold his Thai cartoon magazine *Comic Quest* after four years, Suranit had an idea of making a knowledge cartoons series. He and his staff decided that the first series should be about Thai history. The result was a successful comics, *King Naresuan the Great*, which became the best seller of the series and has been reprinted several times. Consequently, E.Q.

Plus has expanded its cartoon collection into world history (e.g., Cleopatra, David Livingstone), classic novels (e.g., Alice in Wonderland, Dr. Jekyll & Mr. Hyde), folktales and myths (e.g., mermaids, centaurs, the legend of Camelot), science knowledge (e.g., global warming, the dark side of the Internet), and also entertainment-oriented cartoons under different associated publishing companies.

E.Q. Plus is now the biggest knowledge cartoon publisher in Thailand in terms of sales volume. However, Suranit estimated that knowledge cartoons only contribute to about 10 percent of the whole cartoon market in Thailand. Out of that 10 percent, Thai knowledge cartoons only occupy 40 percent, the rest belonging to Korean knowledge cartoons, and about 5 percent from Japan.

E.Q. Plus seems to have a systematic means of producing its cartoons. For each book, the production team of three to five is divided into the academic team who does the research and checks the veracity of the story with historians, and the art team who does the drawing. It should be noted that none of EQ Plus knowledge cartoons shows either the authors or the artists on the cover. Suranit also said that, unlike most publishers, the artists at E.Q. Plus are considered full-time employees, and each has an agreement with the company to not work for other publishers (Suranit, interview, 2008).

## LET'S MAGAZINE

*Let's Magazine* was founded in 2004 by a group of freshmen at the Department of Communication Art, King Mongkut Institute of Technology Ladkrabang, who called themselves "Let's Gang." The leader of the group is Tanyaluck Trechasreesutee, whose family's business is publishing a movie magazine, *Star Pics* (which is also the official publisher of the magazine), who is currently serving as the magazine's executive editor. With the publishing capacity as a backup, the magazine was started as a hobby and channel for Tanyaluck, who, as a high school student, regularly sent his works to Thai cartoon magazines and his friends to hone their skills. Payment for staff members was a free meal. After the first issue was launched, Let's Gang was hired to draw the cartoon version of a best seller biography of Wongtanong Chainarongsingha, the founder of A Book Publishing (a major publisher of graphic novels). As a result, the name Let's Gang became known among cartoon readers (Tanyaluck, interview, 2008).

At present, *Let's* is a monthly cartoon magazine, consisting of six regular series, plus feature articles and columns. Although *Let's* has not published many issues, observers of the Thai cartoon industry see a bright future for the magazine, because of the publishing capacity of the company and dedicated staff.

## THAI COMICS

*Thai Comics*, Thailand's first cartoon magazine composed of cartoons drawn only by Thai cartoonists, was first published in 1993 by Vibulkij Publishing Co., Ltd., a major publisher of manga in Thailand. Vibulkij's Editor-in-chief Worawut Worawitayanont estimated that after more than 200 issues in sixteen years, *Thai Comics* has produced more than thirty Thai cartoonists and seventy to eighty Thai cartoon series. Some of the most famous Thai cartoonists or series got their starts at *Thai Comics*, such as, Chaiyant Suyawej (pen name, "Tapone"), who went on to create several hit series such as *Lookmai* (Tricks), *Takraw*, *Han Soo Pi Narok* (Devil Fighter), and *Yan Man*; Eakasit Thairat, whose short cartoon story "*The 13 Quiz Show*" was made into a critically acclaimed feature length film called "13 Beloved"; Taweesak Wiriyawaranont, who made a name for himself with his two series *Dekja Hansa Gun Noi* (Have Fun, Children) and *Khun Suek Pu Pitak* (The Protector Knight); and *Gang Za Kata Saab* (The Mischievous Gang) Part 1 and 2, both of which have been made into mobile java games, and represent the first RPG mobile game created solely by Thai programmers.

*Thai Comics* is now a monthly cartoon magazine with about ten series per issue, all written by Thai cartoonists. Worawut revealed that through sixteen years, the sales have always been moderate—not exactly a profitable business, although some profit can be gained from individual series. However, he maintained that it was his and his company's main purpose to use *Thai Comics* as another channel for Thai cartoonists to create their works (Worawut, interview, 2008).

## NOTES

1. Author's translation.
2. I assume that "amateur" meant anyone who was not a royal artist, since there was not a professional artist at that time.
3. Any cartoonist discussed in this paper might have at some point done works with other publications than the ones mentioned.

4. Because he is better known as Chai Rachawat, I opt to call him by his pen name.
5. Author's translation.
6. Author's translation.
7. Author's translation.
8. Author's translation.
9. Author's translation.

**4**

# The Swerving Status of Cambodian Comic Art

## JOHN A. LENT

Like other parts of Southeast Asia, Cambodia's history of visual humor and narrative reaches back centuries, in this case, through Angkor Wat paintings traceable to 800; its heyday of contemporary comic art is of the recent past, and its spirited attempt to revive the medium now is in the hands of a few cartoonists and aficionados. Strikingly different relative to Indonesia, the Philippines, and Thailand is the late start-up date of Cambodian comic books in the mid–1960s.

## Political Cartoons

Cambodian political cartoons preceded the comic books, having begun shortly after the birth of the first Khmer-language newspaper, *Nagara Vatta,* in 1936 (Soth and Sin 1982). They, along with satire generally, became prominent in the 1960s in magazines directed by Norodom Sihanouk, former king and the head of state (Marston 1997: 60), namely, *Phseng-phseng, Kambuja,* and *Le Sangkum.* The monthly *Phseng-phseng* had a circulation twice that of any other Cambodian periodical. The other two monthlies were meant for a foreign readership after Sihanouk took Cambodia in a direction away from the United States. Huy Hem, Nhek Dim, and Khut Khun were the magazines' featured cartoonists, their works mingling with an array of foreign cartoons that supported Sihanouk's foreign policy. Marston (1997: 61) said Sihanouk's favoring of political cartoons was a logical extension of his personal style and the character traits he identified with, such as wit, sophistication, and irreverence toward world powers.... The Cambodian artists' work seemed intended to convey the message that Cambodia had wit and sophistication comparable to that of other nations, just as it suggested that Sihanouk's policies were those of someone of wit and sophistication.

The cartoons also served to offset American cartoons opposed to Sihanouk, a few of which were described by *Kambuja* as reminiscent of the "Nazi Propagandastaeffel between 1940 and 1945" (*Kambuja* 1965: 89, quoted in Marston 1997: 61). After Sihanouk was deposed in a 1970 coup, the works of Huy Hem and Nhek Dim disappeared from newspapers and magazines. In fact, the newspapers no longer carried many political cartoons, and what were used, ceased to be hard-hitting or particularly sophisticated.

During 1970–75, when the Khmer Republic was in effect, cartooning thrived, with Sunday editions of *Nokor Thom*, adorned with full-sized front covers of satirical cartoons; their popularity led to increased use of cartoons in other newspapers. Marston (1997: 61) identified the two most important cartoonists of this time as Ung Bunheang for *Nokom Thom*, and Hul Sophon for *Koh Sântepheap*. Ung Bunheang, still a university student, was especially adept at drawing large panoramic cartoons, while the older Hul Sophon rendered cartoons in a "dark and mythic style" (Marston 1997: 61). Under the 1975–79 Democratic Kampuchea (Pol Pot's reign of terror), cartoons ceased to exist in the very few newspapers permitted.

A haven for cartoons in the subsequent People's Republic of Kampuchea (1979–89) was *Kampuchea*, widely distributed mainly through the workplaces; except for the years 1987–89, *Kampuchea* published the government's socialist line. This was understandable because in its first months, the newspaper depended on Vietnam (whose troops defeated the Khmer Rouge) for printing, editorials, and advisors. Gradually, *Kampuchea* became more Cambodian, more open, and an important training ground for future generations of journalists. It also developed its distinctive style of cartoons, drawn largely by Im Sokha, who joined the newspaper staff in 1981. Initially, he drew illustrations for serialized fiction; his first satirical cartoons appeared in 1987.

Unusual about cartoons in the late 1980s was that they were drawn and submitted by readers or they were ideas from readers drawn by Im

Sokha (see Marston 1996; Chongkitthawon 1990). Im Sokha even described himself as an "illustrator who gives form to other people's idea for hire" (Marston 1997: 62). The cartoons, according to Marston (1997: 64), had

> some claim to being the discourse of the mass readership, framed with reference to the elite discourse of the paper as a whole. These cartoons were never truly political and did not criticize specific political issues or state pol-

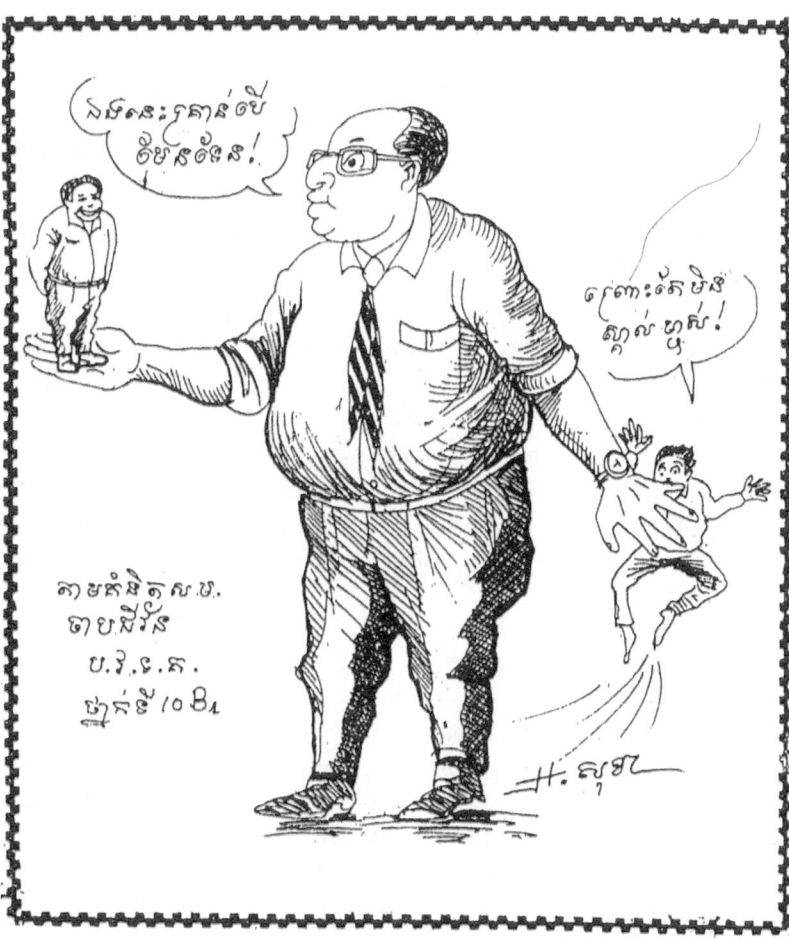

Im Sokha, *Kampuchea*, November 11, 1989. The cartoon represents the artist's uncluttered style at that time and pokes fun at hierarchy and clientism (courtesy John Marston).

icy.... Em [*sic*] Sokha's cartoon style, developed in this period from a somewhat stilted realism to light, uncluttered sketches serving their satirical points efficiently; part of the wit derived from the impression that the cartoons were drawn quickly and effortlessly.

Writing in January 1990, the bureau chief of Thailand's *The Nation* said "anything goes" relative to *Kampuchea*'s cartoons, but he qualified his comment, saying that none of the nation's six newspapers, including *Kampuchea*, ever ran cartoons critical of "the Cambodian leadership or their special relationship with Hanoi" and the Communist Party (Chongkitthawon 1990). He explained:

> Observers said that there is a thin line dividing between what the authorities would tolerate and what they wouldn't. Each political cartoonist instinctively knows how far he and his cartoons can go....
> They also refrain from attacking high-level officials suspected of involving in corruption. But they frequently hammer on corruption by low-ranking officials [Chongkitthawon 1990].

Favorite individual targets of these small (usually four-page) newspapers were Pol Pot for his murderous rampage in the 1970s and Prince Norodom Sihanouk for his role as resistance leader. Top societal topics were modernity and its impact on Cambodian people and their lifestyles, delayed payment of government employees, and dodging military service by wealthier men. Most of *Kampuchea*'s cartoons in 1989, according to Chongkitthawon (1990), "stressed the disparity of the haves and have-nots, the uneven development of the cities and the rural towns, the indifference of government officials toward public problems, and chronic red tape in government offices."

*Kampuchea*'s fate as a vehicle of political cartoons changed with the paper's new editorship in May 1990. Gone were readers' cartoons or their satirical ideas, and although Im Sokha grew in stature as a political cartoonist, his work closely followed government policies and became more doctrinaire. As Marston (1997: 66) wrote, it was during this time that Im Sokha began to caricature Sihanouk and other political leaders of the opposition and was "called upon to make visual references to the brutality of the Khmer Rouge [and] to colour his work with a dark, sinister quality, characteristic of his work in other contexts."

The nation changed still again between 1989 and 1993. Constitutional reforms occurred in 1989 at the same time the country underwent another name change to State of Cambodia. Peace negotiations began subsequent to the United Nations' monitored free elections in 1993. With relaxation of some restrictions on freedom of expression, independent newspapers sprouted, and with them, a number of political cartoons. Dodd (1993) reported in July 1993, that newspaper cartoonists were having a "field day—lampooning corrupt politicians, girl-crazy U.N. peacekeepers and even the once-feared Khmer Rouge." The country's co-presidents, opposition leaders, and former Vietnam-installed "corrupt and fat" ministers, all were presented in unflattering caricatures (Dodd 1993). Newspapers were "much more explicitly political" than in the freest days of *Kampuchea*.

Im Sokha freelanced for these post-election newspapers, including *Sântepheap* (Peace), where his cartoons took up the full front and back covers, partly to attract newsstand customers. For a while, he lived in Bangkok, employed by *Reasmey Kampuchea* (Cambodian Rays of Light), a Khmer-language newspaper funded by a Thai media company. Marston (1997: 69) recalled being told that another cartoonist who replaced him on *Sântepheap* was "tracing heads from Em [*sic*] Sokha's caricatures onto his own pictures." Im Sokha remained very productive, doing cartoons simultaneously for competing newspapers, always with high quality. He told Marston (1997: 70) that he achieved this by following the editors' instructions; basically, he illustrated their ideas. Most Im Sokha cartoons dealt with domestic issues and relied on traditional Khmer iconography.

The importance of political cartoons and Im Sokha in the post-election period was summarized as

> given the conspicuous position political cartoons were given on the front pages of the newspapers, and that a four-page newspaper might also have one or two illustrations by Em [*sic*] Sokha accompanying serialized fiction on the inside pages, the impact of his graphic style upon journalism was unmistakable [Marston 1997: 70].

Rather quickly, the tide for political cartoons changed. By the mid–1990s, according to Marston (1997: 73), there were many fewer cartoons, virtually none on front pages, and newer cartoons "avoided the degree of stylized distortion which had been common in the past." He concluded that political cartoons had ceased to be an "active strategy in the negotiation of public discourse."

Political cartoons (and other forms of comic art) were nearly nonexistent in three major Khmer-language and two English-language dailies I scanned during the latter part of June 2010. The dailies were very bland artistically; they did not carry domestic or foreign comic strips, nor any illustrations of stories. All dailies had substantial numbers of pages with enough space to accommodate cartoons. In fact, only *Kampuchea Thmey Daily* published locally-drawn political cartoons, usually two daily, most often at the bottoms of the same pages. They were two- or three-columns wide, in the same rough style, and on domestic situations. Neither *Rasmei Kampuchea Daily Newspaper* nor *Koh Sântepheap* used any form of cartoon. The English-language tabloid dailies did not fare any better. *Phnom Penh Post* had two syndicated gag cartoons, and *The Cambodian Daily*, a United States political cartoon by Tom Toles.

## Comic Books

The origin of Cambodian comic books usually is traced to the 1960s. Uth Roeun claims to have created the first comic book in 1963 which was published a year later. He could not recall the title, but did

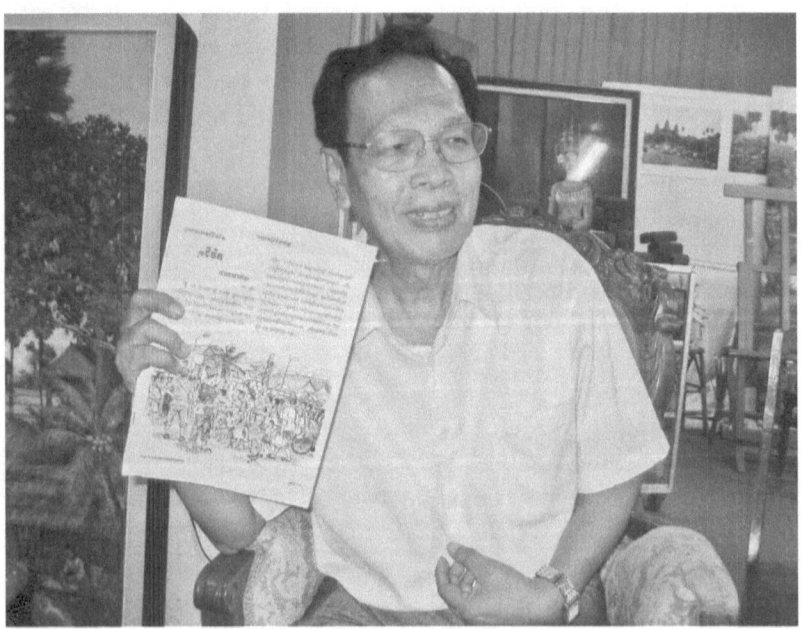

**Uth Roeun, Phnom Penh office, June 23, 2010 (photograph by Xu Ying).**

identify one he did in 1964, *Preah Thoung Neang Neak*, that probably changed his life. Uth Roeun (interview, 2010) said,

> The content was about Muslims [at a time that Sihanouk was trying to unify the country by promoting respect and acceptance of all ethnic and religious groups]. The police interrogated me, arrested me, and detained me for a day. In the process, I missed an exam at school because I did not have time to study. So, I quit my studies and drew fulltime. This was in 1964, June or July.

Uth Roeun said his first comic book was very popular; 20,000 copies were printed and he was paid 4,000 riel [U.S. $400 in currency exchange rate then; equivalent to U.S. $2,000 today]. Throughout the 1960s, he and the few other comic artists were paid 2,000 to 4,000 riel per book. "I was very excited I could make 2,000 riel on a book and spent the money on drawing supplies and books so that I could do a second or third comic" (Uth Roeun, interview, 2010).

His early comics drawings were more realistic than "cartooney," he said, adding that "other artists drew temples [of Angkor Wat], not comics" as he did. Uth Roeun (interview, 2010) said Hul Sophon was the other artist drawing comics but that he only drew covers. However, Uth Roeun also did covers just as Hul Sophon drew inside pages, evidence of the latter were his 1980s' comics (Weeks, interview, 2010). Uth Roeun has said he tried to create Cambodian-style comic books, translating the "people and landscape of Cambodia into the visual language of comics" (Nguyen 2010). When I asked him about his "Cambodian style," he took out a sheet of paper and scrawled a Western cowboy-like figure shooting a Cambodian-garbed person, against a background of local landscape (Uth Roeun, interview, 2010). It appeared to be bande dessineé style converted to Cambodian by the depictions of characters, backgrounds, and language. The only reason he remembered for his pioneering in comics was that he wanted Cambodia to experience this medium, as he had earlier when he read French bande dessineé.

Uth Roeun quit drawing comics before the onset of the Khmer Rouge period. He said:

> The Khmer Rouge forced me to draw, to draw plans for them. I had been conscripted as a soldier during the Lon Nol times. I had no other choice. I was not able to draw comics then. The Pol Pot government asked me my background. I said I was an artist. The government said you are an artist, then you must draw. There was no money paid, just food given. I drew pic-

tures for the Khmer Rouge. If they were building a dam, I did the drawing of it. My fingers were red from exerting myself while drawing for the Pol Pot regime. Because I had a problem with my leg, I served by drawing soldiers, Khmer Rouge plans. I was too skinny to work in the rice fields; I was very thin and could not do hard, physical work. But I could tell stories, legends, in pictures [Uth Roeun, interview, 2010].

During my interview with him, Uth Roeun brought out a partially-illustrated manuscript about his Pol Pot days that he hopes to finish and publish for the French and overseas markets.

The earliest surviving Uth Roeun comic book is *One Night for You*, printed in 1966. He subsequently created about forty comic books (Nguyen 2010). Others of the 1960s and early 1970s that survive and were later reprinted were adaptations of classical stories such as the twelve-volume, uncredited *Reamker Part 5*; comedy, an example being Chuon Ra's *Mr. Soy Visits Heaven*; romance; and drama. The 1960s–70s comics were screen printed in A5 format, with color covers and black-and-white interiors. Weeks (n.d.) felt authors could make a reputation for themselves, receive credit for their work, and perhaps for the only time in Cambodian comics history, make a living wage from drawing comics.

The Khmer Rouge era was definitely not conducive to publishing comic books. The little publishing of any sort that was done was propagandistic; artists themselves were not available, most singled out for harassment and punishment in the prevailing, anti-intellectual atmosphere.

The socialist decade (1979–89) that followed yielded a number of comics, although early in that decade, producing comics or any printed materials was a challenge, because resources were in short supply. In some cases, hand-written novels were rented and copied, and at least in the case of Sin Yang Pirom, the novels she wrote and illustrated became comics (Weeks, n.d.).

As the public craved more entertainment in the latter half of the 1980s, humorous and traditional stories were increasingly told in comic books. Marston (1997: 76) remembered:

While some of these were government-produced and many have provided the prototype for the others, most were independently produced, and probably among the first independently produced publications to come out as socialism began loosening. These comic books were for sale in the markets and seemed very popular during my first visits to Cambodia in 1989 and 1990. However, I did not see them in Cambodia after 1992.

Uth Roeun was prominent in this renewal of a comics tradition with his adaptations of the classic *Torn Chey* (1985, Ministry of Culture), the story of a boy trickster who matches wits with feudal authority and the romance *Tum Teav* (1986, Ministry of Culture), and an original story featuring a soldier, *New Life in Kompong Preah* (1986, Ministry of Culture). After *Torn Chey*, other artists availed themselves of Ministry of Culture financing and publication because of very limited printing facilities. Included were Im Sokha with the horror story *Snae Neang Klaa* (Romance of the Tiger Lady) and Em Satya with the legend, *Sovannasam*. Two other creators who stood out in the 1980s were Sin Yang Pirom, who wrote romance novels (usually in the evening after her day's work in her commune council), and Or Yuthea, known for his romance and drama titles, one of which was *Manaet Star* (Weeks 2011:8).

Besides those of romance, horror, legend, and drama, another genre of the 1980s and 1990s was based on song lyrics. Examples were *Kompong Thom Chamrong Chet* (Kompong Thom Is Where My Heart Resides) and *Lueq Srae, Choul Bar* (Sell My Rice Field and Go to the Bar). In each case, the comic book's plot was based on a popular song of the same title; a lyrics page was included. Weeks (interview, 2010) gave another example of a comic book that ended with the lyrics of Sin Samauth, whom he called the "Elvis of Cambodia."

All of the comics were non-controversial, even omitting mythic and religious imagery as proscribed by the government. Weeks (2011:8) described the comics as "escapist…, depicting fashions unavailable in local stores as well as lifestyles and situations often well beyond the average income." As for production of comic books in that era, Weeks (2011:8–9) said,

> After an initial printing, comics were often sold to a secondary printer or "middleman" (an average price might be $300 USD). This was generally considered to be a transfer of ownership of the work, as Cambodian copyright law was in its infancy. Some artists have disputed they ever gave up the rights to their work. Some classic comics continue to be reprinted over a decade later, often with the creators's [*sic*] name deleted.

The transition from a socialist to a free market economy in 1989 beckoned forth a resurgence of comics production when the government permitted private printing presses to operate. However, soon after, new

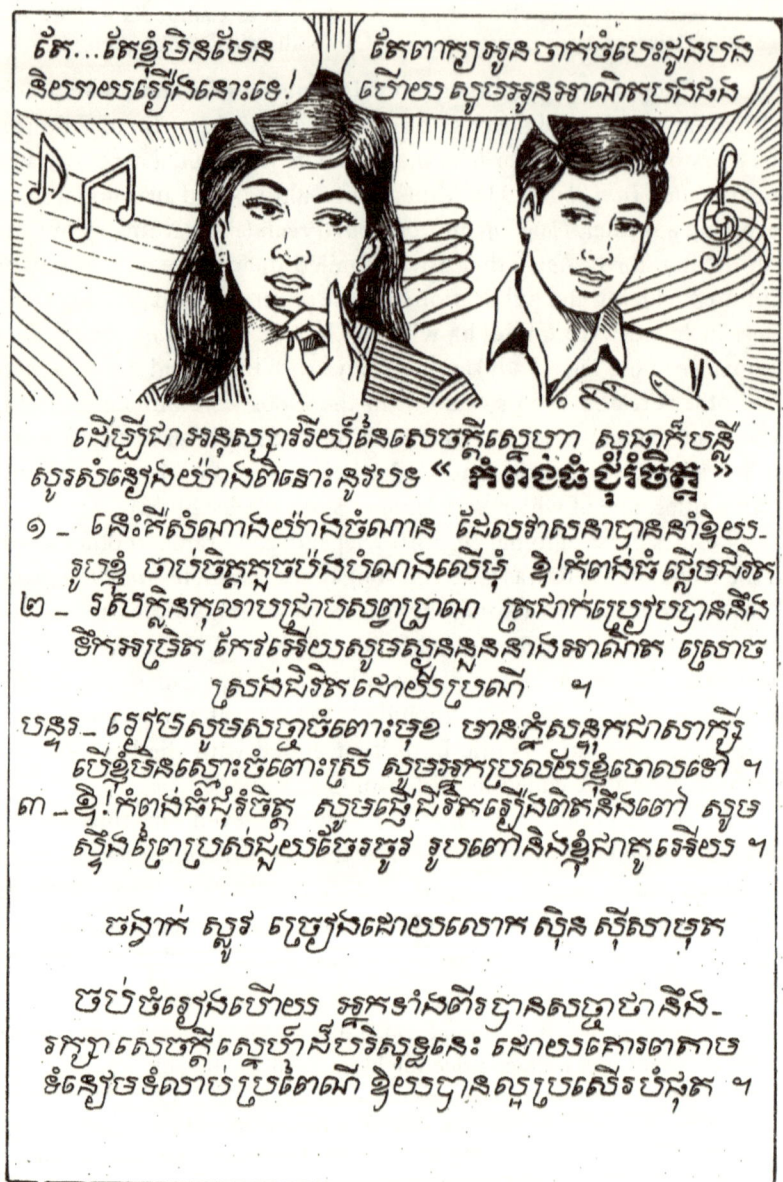

Unknown authors, *Kompong Thom Chamrong Chet*, 1980s or early 1990s example of song lyrics.

works had to take a back seat to "cheap, unauthorized copies from prior years" (Weeks 2011:10), and by 1993, most artists were no longer independently published. They moved on to other careers in illustration, painting, and sculpture. Em Satya and Im Sokha did newspaper political cartoons, Sin Yang Pirom became a merchant, and others illustrated children's books, particularly the popular *Tam Tam* and *Mom & Mab*, magazines, and textbooks. Besides the takeover by reprinted comics, other explanations given for the decline in sales were a lower literacy level and the popularity of television and karaoke.

Bootlegged reprints usually of 1980s' comic books have prevailed. They are sold mainly in a very crowded open market in Phnom Penh, which I visited in June 2010, accompanied by John Weeks, who provided explanations of the comics and their printing and distribution methods. Two comics stalls next to each other were located on the second floor of the market. At the first stall, reprinted comics were sold only in bundles of what appeared to be ten to fifteen copies of an individual title; purchase of a single copy was not possible. Weeks explained that the bundles are sold to wholesalers who then take them to the provinces for re-sale. That stall also sold children's and joke books in A5 (digest) format, as well as smaller song lyrics books. The second stall sold individual reprints at 500 riel (about 12.5 U.S. cents) a copy.

Reprinted comic books do not list a date of publication and all end with the emphatically-stated "The End." Some are redrawn (even traced) by a contemporary artist, thus, making it difficult to determine original authors. Weeks (interview, 2010) gave the example of *The Fallen Areca Flower*, which he thought might have been by Em Satya. The reprint simply lists So Sakin as translator and Chea Savann as drawer. These comic books are reprinted until the screen is almost worn out; one book thought of as the Cinderella story of Cambodia was barely legible because of a very light impression due to an overused screen. Weeks (interview, 2010) said reprint publishers normally do not have a long-term commitment to bringing out comics—"they come and go."

Efforts by Westerners and the Cambodian diaspora helped to salvage comics production during the free market economy, especially in the 2000s. Non-profit, non-governmental organizations, and, in some cases, Cambodian agencies, have kept comics publishing alive by commissioning titles on educational and social consciousness-raising topics such as HIV/AIDS, water safety, labor issues, anti-corruption, and children's rights. Some recent titles and their sponsors are *Taste of Life* on health (BBC), *Wrath of the Phantom Army* (Heritage Watch), *The Factory Gates* on factory labor (Better Factories Project), *Life's Choices* on anti-corruption (PACT Cambodia), and *Waiting for Promises* on commune councils (Equal Access).

A major publisher of the outreach comics is Our Books, a Phnom Penh-based, non-profit organization with a mission to sustain Cambodian comics. Founded in 2006 by John Weeks and Lim Samgepheat, Our Books facilitates workshops and exhibitions, publishes graphic novels, NGO-funded comic books, and a few reprints of old Cambodian comics, and maintains and adds to a digital archive of about 300 works. Weeks, an American who had worked at U.S. comics companies before going to Cambodia in 2000, saw as his purpose to track down and preserve old comics, interview veteran cartoonists, and make Khmer comics accessible to the world (Weeks, interview, 2010). Weeks is relentless in his efforts to preserve comics as an important dimension of Cambodian culture. He said, "If the [printing] work has to be cheap and dirty, I will do it that way, because I feel I have to get the stories of veteran cartoonists out as they are getting old" (Weeks, interview, 2010). Besides the archive, Weeks also has the only comics web in the Khmer-language (qdcomic. com), which he started in 2003. He described Our Books as "sort of a design studio," adding, "We operate on a shoestring. We are like an NGO for comics." Our Books has a pool of twenty to thirty cartoonists on whom they depend to write and draw NGO-sponsored comics, which, Weeks said, "pay the rent." The office staff consists of a manager, sketch artist, graphic artist, and two web designers. Concerning his organization's publishing activities, Weeks (interview, 2010) said:

> Almost all Our Books comics are published for NGOs on development topics. We also published the soap opera-like *Flower of Battambang*, [which is] pure romance. It was done by Em Satya who drew some parts of the book in 1989. The remaining pages he finished three years ago [2007] after suffering a stroke.[1] We'd like to do a second version of *Flower of Battambang*, because the Khmer-language edition of one thousand copies sold out. When we do a Khmer book, we also try to bring out an English version.

Weeks is indefatigable in his work to advance comics. In the absence of a cartoonists association, Weeks takes it upon himself to provide resources to cartoonists and to bring attention to the medium. In 2005, he tried to start an animation studio[2] after holding a workshop, and in

2009, he organized ComicKaze, an event where fifty cartoonists and students created a twenty-four-page comic book within a full day (Pham 2009). He also was actively involved in the establishment of the Comic Special Interest Group in the Federation for the Development of the

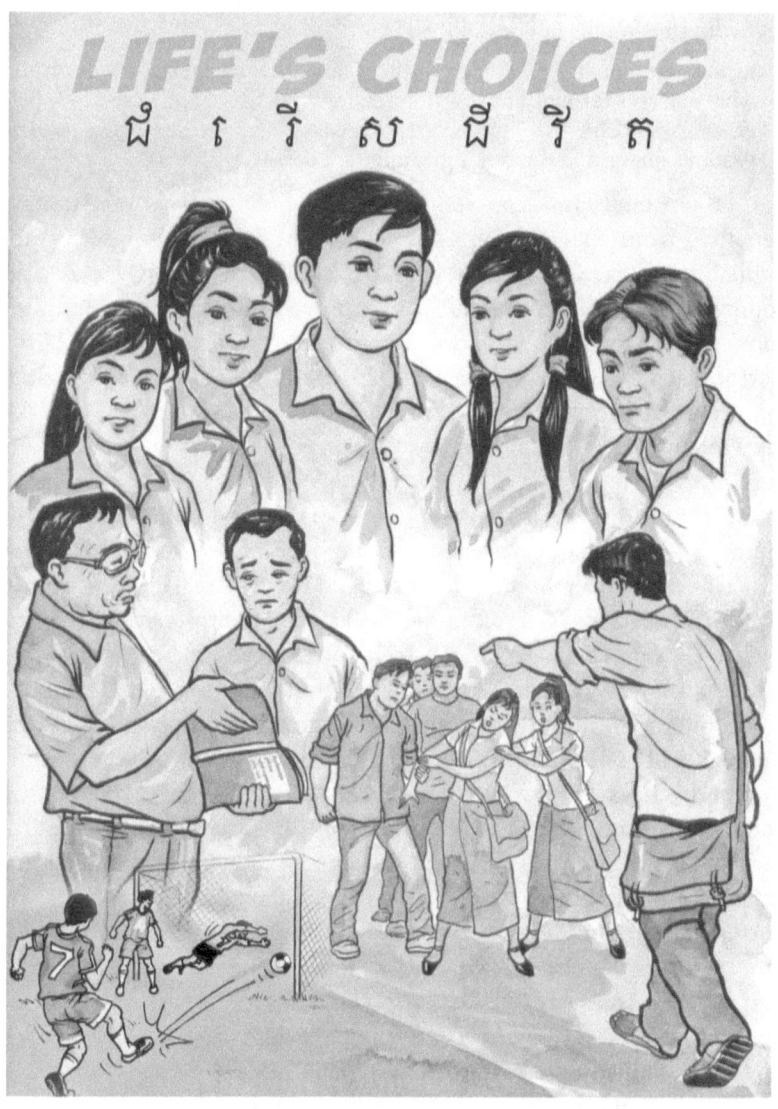

*Life's Choices*, **an anti-corruption comic (Our Books, 2006).**

117

Book Sector in Cambodia, which often met during 2004–06. Two major activities of the group were the sending of a delegate to a world comics conference in Korea (2005) and the hosting of Indonesian artist Beng Rahadian. Actually, Weeks (2011) said members of the group and others formally incorporated Our Books in 2006. The role of Our Books, according to Weeks (Pham 2009), is

> to facilitate, not direct. Ultimately [the local artists] are the ones to determine what emerges through the drawing sessions [such as ComicKaze]. We provide the opportunities, and the artists take one step further to give us ideas to move forward in developing Khmer comics.

Other small comics operations and also individual cartoonists have benefited from NGO commissions. Artist Makara Soeung set up the publishing house Grand Arts with U.S. $800 in 1998; since then, the company has produced about one hundred publications, including comics, many for NGO and government agency projects (Nguyen 2010). Cartoonist Try Samphos (interview, 2010) has occasional commissions to draw small segments of books for groups such as Road To Read and the French SIPAR, which she says, ask her "to draw a style that is not hers."

Help for the advancement of comics has come from Phouséra Ing (Séra), a Cambodian cartoonist residing in France, Cambodian Chan Keu Tian and a team of French artists, and the Centre Culturel Français Phnom Penh. Séra is credited by Weeks (2011) with creating the first original Cambodian graphic novel, *Impasse et Rouge* (1995, Albin Michel); however, although the story is about and is set in Cambodia, it was published in Paris. He authored other graphic novels (*Eau et la Terre*, 2005, Paris: Editions Delcourt) with the intent of not allowing Cambodia and its 1970s' holocaust to be forgotten. Perhaps Séra's most enduring contribution were the workshops he conducted for budding cartoonists in Phnom Penh and Battambang, beginning in 2005 and extending to 2008. The workshop project, called *[Re]Générations*, was born, according to Séra (Nguyen 2010), "from a desire to breathe life into comics in Cambodia." He added, "I notice that the youth I meet are hungry for images and the ability to use them for self-expression. I do not impose anything big. I do nothing more than propose a framework. Then I accompany the current" (Nguyen 2010).

Emanating from Séra's workshops have been exhibitions of students' cartoons and the publication in 2008 of *[Re]Générations: La Nouvelle*

*Bande Dessinée Khmère*, showcasing comics created by workshop participants from 2005–07. It was the first anthology of comics in Cambodia. Nguyen (2010) described the books as revealing

> a diversity of content and techniques previously unseen in local comics. Featured strips depict the daily life and struggles of Cambodians, providing testament to the power of using comics to relate the country's stories. Some using watercolours, some simply using pen, the artists have developed their own individual styles, each finding distinct forms of expression. Specific influences, whether foreign or domestic, are difficult to pinpoint.

Exhibitions of Séra's own cartoons have been held in Phnom Penh, sparking even more interest in comics.

Three artists from France, joined by Cambodian Chan Keu Tian, taught what might have been the country's first comics courses to children at Krousar Thmey orphanage (New Family, a non-profit organization in Siem Reap) in 2001. The team, including Sylvain-Mozie Rondet, Lisa Mandel, and Lucie Albon, self published six volumes of comics in Khmer and English drawn by the students, entitled *Lakhom Kou* (Drawn Theatre). Rondet and Mandel together returned in 2002, 2003, and 2004 to teach at Phare Ponleu Selpak, an art school in Battambang. Mandel was in Battambang also in 2005; from that workshop, she produced a color comic, *Histoires de fantômes qu'on rencontre la nuit* (2005, Tam Tam). Her teaching stint in 2007 will result in a book of her works and those of her students. The visiting artists earlier had published reminiscences of the first workshop under the title *Sept mois au Cambodge* (Paris: Glénat, 2003).

The Battambang workshops taught by these artists were part of the Phare visual arts school, run by an NGO. In 2009, Phare established a graphic arts studio and publishing house, Sonleuk Thmey, which contracted five Phare graduates as their illustrators and designers, guided by a French graphic designer. Paid a salary along with fringe benefits, they work on commissioned projects. In March 2010, Sonleuk Thmey published the graphic novels, *Nos Coeurs* and *Au Commencement*, edited by Séra, illustrated by former workshop participants Nuong Sakal and Chea Sereyroth, and funded by VALÉASE.[3] Nguyen (2010) said the graphic novels featured "modern drawing techniques and bold storylines" and represented "a remarkable achievement for comics in Cambodia."

Centre Cultural Français Phnom Penh was the venue of comics

exhibitions that became popular in the 2000s. The first, Bande Dessinée au Cambodge in 2004, focused on fifteen overseas and local Khmer artists. Part of the exhibition was a forum that led to the formation of the earlier-mentioned comics interest group. In April 2005, Séra presented illustrations from his *Eau et la Terre* at the cultural center and two years later, again at the center, his launch of *Les Lendemains de cendres* (Following Days of Ashes) took place. Three other exhibitions in 2007 were "(Re)Générations" at the National Library and one each in Phnom Penh and Siem Reap when Em Satya's *Flower of Battambang* was published.

The training provided at the workshops held by Séra and the French team has been acknowledged by young cartoonists such as Try Samphos, Chan Pisey, Nhek Sophaleap, and Prak Ke. Chan Pisey received training at a Séra seminar, as well as the Phare Art School in Battambang, while Nhek Sophaleap, after studying with Séra, took his works to Paris for exhibition.

Most young cartoonists, as did their predecesors, came to cartooning the hard way. Séra fled Cambodia as a teen in 1975 when Pol Pot's forces took over Phnom Penh; he has managed to survive financially in Paris by teaching and working as a hotel night porter (Mahr 2008). Chan Pisey left her Battambang home while in her late teens to help support her family. In Phnom Penh, she did odd jobs until she received an advertising contract in 2003 (Surewicz 2008). With two children and pregnant with a third, she said she draws when she has time, usually at night (interview, 2010). Prak Ke as a child begged on the streets in Bangkok. The police sent him back to Cambodia where he was placed in an orphanage. Fortunately, the orphanage has connections to a Battambang-based NGO that operates three art schools; at sixteen, he enrolled in Phare's art school (Nguyen 2010). Try Samphos loved drawing as a child, but her parents steered her away from an art career, fearing she could not make a living. After receiving a degree in management, she sharpened her artistic skills by attending workshops. Since then, she has been a graphic designer and comics artist, and the author/illustrator of six self-published children's books, one in comics style.

Although the young cartoonists have had to contend with many obstacles and must continue to work hard, they appear to be enthusiastic and confident. As an example, Moeu Diyadaravuth of Our Books regularly stays up until 2 a.m. to finish freelance projects, study English, and work on his own comics, explaining, "We like to draw; we hope the future will be better and we will be part of that."

Cambodian comic art has certainly survived under very difficult economic and political circumstances and hangs on with support from foreign NGOs and artists. However, the string from which it is dangling is worn thin and stretched to the limit.

## NOTES

1. Em Satya's book sat in his drawer for nearly twenty years before he showed it to Weeks.

2. There is at least one animation studio in Cambodia, Phare, that produced "Little Boy Drinking Bad Water," a TV commercial showing the digestive tract when one has diarrhea. It was funded by 1000 Fountains, a French company (Weeks, interview, 2010; see also Nguyen 2010).

3. With the ending of the VALÉASE project, Séra does not know where subsidies will come from for future workshops and publications. Others who have depended on such funding have been left with unfinished projects. Chea Sereyroth was preparing another graphic novel in 2010 with no concrete publication plans (Nguyen 2010).

# 5

# Cartooning in Vietnam

## A Brief Overview

### JOHN A. LENT

Vietnamese comic art may have traversed a bumpier road than its Southeast Asia neighbors. Not only did the country's cartoons and comics contend with colonialism, western and Japanese comics invasions, lackadaisical government and public acceptance, and the onslaught of new media, but also severe cultural disruptions brought on by long periods of home-front warfare and authoritarian regimes.

## Political and Social Commentary Cartoons

Colonialism left positive and negative imprints on the development of cartooning. Early twentieth century cartoons drawn by Frenchmen such as André Joyeux and A. Cézard cruelly mocked Vietnamese and Chinese people, but they also skewered colonial society, particularly its racial order, and left a pattern for criticism that local cartoonists subsequently followed. Regarding the latter, Vann (2010: 83) wrote that the colonists' cartoons were eventually used in the "anti-colonial, nationalist and communist movements." He explained:

> However, when the colonised adopted the coloniser's art of caricature, the medium became a method for critiquing the empire without using racial stereotypes. This art form also served as a way to communicate social and political criticism to a population with a relatively low level of education and literacy.... In this way, the earlier phase of colonial cartoons, despite their obvious racism, paradoxically contributed to the rise of a Vietnamese tradition. During the various phases of Vietnamese revolutionary upheaval from the 1920s to the 1970s, there was a clear connection between the prop-

aganda of the nationalist and communist movements and the earlier development of cartoon and caricature in the colonial era [108].

Thus, colonial cartoonists, such as Lelan in the 1890s and Cézard and Joyeux a decade or more later, were the models and in some cases, teachers of Vietnamese cartoonists of the 1920s and 1930s. Joyeux's influence particularly stood out as he taught art and was the inaugural director of Vietnam's first art school (*école de dessin,* or drawing school) in Gia Dinh near Saigon. His colonial cartoons (several dozen) were drawn while he lived in Saigon but were published in Paris as *La Vie large des colonies* (The Colonial Good Life) in 1912. Cézard's *Album* of harsh cartoons appeared in 1909 and were based on his stay in Hanoi.

Cartoons played a role in the anti-colonialist period, with, as in the Philippines and Indonesia, the nationalist leader credited with drawing the first political cartoon. Ho Chi Minh's cartoon about the people's

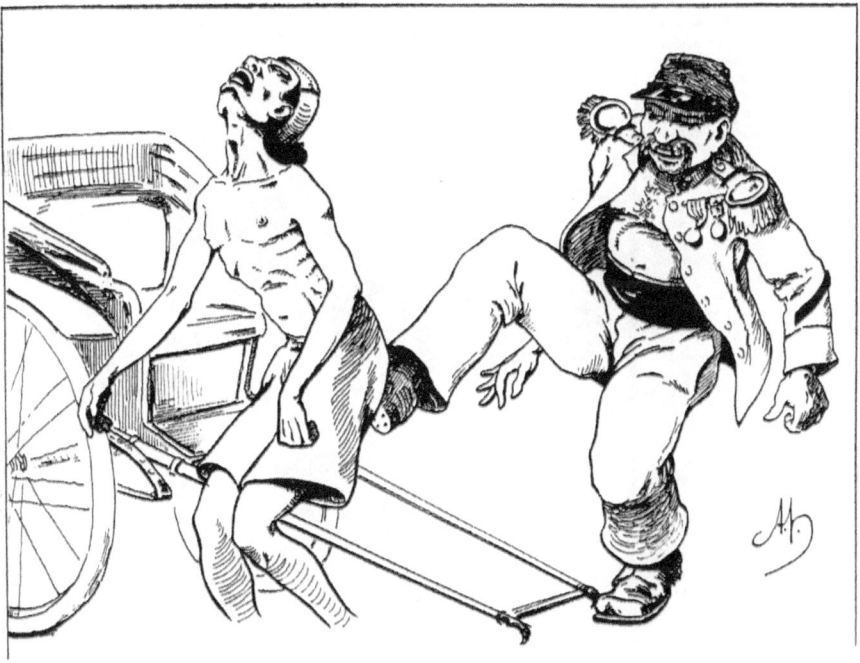

"Tarif Militaire" by André Joyeux, 1912. The cartoon shows a French colonialist violently kicking a trishaw driver, illustrating French harshness against Vietnamese.

123

0, 125 — NĂM THỨ BA                                    THỨ SÁU, 23 NOVEMBRE 1934

# PHONG HOÁ

## RA NGÀY THỨ SÁU

DIRECTEUR POLITIQUE          DIRECTEUR NGUYỄN TƯỜNG TAM          ADMINISTRATEUR
NGUYỄN XUÂN MAI                                                  PHAN HUY NINH

## QUỐC HỒN
## QUỐC TÚY

Từ ngày báo Nam-phong đổi ra báo Tây-phong, ông Nguyễn-tiến-Lãng ra tay gây dựng cơ đồ cho bá lão hủy đấy. Ông ta và bọn đồng chí của ông ta cố nói theo gót người anh thứ nhất của bá lão, để hết tài năng để bênh vực cho cái thuyết dung hòa hai cái văn minh Âu, Á.

Người thì bảo nước Nam ta có cái tổ truyền kim đan, trong có đáng, lâu gặp nhau. Hàn gọt quá. Trước kia, ta được hấp thụ văn minh Tàu, bây giờ lại được hấp thụ văn minh Tây, trời cho ta được cái may kỳ lạ ấy, ta lấy những điều hay của hai văn minh để lập thành một nền văn minh mới, dung hòa thành ra một nước văn minh mới hoàn toàn mới phải.

Người thì bảo dương khí mới, văn tranh, không nên vội bỏ bút lông. Bởi đấy là quốc quốc túy, là đạo xưa nay, chữ cũ đạo vợ chồng, đạo cha con, hiểu theo cái nghĩa hẹp của Nho giáo. Theo mới là sự lập bập, như chiếc đòn ra khơi, như bè bèo nơi có cả, không biết đâu mà đến. Giữ như khư lấy phong cũ, ấy là có căn bản, không sợ gì nữa, dầu ở cái nhà ta nát, hẹp hòi tối tăm, chật hẹp còn hơn là ra nơi đồng rộng mênh mông. Bởi ông Lãng thật có tính chất một người Annam...

Ngày xưa ngày xưa — nghĩa là độ mươi năm nay. — phần đông còn cho văn minh Tây phương là vật đối với văn minh vật chất, đằng sự khờ không kính. Chỉ có văn minh mà của Tây ta, mới đáng là văn minh tinh thần. Dần dần bọn có nói lý ngày ra rằng hay trực không phải chỉ biết ăn. Ăn nhau ở biết nhau ở...

(Xem tiếp trang 7)

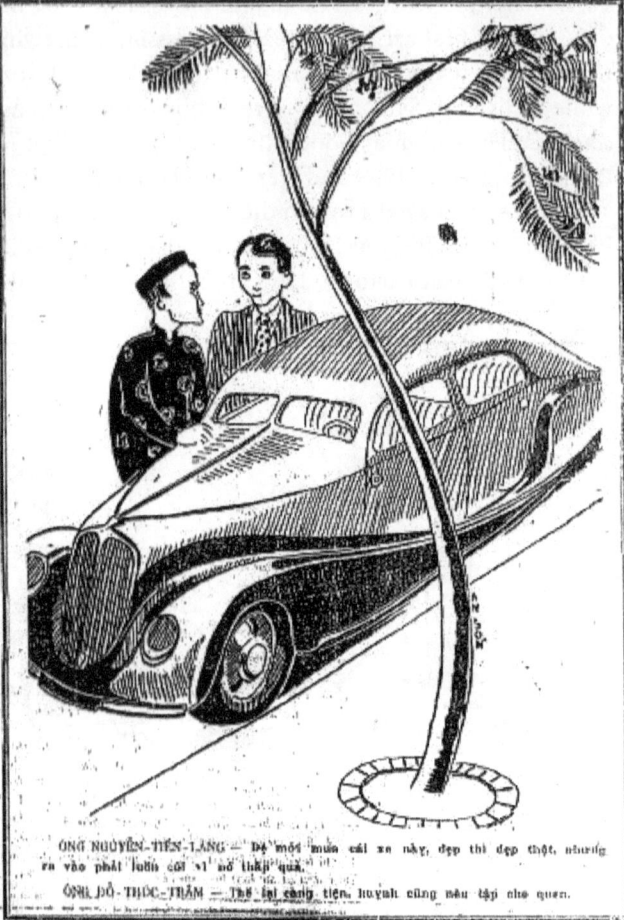

ÔNG NGUYỄN-TIẾN-LÃNG — Đệ một muốn cái xe này, đẹp thì đẹp thật, nhưng ra vào phải luôn cúi vì nó thấp quá.

ÔNG ĐỖ-THÚC-TRÂM — Thế lại càng tiện, huynh cũng nên tập cho quen.

---

Xin xem ở trang 8-9 bức tranh

## NON BỘ PHONG-HÓA

---

Front cover illustration in *Phong Hoa*, 1934 (courtesy Do Huu Chi).

opposition to the French appeared in his revolutionary *The Pariah* in 1922 (Pham 2008). The earliest ongoing cartoon characters, Ly Toet and Xa Xe, humorously portrayed the difficulties of colonial life, serving as "a way for the Vietnamese elite to comment upon colonial modernisation's intense disruptions of Vietnamese society" and creating a "safe space for subtle political commentary" (Vann 2010: 108). Ly Toet was a thin, elderly man in traditional dress, seen muddling his way through various adventures in colonized Hanoi; his sidekick, Xa Xe, was short and stout. Ly Toet was created by Nhat Linh (pen name, Dong Son); Xa Xe by Nguyen Gia Tri, one of Vietnam's important painters. Nhat Linh was chief editor of the newspaper *Phong Hoa* (Corruption), where he relocated his character in 1932, after it first appeared in the weekly *Phu Nu Thoi Dam* (Woman Today) two years before. *Phong Hoa* was started by Tu Luc Van Doan (Independent Writers Group), also led by Nhat Linh. After a few years, when the government closed *Phong Hoa*, the writers continued with the weekly *Ngay Nay* (Today), where Xa Xe appeared. But, for most of the time, the characters appeared together; they were very popular, and were adopted by other artists (Chi 2010). Chi (2010) wrote that other cartoons appeared in the 1930s–40s, including the sequential strips in the weekly newspaper *Loa* (1934–36).

Distinctions between political cartoons and illustrations have not always been clear in Vietnam, especially during the thirty years of war, first with France and then the U.S. Seldom humorous and often propagandistic, these drawings depicted military life and maneuvers and various government campaigns (such as the "Cultivation Revolution" of the 1950s); sometimes, they were prominently displayed on the covers of periodicals such as *Thep Moi* (Modern Steel), *Van Nghe Ouan Doi* (Arts and Literature of the People's Army), and *Thieu Nhi* (Youngster), and others.

During wartime, many famous painters drew illustrations, and, in some instances, for magazines and books; among them were Si Ngoc (Nguyen Si Ngoc), a drawer of simple and clear compositions; Bui Xuan Phai; Duong Bich Lien; Dang Duc Sinh; Van Da (Nguyen Van Da), who drew for regiment and division newspapers during the first war of resistance, and Huy Toan (Le Huy Toan), a military illustrator of *Arts and Literature of the People's Army*, who was known for his realistic battle scenes. Two artists more identified with cartoons were Mai Van Hien, distinguished by his "humorous and optimistic approach," and Phan Ke

An, who, during the first war of resistance as a cultural militant in the Press and Propaganda Service, did satirical drawings under the signature of Phan Kich (*Tran* Van Can *et al.* 1987: 73–74).

The popular political cartoonist during the war with the United States was Nguyen Hai Chi, who used the pen names Tran Ai and Cap, but was better known as Choe. His career, interrupted by arrests and long term imprisonment, epitomized the unstable and uncertain nature of Vietnamese society in the late 1960s and 1970s. Choe started as a cartoonist in 1966 at age twenty-two; he did satirical drawings while serving as a sergeant in the military. Thuc-sinh (1984: 9) described his work as seemingly "crude," but, "to a people with no journalistic tradition, only recently emerged from centuries of 'mandarinal' bureaucracy and one hundred years of colonial censorship, his sharp and often grotesque depictions of those he deemed responsible for the state of his country were startling." He spared no one and nothing, striking out against foreign leaders such as Nixon and Kissinger, but reserving his main attacks for the North and South Vietnamese authorities. The *New York Times* (quoted in Thuc-sinh 1984: 9) described one of Choe's drawings just before his 1975 arrest as showing "an unmistably Thieu-like figure confronting the Communists, holding a rifle under his arm. But the rifle was pointed at figures representing the Vietnamese people, not the Communists."

Choe's funny, sarcastic cartoons about Vietnam, its people, and their lifestyles gained him fame not only at home, but also abroad, as they appeared in periodicals such as *The New York Times*, *Asahi Shimbun*, *Newsweek*, and others. His lifetime production was more than fifteen thousand cartoons, mainly targeting corruption, social vices, violence against women, and, of course, war (*NhanDan Online*, November 10, 2009).

Choe held the dubious distinction of having been arrested by both the Saigon-based Thieu government and the Communist forces. On February 4, 1975, during Thieu's last months in power, he was arrested as a Communist agent. The police denied the arrest, but the *Saigon Post* wrote in the space normally saved for Choe's cartoon: "Following the arrest of our cartoonist Choe by the national police, his column is left vacant beginning Thursday. We hope that he will be freed soon to resume his work for our readers' service" (Thuc-sinh 1984: 9). Choe continued to draw after the collapse of the South Vietnam government

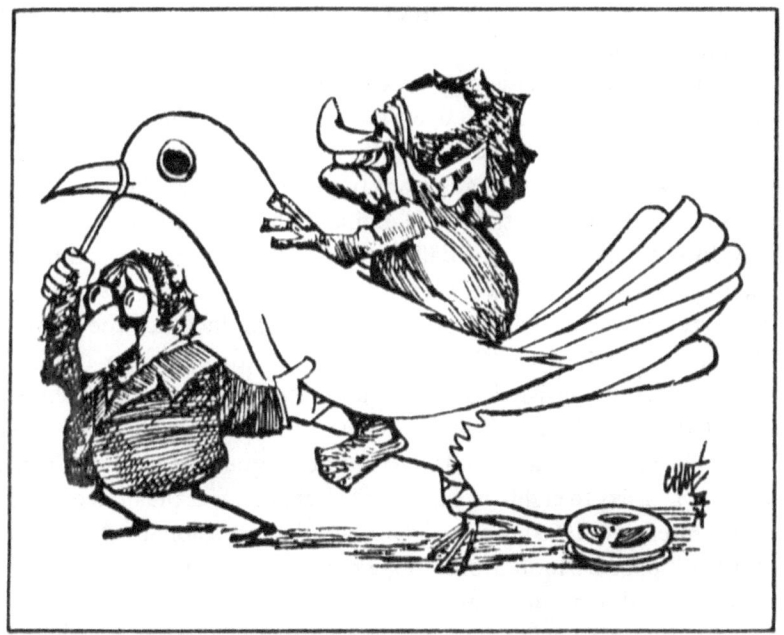

A cartoon by famous cartoonist Choe (Nguyen Hai Chi) showing the Watergate-weakened Nixon and his secretary of state Kissinger searching for peace in Vietnam after the 1973 Paris agreement. *Song Than*, July 14, 1974.

on April 30, 1975, publishing as "Ta" in *Tin Sang*, one of only two surviving dailies. The following year, he was one of sixty South Vietnamese writers and artists rounded up by the police between April 4–8 and taken to Le Van Duyet prison for interrogation. Half of the detainees were released, but Choe was among thirty "dangerous reactionaries and counter-revolutionaries" who were sent for re-education in the central highlands. He was held without charges or trial for many years. Thucsinh (1984: 9) wrote, after Choe had been imprisoned for more than eight years, that he was "reported to be suffering from severe paralysis of the right hand. If this gets worse he might even be released. But perhaps he is ambidextrous."

Upon his release, Choe's jail time qualified him to resettle in the U.S., but he decided to stay in Vietnam, continuing to draw cartoons for the dailies *Lao Dong* (Labor) and *Cong An* (Public Security), under the pen names Tran Ai and Cap, and publishing books of his works such as

*Lai Rai Ve ... Viet* (Drag on Painting ... Writing) (Tuc, n.d.). He died in 2003 after a long illness.

Strips continued to appear throughout the 1970s and 1980s, such as the two-page cartoon by Nguyen Tai, published in *Thieu Nhi* (youngster). Political cartoons and illustrations have not fared well in more recent years, though the situation was better in 1993 than 2010, the dates of this author's research trips to Hanoi and Ho Chi Minh City, respectively. In 1993, all three Hanoi dailies carried illustrations, often humorous, despite very limited space (four pages) because of paper shortages. The party paper and the largest daily, *Nhan Dan*, included the column "Chuyen Lon ... Chuyen Nho" (Big Story ... Little Story) on Tuesdays and Saturdays; it consisted of a brief and funny, illustrated comment on societal issues such as pollution, lake and road safety, etc. Two other days of the week, the paper had what one department head called "black *Nhan Dan*," a six- to eight-inches short feature that was illustrated (Kong Ngoan, interview, 1993). Kong Ngoan said that occasionally, *Nhan Dan* ran a front page cartoon promoting a government campaign and, very rarely, one tied to a critical article.

The sixteen-page Sunday *Nhan Dan* used tiny illustrations/cartoons of one column or less on nearly every page; there were twenty-one in an issue I scanned. Kong Ngoan (interview, 1993) said the number of cartoons in an issue depended on the articles' contents, while another staff member said cartoon usage was totally at the discretion of the editor (Phuong Ha, interview, 1993). Illustrations and cartoons were minuscule because of lack of space, a cartoon taking up the equivalent of 200 words. Kong (interview, 1993) said that "we must inform about many things each day. The decision to use big or small drawings depends on the day's problems in the news." The number and size of cartoons decreased sharply also because of fewer governmental campaigns to promote and a policy of not lampooning foreign leaders, in line with Vietnam's hopes of developing friendships in the international community. Seven artists, all graduates of the art university, were fulltime employees of *Nhan Dan*; they had the added responsibility of designing and laying out the newspapers. They were paid abysmally (Kong Ngoan, interview, 1993).

Hanoi's second largest daily, *Tienphong Chu Nhat*, though oriented to youth, did little better relative to cartoons. In a typical week, perhaps three or four cartoons appeared, as well as some short story illustrations drawn by the company's three fulltime artists, Van Thanh (Viet Tuen),

Trung Dung, and Pham Tien Binh, and occasional freelancers, some unpaid (Nguyen Thanh Chung, interview, 1993). The paper's sister monthly, *Tienphong Cuoithang*, devoted its last page to jokes with cartoons submitted by freelancers. The city's other daily, *Hanoi Moi* (New Daily), was also four pages. An issue I saw carried a two-column illustration and a tiny seven-panel story of cartoons.

In 2010, the two most popular dailies in Ho Chi Minh City, *Thanh Nien* and *Tuoi Tre*, were nearly devoid of cartoons and illustrations, even though the newspapers contained many pages, most full of advertisements. Occasionally, *Thanh Nien* had a cartoon by "Dad" illustrating a story; the paper's weekly used one illustration on the children's page. *Tuoi Tre's* output was a two-column, color cartoon entitled "Biem Hoa" by Sate, a two-column, color sports cartoon, and cartoons by Nop. However, these cartoons were spaced over a few days and seldom did more than one appear on any given day.

Possible reasons for the dearth of newspaper illustrations are government surveillance and censorship of political content, a shortage of opinion columns to be illustrated, and the public's denial of the importance of cartoons.

## Comic Books and Humor Magazines

The history of Vietnamese comic books is very sketchy. Until now, cartoonists' careers and experiences have gone unrecorded, their comic books and other works in most instances, not preserved. A prevailing attitude that comics are not important culturally and academically and wartime disruptive forces combined to hamper the preservation, professionalization, and serious scrutiny of comic books. What little that is known is the recent research of cartoonist Chi Do Huu, under my tutelage.

Though they most likely existed before, Chi (2010) starts his history during 1965–68 with the publication of the series *Con Quy Truyen* (The Ever-Lasting Monster) as a sixteen-page black and white comic book. He claimed the title was very popular, selling "hundred thousands" of copies.

Current comic book sales pale in comparison, most titles selling a maximum of two thousand to three thousand each nationwide. Of course, readership is beefed up by comics rental shops, which Duong (interview, 2010) said do not affect the market much because "those who want to read a comic book will buy it."

The two largest comic book publishers today are the fifty-year-old Kim Dong Publishing House and Tuoi Tre Publishing House, the latter in existence for about twenty years; both are controlled by the national government, as is all publishing in the country. The procedure is that books, including comics, must carry the name of a company and a government publisher. For example, *Dat Viet*'s company is Phanthi, the publisher, Van Hoa Sai Gon. The company is responsible for commissioning creators, printing, and production, but it must first obtain permission from the publisher on how many copies to print, how often, etc. (Chi, interview, 2010). It takes about two weeks to obtain the permit, which must indicate that the original publisher authorized a reprinting. Duong (interview, 2010) said the government also holds up permits because of sexual, political, and violent content. He and Chi (interview, 2010) said violent content is not a government priority; in fact, only politics is of major concern. Chi (interview, 2010) said,

> We are told not to be concerned with politics, that the government will take care of politics. If we develop comics to a higher level in the future, we will reach abstract ideas that will touch on politics—telling how poor and hard the people's lives are, dealing with social issues. There will be problems with government when that is done. Comics will have to have subtle meanings.

Duong (interview, 2010) said government regulations on what to avoid do not exist, that there are "very general documents, very general laws, and no decrees solely for comic books." This, he said, allowed the authorities "to arrest you at any time." As for sexual content, Duong (interview, 2010) said, "Sometimes, the government will go along with nudity, sometimes not. Naked foreigners are okay; Vietnamese, no. The books can show kissing between Vietnamese, but they cannot be naked."

## Foreign Comics

After 1970, and into contemporary times, much pirating of French-Belgian, American, Hong Kong, and, after 1992, Japanese comics occurred. Chi (2010) wrote that once the titles were imported, the Vietnamese traced the drawings over transparent paper, translated the text, including characters' names, into Vietnamese, gave themselves credit as the authors, and printed the books in black and white the same size as the original comics. Many famous comic books, such as *Lucky Luke, Tin Tin, The Smurfs, Batman, Spirou, Superman, Old Master Q*, and those of the Disney characters, received this treatment.

My sampling of Hanoi comic books in 1993 found a very close resemblance to foreign characters, plots, and styles; they varied in that some were mere translations with credits to original artists, such as Fujiko F. Fujio's *Doremon*; others were blatantly copied, with no mention of the foreign authors. *Walt Disney's Dingo. Ke Bat Coc Vo Tinh* used only Vietnamese names among artists and writers, though Disney was credited as part of the title. The seventy-two-page book featured Mickey Mouse and other Disney characters.

Comic books I found in 1993 were either of an horizontally-elongated 7.5 × 5-inch or a digest size 5 × 7.5-inch format. An example of an horizontal book was *Hoang Tu A Phay Ma Ni*, published as a series, each of sixty-four pages, detailing the story of a Thai prince named A Phay Ma Ni. The artwork was simply drawn and laid out four rectangle panels per page. The vertical, digest size books had sixteen pages each with different panel sizes and shapes concentrated on a single story. Titles found were *Diet Tru Hiem Hoa*, about a female aviator; *Bon San Tim Nguoi Song*, a Japanese-based story, and *Oan Hon Xet Xu*, featuring Western characters. All books were published on coarse paper of a color other than black and white. For example, the Disney *Dingo* comic alternated pages with no regular pattern, between red, blue, green, and brown.

After 1992, when Kim Dong Publishing House introduced *Doremon* without license, manga dominated the Vietnamese comics market. In its first three years in Vietnam, *Doremon* appeared in one hundred episodes with total sales of fifty million copies, a record never surpassed. Of course, such phenomenal success led Kim Dong and other publishers, particularly Dong Nai and Tuoi Tre Publishing House, to publish large numbers of manga. From then on, manga and other foreign titles flooded Vietnam almost unchecked. Of the estimated weekly sales of six hundred thousand comics copies in 2002, 95 percent were foreign-originated, from Japan, China, and the West (Tran Dinh 2002). Because most of the content of foreign comic books was bloody and violent, and to a degree, sexually explicit, parents, educators, and government agencies all

expressed their dismay. Some publishers heeded the critics and suspended the printing of foreign series singled out as brutal; others introduced educational comics from abroad as an alternative.

Vietnam's signing of the Berne Convention in 2004 forced some
publishers to recognize foreign copyrights, but, because of shortcomings
of the national regulators, pirating continued almost unabated. Regulations occasionally facilitated speedier and simpler publishing procedures. One enacted in 2005 allowed companies to publish a book seven
days after registration with the Publication Administration of the Ministry of Information and Communications, without waiting for approval.
The regulatory system failed to stop unauthorized manga and other foreign comics because of a shortage of inspectors and maximum fines
(U.S. $1,829 in 2008) that were set too low (*Thanh Nien Daily* 2008).
Another revision of the law in 2009 mandated that books must be registered with the Publication Administration and that publishers had to
publish only approved content.

Recent efforts to stiffen the regulation of manga were brought about
by outcries by educators, parents, and psychiatrists, the latter claiming
that manga excited Vietnamese teenagers who normally led quiet lives
(*VietNamNet*, September 22, 2008), and that salacious Japanese stories
provided misinformation about sex. A member of the educational psy-
chiatric association urged parents to tell their children about sex, "the
facts of life—that girls should be gentle and charming while boys are
supposed to be brave and strong" (*VietNamNet*, October 31, 2008). Two
publishers, Thanh Hoa Publishing House and Van Hoa-Thong Tin Publisher, were singled out in 2008, both condemned for not respecting
copyright, nor submitting their titles to the Publication Administration.
For example, Thanh Hoa's *Chang Trai Trong Truyen Tranh* (The Boy in
Manga) contained no author's credits, except for a note that the book
was "made by Ly Lien." Other titles, *Ichigo—Ky Niem Xanh* (Ichigo 100
percent) and *Crazy Kiss*, by these two publishers were also sharply criticized for displaying on their covers, scantily-clad characters and females
in their underwear. Particularly worrisome was the books' ready availability at newsstands and book rental shops near schools at the affordable
daily rental price of VND1,000 to VND1,500 (U.S. six to nine cents).
Despite both publishers' attempt to place the blame on a bookstore part-
ner which, they said, did not publish the versions they provided, they
were fined, and the *Chang Trai Trong Truyen Tranh* series was suspended.

## Locally-Originated Comics

It is readily apparent that Vietnamese-originated comic books have faced crippling challenges–from wartime deprivations, rigid Communist Party control from 1975 to 1986, and the dominance by manga and foreign comics.

After Vietnam opened its market to capitalism in the late 1980s, a few comics artists tried to rejuvenate the industry, but stumbled because the popular horror genre was now forbidden and the audiences were diminished (especially for Western comics) because of the decade-long "oriental" education policy of the Communist government.

What was released as Vietnamese after 1992 took on a Japanese flavor, being drawn in a manga style and adapted from anime or manga stories. One of the most famous "local" comic books was *Hero Hesman* by Hung Lan, an adaptation of the anime series "Voltron." From 1992 to 1995, 159 volumes were printed with a peak sales of "several hundred of thousands copies" (Chi 2010). In 2007, as the translated comic book market expanded to again include European and American titles, a collaborative work, *Red Shadow*, appeared, containing Vietnamese stories with indigenous settings and characters and Western-style illustrations. The book was conceptualized and co-written by Nguyen Thi Hong An, who invited Belgian comic writer and illustrator Eddy Coubbeaux to help her complete the project (Tuoi Tre 2007).

There were comic books that took on a local flavor, but most did not last long. Unique among them was *Kien Tini*, published in 2005; it featured character drawings by pre-teens. Another Vietnamese-originated comic found in the bookstore was *Tran Quynh*. A much longer-lived and significantly more local comic book series is *Than Dong Dat Viet* (The Vietnamese Genius), stories about a boy genius Trang Ti and his friends. Started in 2003, the monthly deals with traditional Vietnamese folklore. A typical issue is made up of 112 pages in slightly smaller than digest format, printed in black and white with a color cover. Through tie-ins with Marvel, DC, and Dark Horse, the first thirty-eight issues of *Than Dong Dat Viet* were made available to an American audience. For a while, *Dat Viet* had a companion comic book, *Fan Club*, drawn by its fans.

Also striving to present comic books more representative of Vietnamese society is Vuong Quoc Thinh, who formed the company

Art/Sign Comic and Animation with friends while he was studying architecture. His decision to preserve and present his country's culture through comics came after he questioned why "girls in Vietnam knew a lot about the New Year festival for Japanese girls through *Doremon* but little about the legend of *cay neu* (New Year Tree) of Viet Nam" (*Viet-NamNet/Viet Nam News*, August 4, 2009). Vuong Quoc Thinh attempts to educate children about Vietnamese culture through fairy tales to which his creators add modern touches. Among the seven comic books introduced in 2009 were *Banh Chung Banh Day* (Square and Round Glutinous Rice Cakes) and *Su Tich Dua Hau* (The Legend of the Watermelon). An example of mixing traditional stories with contemporary culture, *Banh Chung Banh Day* is a fable about a young prince who dreams that a god told him how to prepare a special rice dish to offer his father, the king; in the funny comic book, the prince dreams that he has entered a popular television cooking contest.

Few local comic books such as these are available, as a June 2010 visit to Ho Chi Minh City's largest bookstore, Fahasa, attested. Although two long rows were crammed with comic books (and with children standing or sitting on the floor engrossed in reading them), the majority of titles were manga. Others came from China, Korea, and Taiwan. Among them was *Tam Mao*, a copy of China's classic *San Mao*, with no credit to its creator Zhang Leping, copyrighted by Jilin Fine Arts Press of China in 2006 and Tanviet Investment and Development Co. Ltd. of Vietnam in 2009. Some settings in *Tam Mao* seemed to be Vietnamese. Also on the racks were *Full House*, a Vietnamese version of South Korean Won Soo-yeon's comic, with translation rights arranged through Seoul Cultural Publishers, and *O Long Vien* by Au Yao Hsing of Taiwan, with the Vietnamese translation copyright held by Kim Dong Publishing House (Hanoi) through an arrangement with Au. Prices of comic and picture books in Fahasa ranged from 10,000 dong (53 U.S. cents) for local titles, such as *Xi Xon on line* and *Sang Tao Vietnam*, to a high 25,000 dong (U.S. $1.32) for *Tam Mao*. Some local works were more like children's books than comics, such as Do Huu Chi's *Deo Nhac Cho Meo*.

Observers of the comic books scene in Vietnam agree that the industry either does not exist or is still in its infancy. Comics artist Do Huu Chi (interview, 2010) and Nha Nam Publishing and Communications (Ho Chi Minh City) executive Duong Thanh Hoai (interview, 2010) felt the mentality that comics are only for children must be changed to

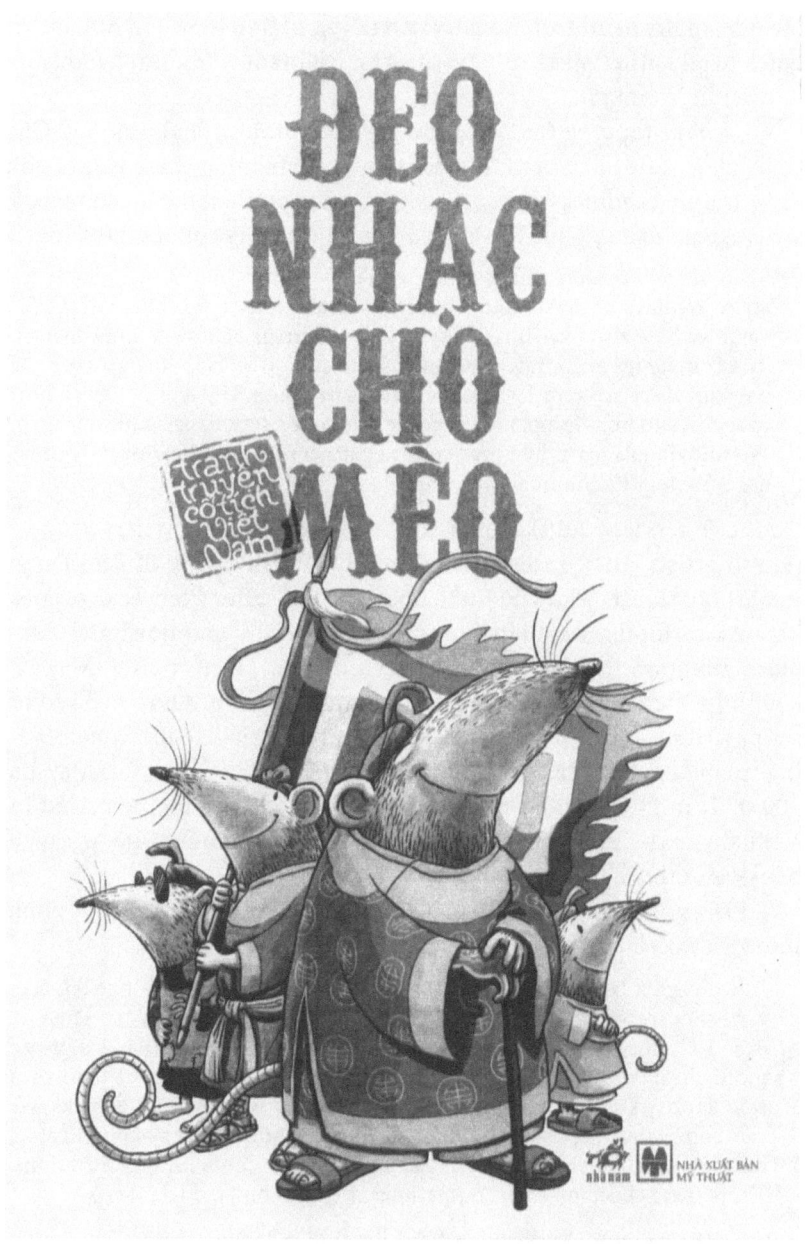

Children's book *Deo Nhac Cho Meo*, Do Huu Chi, 2010, Nha Nam (courtesy of Chi and Nha Nam).

include adults before an industry can develop. But, they and others are quick to add other missing necessities for a vibrant comic book industry to exist in Vietnam.

Perhaps topping the list is the need for professional training. Chi (interview, 2010) deplored this deficiency, saying that there is how-to-draw training online, where artists teach one another, mostly in manga style. About existing university courses on drawing comics, he said:

> Some schools opened courses to learn to draw comics but they taught manga style. We have no one knowledgeable to teach other types of comics. Universities here also have three to four-year programs on how to draw manga. The companies encourage young artists to submit work in manga style. As a result, there are very few creative works by youth. Universities teach how to repeat and imitate, not how to create. We have a serious crisis in education. We individuals learn by ourselves; we get help from professionals, but we are self-taught [Chi, interview, 2010].

Duong (interview, 2010) emphasized a need for trained writers in addition to artists. His concern was shared by Ta Huy Long of Kim Dong Publishing House, who said Vietnamese comics suffer from weak scripts, because cartoonists are not trained systematically and don't give adequate attention to what they consider side jobs (*VietNamNet*, May 12, 2009). In Vietnam, according to one source, artists are not involved in script writing and development; they are given scripts to illustrate, leading to an "unclear structure between episodes" (*VietNamNet*, May 12, 2009). Tran Dinh (2002) reverted to the way comics are perceived in Vietnam as the problem, saying writers want to do adult literary-type books, not those for children.

Piracy also plays havoc with nourishing comics and children's book industries, as Duong (interview, 2010) explained:

> If we reach a large circulation [with the company's children's books], fake publishers recognize our sales and bring out fake books in a hurry. Then we can't sell more, because of the abundance of fake editions that are priced more cheaply. On the fake books, publishers put the names of their own staff as artists and writers, though our artists and writers did the books. We can complain, but nothing happens. The situation is very complicated, bureaucratic. People who sell books on the streets are selling fake editions. There is no check on them. Sometimes, we even buy the fake books.

Besides the previously-discussed Publication Administration within the government, there is also the government-operated Association of Publishers and Printers, but Duong (interview, 2010) said it provides publishers no protection. The cost of obtaining a copyright is only U.S. $500 to 1,000, good for four to five years.

## Humor and Children's Magazines

An important venue for cartoonists is *Tuoi Tre Cuoi* (Youth Laugh), a bi-monthly conceived by Prime Minister Vo Van Kiet in 1984. Most of *Tuoi Tre Cuoi* is satirical, often poking fun at corruption and the nouveau rich, but rarely, if ever, directing the humor at an individual. Though it has contended it is non-political, there have been cartoons that bordered on criticism of government, such as one by Nop years ago, showing an office with a bottomless opinion box placed over a garbage pail (Keenan 1997: 45). *Tuoi Tre Cuoi*, an offshoot of the daily *Tuoi Tre* (Youth), is loaded with cartoons, illustrated jokes, and caricatures on nearly every page. In 1997, when circulation was two hundred thousand copies, the magazine was important enough to inspire the creation of a popular stage show in Ho Chi Minh City. Keenan (1997: 44) wrote that the "magazine and its theatrical offspring are setting the agenda for modern satire in Vietnam."

Children's magazines also have used cartoons and illustrations freely to spruce up inspirational stories, games, and jokes. One I saw in 1993 was the sixteen-page *Nhi Dong*, meant for small children. Currently published is *Thieu Nien*, part of the daily *Tien Phong*, and designed for the eleven to fifteen-year-old age group. Besides numerous drawings attached to entertaining stories and jokes, *Thieu Nien* also carries two-page spreads in color of *Doremon* translated into Vietnamese and a serialized Vietnamese story set in the past, called "Tu-Mac."

## Conclusion

Efforts to spark interest in cartooning in Vietnam have been on the rise since the mid–2000s, with the establishment of some new comics publishing companies, the holding of the country's first press cartoon competitions in 2007, on the occasion of the eighty-fifth anniversary of Ho Chi Minh's first cartoon, and again in 2010; an occasional exhibition; and the setting up of a few training courses (see Bach 2007; *VietNamNet*,

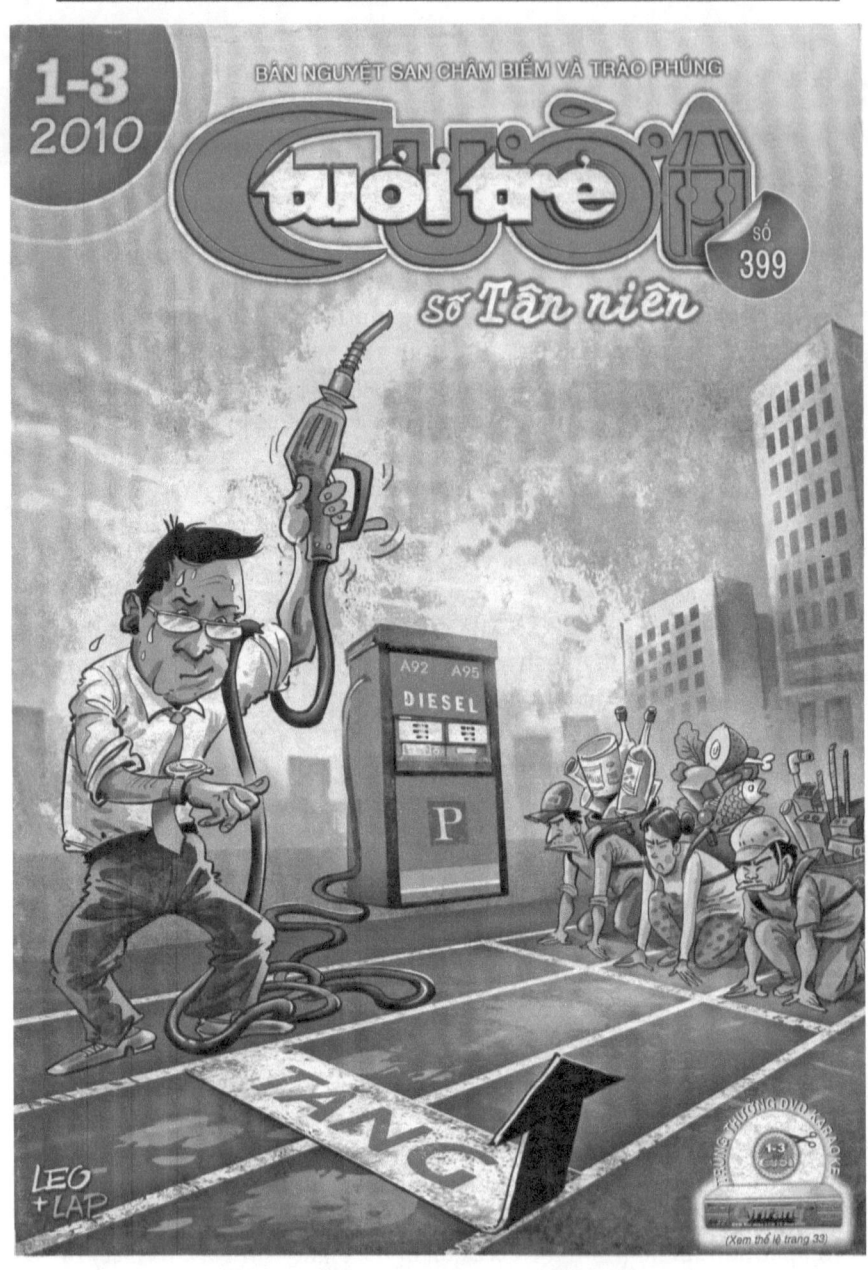

Cover of *Tuoi Tre Cuoi*, no. 399, 2010.

December 12, 2007). Also, with the Internet, cartoonists increasingly are networking and showing their works to the world.

No shortage of talent exists in Vietnam with cartoonists such as Nguyen Quoc Hung, Pham Huy Thong, Ta Huy Long, Nguyen Huu Khoa, Nop, and Chi plying the trade. However, missing are opportunities for them to find venues, and correspondingly, to earn a living. Space in newspapers is more limited than previously, and, because of advancing globalization (a polite word for cultural imperialism), comic books from Japan and elsewhere corner that market.

The profession is also hurt by the lack of serious recognition by the government, the public, and the arts. Perhaps the cartoonist Phan Ke An best summed up the situation: "I feel happiness and self-pity today because cartoons are considered a clown on the stage or an abandoned child of the arts" (*VietNamNet*, December 12, 2007).

# PART II

# Socio-Cultural and Political Issues

# Chinese Cartoonists in Singapore

*Chauvinism, Confrontation and Compromise (1950–1980)*

LIM CHENG TJU

In a 2004 cartoon about of the Iraq war in *The New Yorker*, cartoon editor Bob Mankoff had this to say: "If you don't risk alienating some people some time, you're pandering." Mankoff was talking about the need to do something different when portraying harsh everyday realities, even if it meant upsetting some readers (Manuel 2004).

Upsetting people is also a way to make sure they do not forget the terrible events that have happened. Unfortunately, as pointed out by the nineteenth century French historian Ernest Renan in an 1882 speech, "What Is a Nation?" historical amnesia is an essential element in nation-building: people need to forget the terrible price they paid in the distant past for their unity. The nation is therefore a spiritual principle, the outcome of profound complications (or even distortions?) in history. The desire to live together and the will to perpetuate the value of received heritage are the principles of nationhood (Renan 1996: 41–55).

In the case of the former British colony of Singapore, politicians would like the people to forget the price they paid for independence by eradicating Chinese chauvinism, communism, and civil society in the 1960s and 1970s. However, it is not so much a case of historical amnesia, as the history of those eventful years of nation-building is being taught in schools as part of National Education, to instill pride and patriotism in students, and to remind them that such times of confrontation and political and racial strife should never happen again (http://www.ne.

edu.sg). But for Chinese artists and intellectuals of that period, perhaps they have more forgetting to do today, especially the compromise of their art to serve the needs of a new nation.

After 1965, the year Singapore gained independence, the writing of history was de-emphasized in order for the state to focus on forging a new identity and belonging among the citizens, by having a clean slate, so to speak. Only certain political lessons of the past, useful for the state agenda of promoting unity, were documented. It has only been since the 1980s, when the political leadership realized the usefulness of ethnic history (Chinese, Malay, Indian) in fermenting cultural values and ballast, that more social and cultural history has been written (Loh 1998: 4–5).

However, writings on contemporary art and the study of different cultures in Singapore tend to be dominated by the island state's multicultural character, often blandly portraying the arts and traditions to exist in harmony and in tandem with each other.[1] Recent books have sought to rectify the non-controversial portrayal of the arts in Singapore; among them are *Red Wave: Cultural Revolution-inspired Chinese Literature in Singapore* and *Ask Not: The Necessary Stage in Singapore.*

As for the history of cartoons in Singapore, the tradition is colorful, exciting, and very political. There were various strands to this tradition in Singapore cartooning. Earlier research I did on the cartoons of *The Straits Times* since 1959 reveals a rather pro-establishment view of politics and society in its pages (Lim 1997).

The Chinese press, on the other hand, reveals a more volatile past (Thum 2010). There was a tussle between cartoonists and society in post-war Singapore: the cartoons expressed the spirit of the time and reflected its worldview. But these cartoonists did not simply reflect public opinion in their works. They wanted to shape it as well, in terms of values, morality, politics, and culture. This inevitably brought them into conflict with other political and social forces in the 1950s and 1960s (Lim 2001).

The characteristics of Chinese cartoonists listed in the title of this essay, "Chauvinism, Confrontation and Compromise," cannot be taken at face value. Singapore is a multi-racial society with the majority of its population being Chinese, while the rest are mostly Malay, Indian, and Eurasian. In the 1950s, Chinese chauvinism was seen as a threat to the peace and stability of Singapore, especially to the other races. The

Chinese's political inclinations were also geared towards communist China. All these did not bode well for the independence movement of Singapore in gaining freedom from the British. The latter would not transfer power to communists or chauvinists who could be a threat to the other races.

On the issue of Chinese chauvinism, the historical perception is that Chinese politics, and cartoons for that matter, cannot be too radical in multi-racial Singapore, or too Chinese and that the energies of the Chinese-educated, the Nanyang University (Nantah) graduates from the 1950s to 1970s, must be kept in check. Singaporeans are constantly reminded of the reality that they are living in a Malay world locked in by Malaysia and Indonesia.[2] But this Malay world view can be too simplistic. If one is to accept this argument, and to keep using the concept of multi-racialism to explain how things are done in Singapore, a lot of the state rhetoric will be taken for granted, and the historical reality will be ignored.

The reality then is that not all Chinese cartoonists of the 1950s and 1960s were chauvinists. Some of them were idealists in their attempts to shape the making of a new nation during the anti-colonial process in postwar Singapore. They were Malayans (people who believed in the political future of Singapore and Malaya as one), and not all of them had the same political inclinations or goals to be labeled as agitators who were highly confrontational.

The Chinese community of the 1950s and 1960s cannot be lumped as a whole. The two prominent groups discussed in this essay are the English-educated Chinese elites that made up the core of the People's Action Party (PAP), the ruling party in Singapore since 1959, and the Chinese-educated students, unionists, and intellectuals that the PAP worked with in the 1950s. Their interests were aligned in the 1950s, and even after the political and ideological split within the PAP in 1961, some cartoonists continued to support the leading party.

Thus, the characteristic of being confrontational that is associated with Chinese cartoonists of the 1950s to 1970s is problematic, because it really depends on which group one is referring to in context. Each group was merely fighting for the side it believed in. The pro–PAP cartoonists were no less confrontational or aggressive than those who were against them. Therefore, the negative association of Chinese cartoonists being confrontational needs to be addressed and reviewed.

On the third characteristic of the compromise the cartoonists had to make in the 1970s to the demands of nation-building and social consensus, the compliance of the artists did not come easy. It was marked by actions taken against the Chinese newspapers and the restructuring of the press laws in the 1970s. It was marked by the demise of public activism and civil society in Singapore and by the end of the political pluralism Singapore witnessed briefly in the period of the 1950s and 1960s.

Researchers on Singapore need to move beyond the "us versus them" paradigm of looking at politics and culture in the 1960s and 1970s. It reduces the history of local cartooning to a tempered narrative of resistance and satire. It is a top-down structure that confines all decisions to state initiatives, with the cartoonists merely responding to government actions.

What will be explored in this essay are the steps and decisions taken by cartoonists in the 1970s to continue drawing, to creating their own space. It seeks to examine the fallout of their actions in moving from a position of idealism to professionalism, a move that changed the purpose and outlook of cartoonists in Singapore, and, in many ways, robbed the medium of its power.

If one is to consider cartoonists of the 1950s and 1960s as organic intellectuals, as defined by Antonio Gramsci, and to position them as part of the emerging civil society of that period, then the fate of Chinese cartoonists by 1980 reveals an anti-idealism and anti-intellectual character in Singapore that is still prevalent in most arts today (Gramsci 1972).

A word on the time frame: the years 1950 to 1980 were chosen because they represented the "golden years" of Chinese education in Singapore: 1950 was when the idea of Nanyang University, the first Chinese university in Southeast Asia at that time, was first mooted, and 1980 was the year Nantah was closed. The vibrancy and decline of Chinese cartoonists in Singapore corresponded to a large extent with this time frame.

## 1907–49: Setting the Stage

The story of Chinese cartoons in Singapore began at the turn of the twentieth century with the setting up of *Chong Shing Jit Pao* in 1907 by members of the Singapore branch of the Tung Meng Hui (Chen 1967: 97). The advent of the mass media, new printing technology, and revolutionary interests coincided to introduce cartoons to the Chinese immigrants on a wide scale. The first images to hit the popular Chinese imagination then were political-anti-Ching Dynasty cartoons that supported the revolutionary cause of Sun Yat-Sen. Although its targets were miles away in China, the anti–Ching nature of the newspapers attracted the attention of the colonial government in 1908, to the extent that the British threatened to deport the editors of the paper for advocating "seditious agitation against China" (Yong 1991: 31). The cartoonists, often the troublemakers in newspapers, played their part in stirring up the flames of political discord.

With the overthrow of the Ching Dynasty in 1911, the cartoons refocused their attacks on other problems in China, such as warlordism and Japanese aggression. The May Fourth Movement of 1919 further politicized the Chinese population in China, as well as the overseas Chinese. Among them were artists, writers, and cartoonists.

Such energies found their way to Singapore through imported books as well as the roles played by teachers and artists from China, who were very influential in the cultural life and educational focus of the overseas Chinese in Singapore. Through their writings and drawings, these Chinese-educated intellectuals were creating a sense of identity among the Chinese that was highly politicized, setting the stage for the activist role cartoons would play after World War II during the decolonization period (Kenley 1998).

Before 1946, the concerns and opinions of the overseas Chinese were on the political events in China. Thus, the cultural production of all things Chinese in Singapore, whether they were plays, literature, or cartoons, was very Sino-oriented. With a few exceptions in the late 1920s and early 1930s, artists and writers were responding to the issues and problems in China, such as the Japanese war. Chinese cartoons in Singapore up till World War II focused very much on the political situation in China. In a way, Liu Kang's *Chop Suey*, a collection of cartoons depicting the atrocities of the Japanese Army in Singapore, broke with that tradition in 1946. The focus slowly shifted to local issues and concerns. Cartoons and other artforms were then employed in the anti-colonial movement that was sweeping across developing nations in the postwar years.

From the late 1940s onwards, there were more cartoons on local content appearing in the Chinese newspapers. This paralleled the shifting of loyalties among the overseas Chinese in Singapore, from seeing China as their country to identifying with the future of Malaya and Singapore (Hara 1997).

## 1950–53: Social Awareness and Ideological Debates

By 1950, the major Chinese press in Singapore, such as *Nanyang Siang Pau*, was running socially conscious cartoons that reflected the upheaval in society. In that year, Singapore faced tremendous social and political turmoil. It was still recovering from the post-war recession. Food shortages had persisted with the last "people's restaurant" (cheap eateries for the poor) operating till August 1948 (Singh and Arasu 1984: 97) Unemployment was high, giving rise to an increase in crime and secret society activities (Turnbull 1989: 227). The Malayan Emergency against the Malayan Communist Party (MCP) was declared in 1948, which affected the economy and stability of Singapore (Singh and Arasu 1984: 120, 135).

With the unification of China by Mao Zedong under communist rule in 1949, the Chinese community in Singapore came under further scrutiny. An Immigration Bill was passed in Singapore that year to restrict the immigration of Chinese communist sympathizers. The leader of the Chinese community, Tan Kah Kee, left Singapore for China for the last time in 1950 as the British did not allow his return (Turnbull 1989: 240–41). Chinese schools, seen as the breeding ground for communism, came under attack. In May 1950, the School Registration Ordinance was passed, which allowed the search or closure of any school used "as a meeting place by an unlawful society" or for spreading "political propaganda." The following month, two leading Chinese schools were closed for two months. The police found subversive materials in the Chinese High School and Nanyang Girls' High School. Sixty-seven students and seven teachers were expelled (Singh and Arasu 1984: 120). Against such a backdrop, Tan Lark Sye, chairman of the Hokkien Huay Kuan, first mooted the idea of setting up a Chinese university (Kee and Choi 2000: 36; Wang 1997).

It is not surprising then that images of social injustice and cruelty filled the cartoon slots in *Nanyang Siang Pau*. With the increased confidence among the Chinese community in the emergence of China as a renewed power in Asia and possibly the world, they were concerned about the political future of Singapore. It was a fact that the China-born and Chinese-educated population was excluded from the political process in the early 1950s. Only those who were Straits-born or naturalized British subjects educated in the English medium were participating in the Legislative Council (Turnbull 1989: 240). If the Chinese-educated did not have their say in the upper echelons, they took their message to the streets.

The Chinese cartoonists were concerned with values and moral issues, given the poverty and rampant crime in 1950s Singapore. The pre-war Societies Ordinance, which was enacted to curb the problem of secret societies and was held in abeyance after the war, was reinstated in the late 1940s (Turnbull 1989: 227). A particularly potent image appeared in the March 31, 1950 edition of *Nanyang Siang Pau*. A man is seen drowning in the sea. As he was about to be saved by a Samaritan, two evil-doers in the background are seen lifting stones to throw at them. This theme of the good being "rewarded" for their good deeds is a recurring one.

Morality and relationships between men and women were other concerns. Marriage as a business transaction, buying sex with money, and indulgence in yellow culture were already social problems before the war. Cabaret culture was prominent in the 1930s when three popular amusement centers, the New World, the Great World, and the Happy World, opened cabarets for dancing, merry-making, and other extra-conjugal activities after the dance halls were closed (Rudolph 1996: 26). Tan Kah Kee wrote about the evils of dance halls in his memoirs (Ward, Chu, and Salaff 1994: 281–83) and cartoons in the 1930s had already pointed out this social ill.

A rather humorous example of this sort of cartoon is from 1951. It shows a man looking at pictures of naked women, instead of working. This has obviously affected the productivity of the company as the chart in the background shows that profits are going down. Another (pictured) is a straightforward depiction of the transaction involved between sex and money.

The problem with such a simplistic portrayal is that readers could

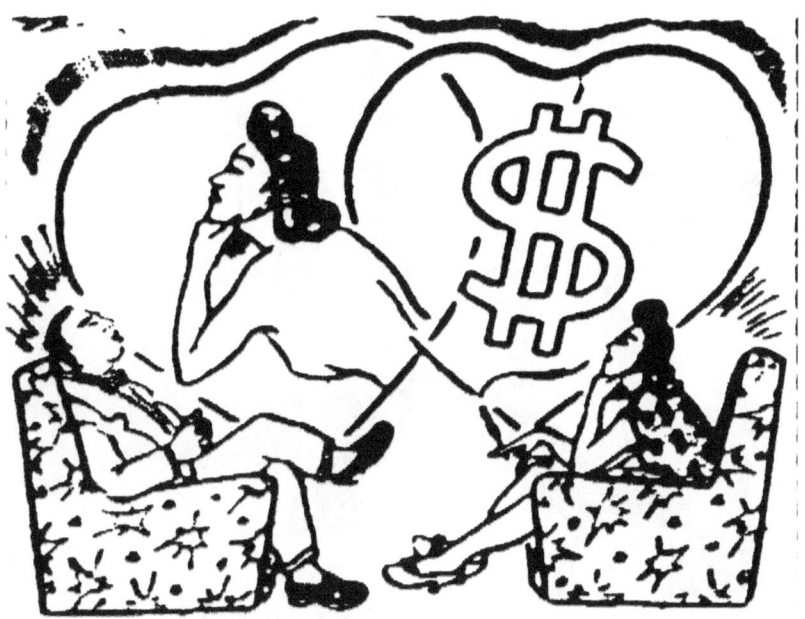

**"Great Minds Think Alike," artist unknown (using pen name),** *Nanyang Siang Pau,* **January 11, 1950.**

mistake the cartoons as merely reflecting the latest relationship trend and view them as endorsement of such social behavior. With no way of confirming the intentions of these works, there is a danger that the depiction of the naked female body in so-called moralistic cartoons is an excuse to exploit it further. This is not unique to Chinese cartoons in the early 1950s as a cartoon from *The Straits Times* in 1951 showed similar depictions and possible exploitation of the female form to satisfy the male readership.

This is the limitation of the single panel cartoon—by reflecting the social reality to comment on it, the work might reaffirm that reality. This possibility is supported by the kind of logo cartoons that accompanied regular columns in the leisure page of the newspaper. For example, the image used for the column "Take a Break" shows a man having drinks with a sexy-looking woman. Both of them are dressed in Western clothes. The cartoon used for the heading of the leisure page itself, "Other Business," reaffirms the paternalistic patterns of society. It shows a man relaxing at home, sitting in a sofa, and smoking his pipe. In the

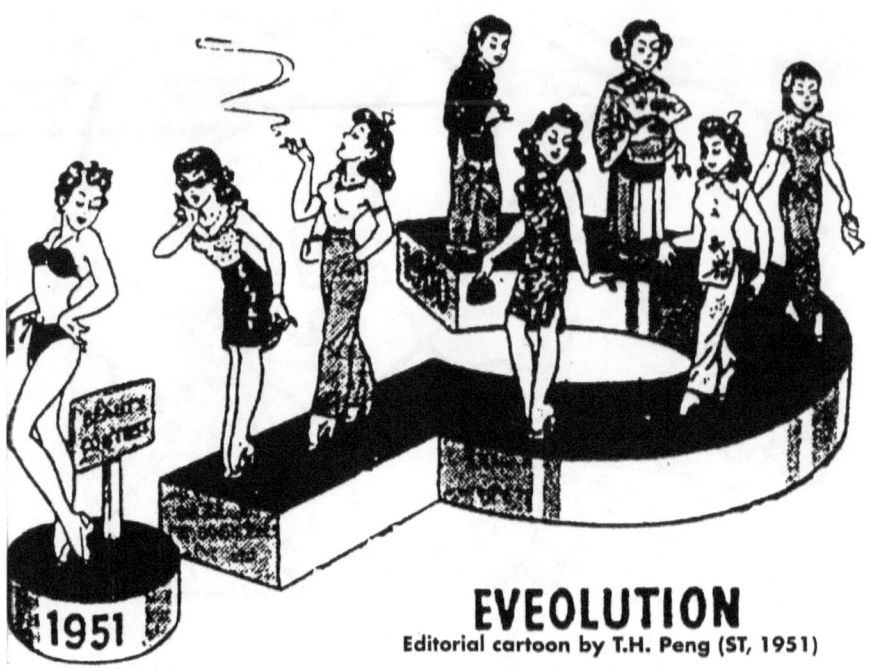

EVEOLUTION
Editorial cartoon by T.H. Peng (ST, 1951)

"Eveolution," Tan Huay Peng, *The Straits Times*, February 6, 1951.

background, the housewife is drawing the blinds to make it more comfortable for the husband. In both cases, these images of supposed modernity (as indicated in their Western dress and attitudes) contradict the new values other cartoons were supposedly promoting. The unintentional messages of these two logo cartoons reveal more about social attitudes back then as they appeared almost every day with the columns. While other works reflected society, these two cartoons could be shaping social norms subliminally as they were a constant feature of the paper.

While the end results of such moralistic cartoons were debatable, one perhaps could argue that this burst of moral outrage was a result of the urgency of strengthening the Chinese spirit and moral fiber overseas in the light of a "new" hope for China in 1949. However, we have just seen that there were inconsistencies in the promotion of values in early 1950s print and visual culture, especially in the usage of cartoons.

Although the impetus for this new values movement in cartoons could be attributed to the political changes in the homeland, this was different from the China-oriented moral attitudes of cartoonists of the 1930s. The Chinese cartoonists and intellectuals of the 1950s were more concerned about the social issues of Singapore and the rest of Asia. Thus, other than cartoons about the widespread poverty and rising inflation, there were works that were more internationalist in outlook, such as those showing an interest in the Korean War.

## 1953–55: Getting Political with "Mr. Nonsense"

It was when cartoonists brought local politicians into their world of caricatures and satire that the medium got into trouble. In 1953, Chung Cheng High School art teacher Qiu Gao Peng was invited by *Nanyang Siang Pau* to produce a weekly strip every Monday. Qiu, who used to draw anti–Japanese cartoons during the Sino-Japanese war in China, brought along with him the idea of using cartoons as tools for social change when he came to Singapore in 1948 (Qiu, interview, 2001).[3] He had been contributing cartoons to *Nanyang Siang Pau* since 1950, creating a "Sanmao"–like character called "Wang Er."[4] His 1953 comic strip, "Mr. Nonsense," proved to be a hit and attracted new readers as it tackled hypocrisy in society, and even sensitive topics such as the constant strikes in early 1950s Singapore (Wang 1992: 73). It was a good time for cartoons to take more chances as some of the Emergency Regulations were lifted in 1953 (Gillis 2002: 235).

Because of his background and experience in drawing anti–Japanese cartoons in China, Qiu was by far the most political of the early 1950s cartoonists. The two cartoons he did as covers for *The Literary Post* in 1955 prove that. One cartoon shows a typical temple scene of a female worshipper making offerings to a Chinese deity. However, if one looks closely at the label attached to the lady, it says "election candidate." The label attached to the pig offering says "election promises" and a Chinese deity opposite has a label "voters." This is a rather clever depiction of the April 1955 general election in Singapore, the first that gave the people the chance to elect their own ministers.[5] The electorate was enlarged as a result of automatic registration which revealed that the majority of first-time voters were working-class Chinese (Singh and Arasu 1984: 123). Thus, it was fitting that Qiu used such a familiar Chinese activity to illustrate the election. This cartoon also has a subtext of empowerment for the Chinese voters, showing that power lies with the people. That would include cartoonists like Qiu, who then had the power to comment on the politics of Singapore. It could also be a reminder of the election promises made during the campaign trail, such as the ones David Marshall, the chief minister-elect, had made. He told voters that he would persuade the colonial administration to revoke some of the Emergency Regulations if he came to power. Of particular interest to the Chinese was the Banishment Ordinance that was used to deport undesirables, a law that they had hoped would be abolished (Drysdale 1984: 105). But that was not to be.

Qiu expressed his opinion of the politicians in a subsequent cover for *The Literary Post*. At a first glance, it is a rather harmless and humorous cartoon on the absurdity of wearing hats that are too big for one's head. But taking into context the political turmoil in the streets of Singapore in the immediate months after the election, this image could be a criticism of the newly elected leaders for taking on a job too large for their shoulders, and failing to fulfill election promises. It was a task too big for them to handle, and by wearing such a big hat of responsibility, they were blinded and could not see where they were going or what they were supposed to do.

However, in October 1955, Qiu crossed the line when he caricatured David Marshall in a "Mr. Nonsense" cartoon strip, showing the chief minister to be more of a glory hound than one interested in solving the social problems that plagued Singapore that year. Workers and students' strikes were rampant in the 1950s with 275 workers' strikes in 1955 (Singh and Arasu 1984: 151). Chung Cheng High School students were involved in the Hock Lee Bus riots and some of the student leaders were arrested.[6] The government threatened to close the schools if the students supporting the strike were not expelled. Qiu, being a teacher at Chung Cheng High School at that time, would have known of the clash between the government and the students, thus explaining his critical attitudes towards Marshall.

The next "Mr. Nonsense" cartoon that appeared in the October 31, 1955, *Nanyang Siang Pau* went a step further and compared the political leaders of Singapore to pigs and even dictators such as Adolf Hitler. That was the last appearance of "Mr. Nonsense" in *Nanyang Siang Pau*—it was rumored that political pressure was placed on the editors to remove Qiu from the papers (Wang 1992: 74).

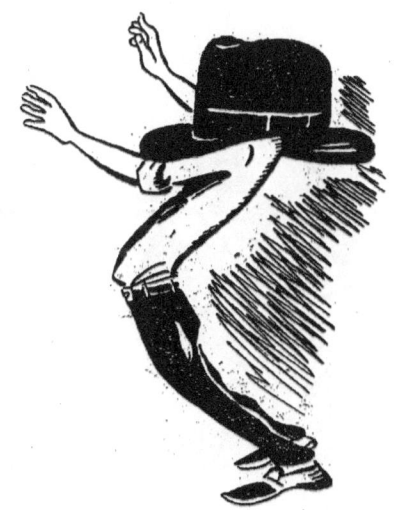

文藝報副刊

「大帽子」

丘岳作

·零售每期二角·

4.5

"Big Hat," Qiu Gao Peng, *The Literary Post*, August 10, 1955.

However, there was inconsistency in the censorship of Qiu's "Mr. Nonsense" from the Chinese press. The English press, on the other hand, seemed to have more leeway in dealing with political issues and caricatures. David Marshall and his Labour Party were a constant feature in the cartoons of Tan Huay Peng, being made fun of for their incompetence in a rather witty way. Even Tunku Abdul Rahman, the future prime minister of Malaya, was portrayed in drag, all tarted up in a cheongsum,

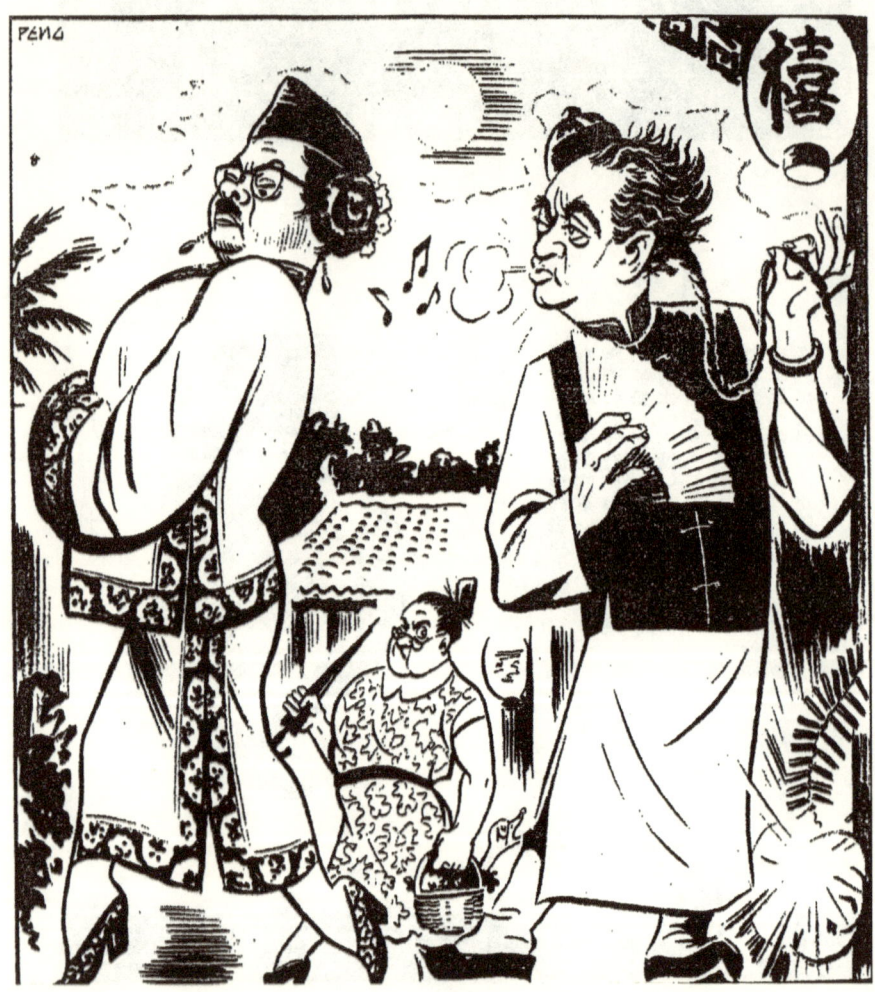

"Chap Goh Meh," Tan Huay Peng, *The Straits Times*.

154

being wolf-whistled by Marshall in a game of merger courtship. From such evidence, one can gather that more freedom was given to the English papers because the colonial rulers had deemed that it would be the English-educated who would inherit Singapore from them. They were the favored sons of the British Empire.

## *1955:* Selection of Woodcuts and Cartoons by Singapore and Malayan Artists—*The Impact of Lu Xun, Lim Hak Tai, and the Nanyang Academy of Fine Arts*

What happened to Qiu and the cartoons he drew in defiance of the authorities was the exception rather than the rule. Most Chinese cartoons were not so direct in their criticism of imperialism and political incompetence. Despite this setback for cartooning, 1955 was a good year for Chinese cartoons in Singapore. It saw the publication of *Selection of Woodcuts and Cartoons by Singapore and Malayan Artists*, a landmark book in the history of Chinese cartoons. Edited by Ho Kah Leong and Ong Shih Cheng (pen name Ong Yih), it was the first cartoon collection about the immediate experience of local living, focusing on issues of morality, values, Chinese education and hardships in colonial society. The woodcut section of the book was edited by Ho while Ong handled the selection of cartoons (Ho, interview, 2001).

Ho and Ong were good friends studying at the Nanyang Academy of Fine Arts.[7] Both wanted to promote woodcuts and cartoons, partly inspired by the example of Lu Xun in the 1930s, who saw both media as "sister arts" to bring about changes and improvements in society. *Selection of Woodcuts and Cartoons* was to provide art for the masses, who might not have the time or means to view it in galleries or see it in the newspapers. One thousand copies of the book were printed and sold at S$1 (Ho, interview, 2001).

In an interview I conducted with Ho in 2001, he said that in the 1950s, cartoons were drawn to reflect the concerns of society. He and Ong wanted to do the book because both of them believed that there was a social need to develop the community by using art to deal with issues of the day.

It is important to take a look at where these ideas came from. The relationship between cartoons and politics was already firmly established right from the beginning, since the first appearance of Chinese cartoons in Singapore in 1907. By the 1930s, the cartoon was seen as an artform that could serve the needs of the people. Cartoonists-cum-activists introduced the ideas of Lu Xun and social realist works to a new generation of artists. This view of art was reaffirmed at the first graduation ceremony of the Nanyang Academy of Fine Arts, the first arts academy in Malaya, in 1940. The principal, Lim Hak Tai, stressed that "the purpose of art should not be anything beyond and above social realities" and that "art should have the spirit of resistance so that it can become a forceful weapon" (Fan 2000: 22). This role of art to express the needs of the people was one of the six stated objectives of the academy. When the academy was reopened after the war, this remained a key objective of the school as evidenced in the introductions of its various graduation catalogues in the late 1940s and early 1950s.[8] There was an additional external factor that laid the seeds of social realism in Singapore in the 1950s—Mao Zedong's "Talks at the Yan'an Forum on Literature and Art" in 1942 (McDougall 1980). The message was clear: art should not be done for art's sake.

Thus, the students of the Nanyang Academy of Fine Arts like Ho and Ong were attuned to such ideas about art and society. In *Selection of Woodcuts and Cartoons*, the more interesting cartoons were those on social issues such as Chinese education. In 1953, Tan Lark Sye, chairman of the Singapore Hokkien Huay Kuan, proposed the establishment of a Chinese language university, in light of the difficulties faced by Chinese students to pursue a university education in China after 1949 (Kee and Choi 2000: 28). The British viewed returning students with mistrust. In 1955, the recruitment of the first batch of pre-university students began. However, the government viewed the yet-to-be established Nanyang University with suspicion, given the radical left wing activism of Chinese students in the 1950s. There was discussion to introduce bilingual education in Singapore, which took effect in 1956. Chinese educators and students saw this as a threat to Chinese education and culture. The cartoons in *Selection of Woodcuts and Cartoons* reflected such concerns. One shows a boy giving up his Chinese book to carry an English book as he could not handle both their weight in his bag. This cartoon, drawn by Qiu Gao Peng, first appeared in *Chinese Students*

*Weekly.* Ong was an ex-student of Qiu when he studied at Chung Cheng High School. He asked his former art teacher for permission to reprint his cartoons in *Selection of Woodcuts and Cartoons* (Qiu, interview, 2001). This cartoon on the difficulty of studying two languages is still pertinent today.[9] Qiu's cartoons in *Selection of Woodcuts and Cartoons* reflected his own concerns as a Chinese teacher and they came across effectively.

## Popularity of the Medium in the 1950s

In essence, cartoons were well suited for newspapers as it was easier to reproduce them for print publications, as compared to oil paintings or other media. Poor printing technology did not allow oils to be reproduced clearly in newspapers and magazines.

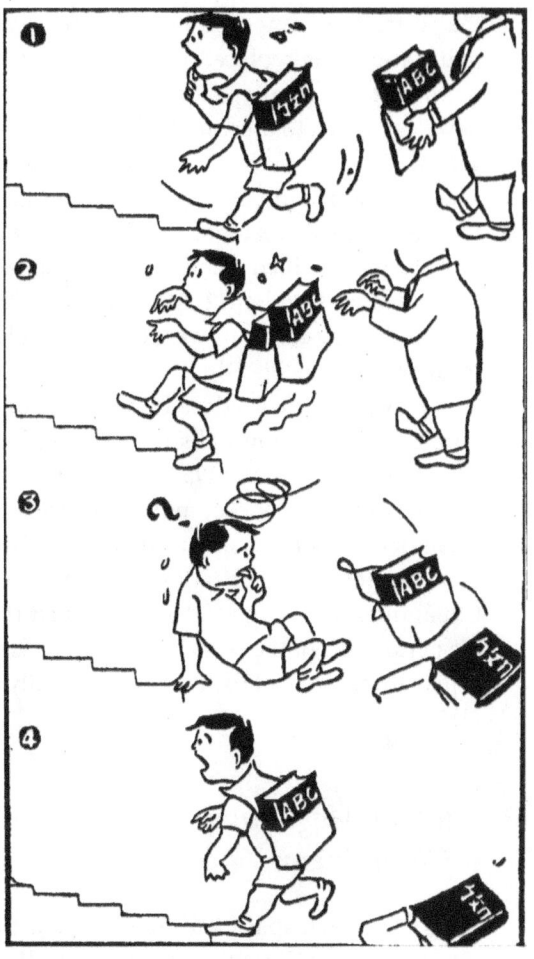

"Bilingual Policy," Qiu Gao Peng, *Chinese Students Weekly*, 1955.

Another reason for the popularity of cartoons in the 1950s was the availability of rich material which could be mined from everyday life. Chinese education was not the only hot topic of the day; the anti-yellow movement in literature and the arts had reached a peak by the mid–1950s as well. After serious magazines were banned in 1948 because of the restrictions imposed by the Emergency Regulations, this void in publication was replaced by the emergence of more than forty "mosquito" or tabloid newspapers in Singapore, which printed sensationalized news, using sex to increase their circulations (Yap 1996: 116). These sold very well, much to the chagrin of students and teachers, who protested against this rise in pornographic materials. This also partly accounted for the moralistic cartoons in *Nanyang Siang Pau* in the early 1950s. Public outcry intensified when a sixteen-year-old female student was raped and killed on October 12, 1953. Yellow culture was blamed for the incident and many cartoons were drawn to fight such corrupting influences in society (Ou 1998: 19).

However, one needs to be careful about attributing altruism to cartoonists who drew moralistic or anti-yellow works. Being an artist did not pay very well in the 1950s. Contributing cartoons to the newspapers and earning extra pocket money (about $5 for each cartoon), especially when one was still a student, were attractive enough for many to submit their cartoons for publication (Ho, interview, 2001; Tan, interview, 2001; Chua, interview, 2001).[10] This explained the abundance of cartoons in the periodicals of the 1950s. These cartoons were able to meet the public's expectations as readers liked such socially conscious works (Ong 1991: 145).

## Student Magazines: Disputing the Image of Chauvinism

Given such space and freedom to articulate their ideas and views about society and politics, many artists did not let the opportunity slip. One of the more popular showcases for cartoons was *Shidaipao*, a current affairs and cultural publication put out by students of Chinese High School (Ng, interview, 2001). Most of the cartoons in *Shidaipao* are signed using pen names. I have been unable to identify them, nor find any artists wanting to claim ownership, perhaps because of the radical anti-colonial nature of these works.

The cartoons in *Shidaipao* contributed to the independence movement of Singapore. They did not just reflect public opinion or sentiment about colonialism, but also played a part in the shaping of what Singapore's political future should be like. An image from 1956 shows the

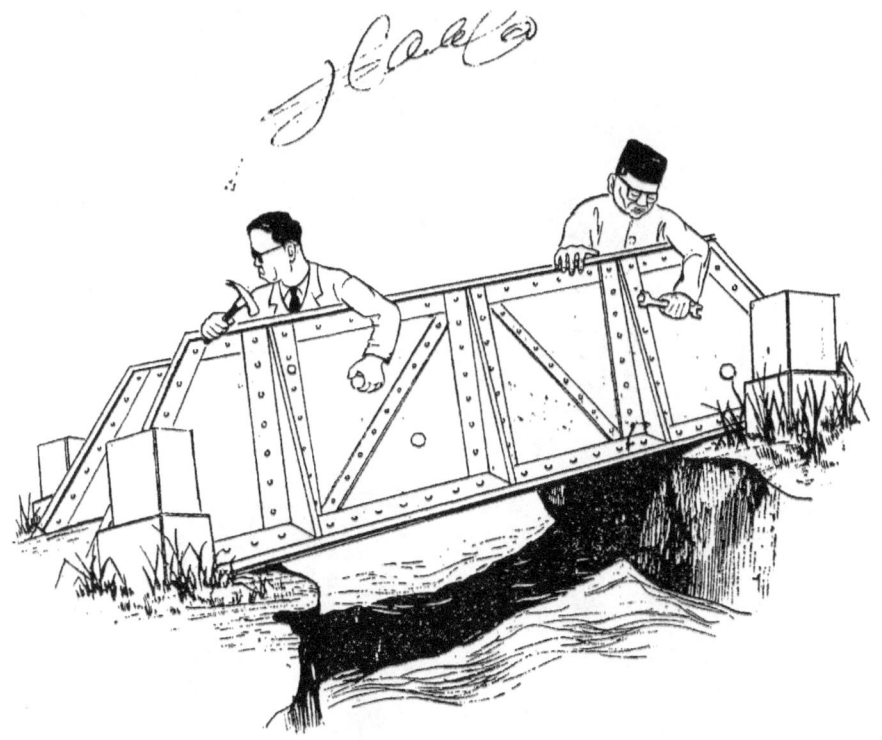

**"Bridge Building," artist unknown (using pen name),** *Shidaipao,* **1956.**

building of a steel bridge by Singapore Chief Minister Lim Yew Hock and Tunku Abdul Rahman, the future prime minister of Malaya, giving support to cross–Straits cooperation in the fight against colonialism.

Thus, far from being Chinese chauvinists, an image that arose because of their concern for Chinese education and culture, these cartoonists were Malayans, people who believe in the political future of Singapore and Malaya as one. A *Shidaipao* cover shows that all races were brothers-in-arms against imperialism and marching towards Merdeka-freedom.[11] Particularly potent is a cover from the September 10, 1956 edition of *Shidaipao.* In "Strength in Unity": each race is helping the other to untie its ropes, freeing themselves from foreign tyranny and oppression. One figure is dressed in Malay clothes. I believe this was drawn intentionally to highlight the cooperation needed by the other races in this struggle, especially the Malay population.

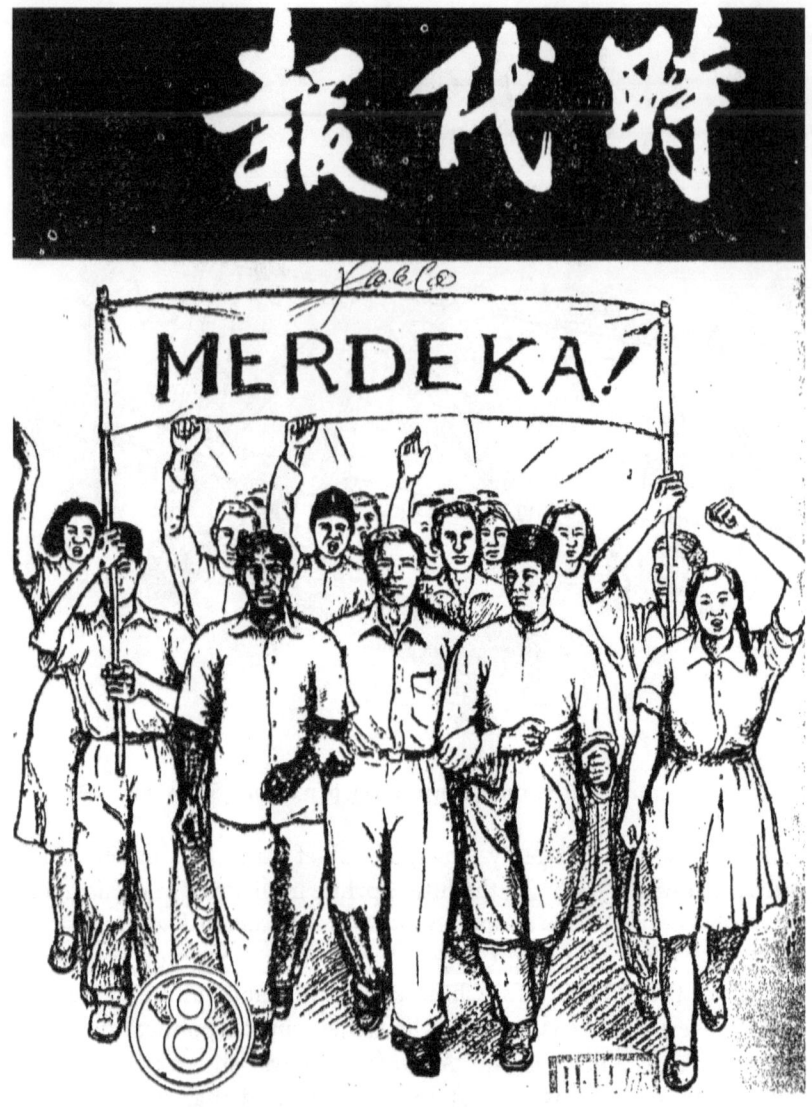

**"Merdeka!" artist unknown (using pen name),** *Shidaipao*, **January 15, 1956.**

The other publication that featured many cartoons during this period was the *University Tribune*, a newspaper put out by the Nanyang University Students' Union. Within these pages, further discussion of Malayan culture and consciousness was held.[12] Students contributed cartoons to the paper that debated the issue of what made a Malayan, and even articles about the role of art and cartoons in Malayan society.[13]

## Anti-Colonial Stance of Chinese Cartoonists in the 1950s

Cartoonists of the 1950s were part of the anti-colonial movement. They were supporters of the strongest contenders then—the PAP—and thus their interests were aligned with Lee Kuan Yew and the English-educated leadership within the party. For example, cartoonist Tan Wee Huan, who drew strong social statements in *Selection of Woodcuts and Cartoons*, contributed a powerful woodblock print for the *People's Action Party 1st Anniversary Celebration Souvenir (27–11–1955)*, which accompanied a Chinese article credited to Lee Kuan Yew. The article, "Our Stance," was a firm declaration of Lee's own socialist beliefs.

The PAP was the main left-wing party in the 1950s. It started with democratic socialist ideals, and its platform to the voters was social justice for all. There was an alignment of socialist interests between the English-educated leaders of the PAP and the Chinese-educated students, unionists, and intellectuals that the PAP worked with in the 1950s. They had common interests and goals in the 1950s, and even after the split within the PAP in 1961, some cartoonists continued to support the ruling party (Yeo and Lau 1991: 142).

Cartoons and other progressive works were thus valued highly by the public and politicians. They were weapons which political parties could harness. Cartoonists were committed anti-colonialists and Malayanists. This account below, related to me by Tan Wee Huan, illustrates the convictions of young artists during these times.

Tan joined *The Straits Times* as an artist after his graduation from Nanyang Academy of Fine Arts in 1955. When the paper moved to Times House at Kim Seng Road in 1958, a visit was made to the premises by the Prime Minister of Malaya, Tunku Abdul Rahman. Merger with Malaya to gain independence from the British had always been the game plan for anti-colonialists in Singapore, even for those of different political inclinations such as David Marshall and Lee Kuan Yew.

The cartoonists had come out strongly in support of a union with Malaya. However, since gaining its independence in 1957, Malaya had looked upon Singapore with suspicion. With its Chinese-dominated society which could upset the racial balance in the peninsula if it were to join Malaya, Singapore was perceived as a little China at the doorstep of Malaya. PAP was especially viewed with mistrust by the Tunku as it was the strongest left-wing contender in the late 1950s. The Malayan prime minister and his party, United Malays National Organization (UMNO), believed that if PAP were to win the 1959 general elections, it would become a Trojan horse for the Malayan Communist Party (Ang 1991: 196). Thus, the Tunku was cool to the idea of a merger in the late 1950s and gave his support to Lim Yew Hock's Singapore People's Alliance, a right-wing party.

On the day of the Tunku's visit to Times House, everyone stood up to greet him as a mark of respect to the prime minister of Malaya. Tan told me proudly that he refused to stand up and remained seated in his chair when the Tunku entered the room (Tan, interview, 2001). Such were the political convictions of artists and cartoonists that fuelled the independence movement.


## 1960s: The Proposed Merger and the Radicalization of Chinese Cartoons in Political Magazines

It was the Tunku's change of mind about the merger in 1961 that led to the split within PAP, which effectively polarized the cartoonists supporting the party. The leftists in the PAP realized that if Singapore were to merge with Malaya, the central government in Kuala Lumpur would not hesitate to purge the leftist elements in Singapore using the Internal Security Act. The Tunku supposedly was convinced by the British to take in Singapore in order to safeguard the security of Malaya itself from leftist influences in Singapore penetrating the peninsula (Lee 1998: 366).

By July 1961, the die was cast and thirteen PAP assemblymen quit the party to form the anti-merger Barisan Sosialis (Drysdale 1984: 283). The Barisan had the support of the trade unions, especially the Singapore General Employees' Union, led by Lim Chin Siong and Fong Swee Suan. Battle lines were drawn not just in the Legislative Assembly, but in the galleries of magazines as well. Artists who supported the Barisan contributed cartoons to the party organ, *Battle Front Weekly (Zhenxianpao)*, and *Fan Xin Pao*, the publication of the Singapore General Employees' Union.[14]

Attacks against the proposed merger, Lee Kuan Yew, the Tunku, the British and the pro-PAP union, and the National Trade Union Congress became the central topics in these cartoons. The strongest cartoons appeared in 1961 and 1962 when the battle for merger was raging. Several metaphors were used against the merger such as the need to burst the merger bluff, symbolized by a balloon.[15] The attacks against Lee Kuan Yew were more acerbic. Lee was portrayed as a lackey of the Tunku, with the British pulling all the strings in the background.

Much inventiveness was shown by the cartoonists who mixed the 1950s social concern of morality and values with challenges against the PAP's political legitimacy and Lee's right to rule Singapore. The Barisan cartoonists questioned the masculinity of Lee Kuan Yew, saying that he was not man enough to lead a new nation.

In one cartoon, we see Lee getting married to the Tunku by a British pastor. It is clear who the girl here was and who would wear the pants

### Tembelang Perchantuman Akan Terbongkar.

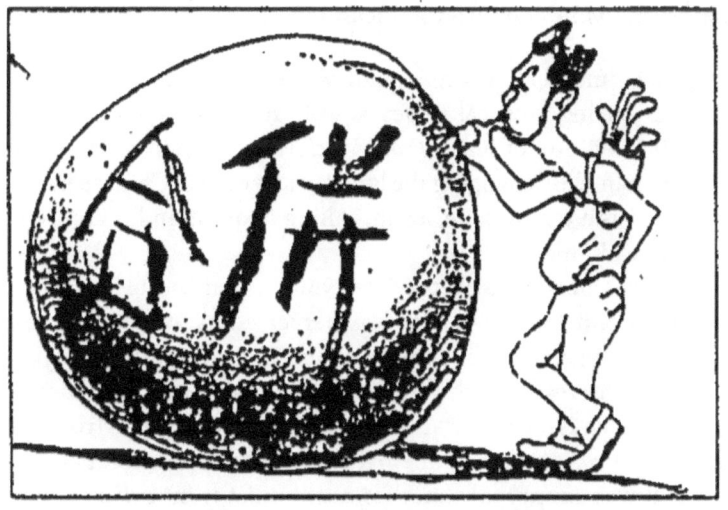

### The Merger Bluff Must Explode.

"The Merger Bluff Must Explode," artist unknown (using pen name). Cartoon on bookmark distributed by Barisan Sosialis, a defunct political party, 1961.

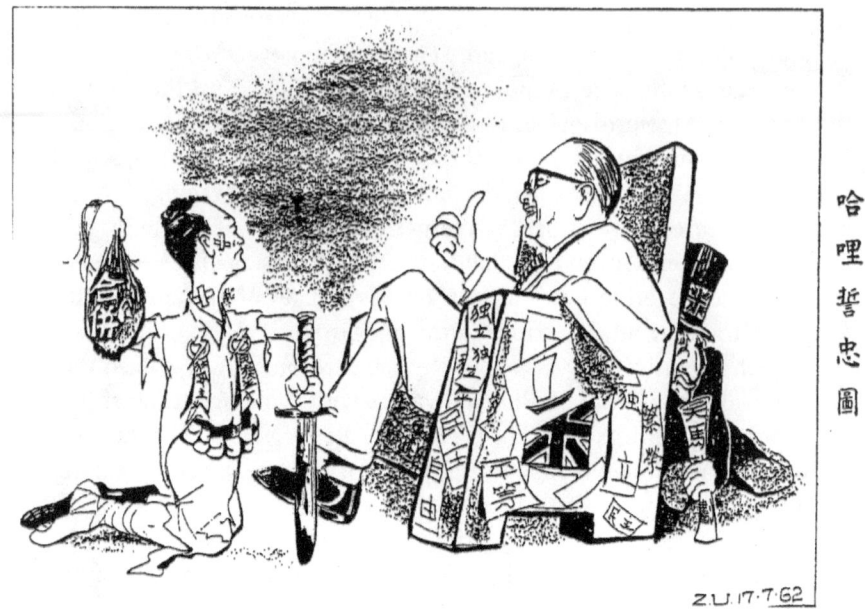

**"Loyal Harry"** (Harry is the English name of Lee Kuan Yew), **artist unknown (using pen name),** *Battle Front Weekly,* **August 1, 1962.**

in this marriage/merger. This metaphor was extended to slogans and name-callings during political rallies as well. A photo taken from the August 22, 1962, edition of *Battle Front Weekly* made a pun of Lee Kuan Yew's Chinese name. By changing the last character of his Chinese name, Lee was labeled as a transvestite, again, calling to question his ability as a real man to lead Singapore.

Such images persisted till the late 1960s, when the merger with Malaysia failed and Lee Kuan Yew was perceived as welcoming new imperialism to Singapore. The power of such images and messaging should not be underestimated. While we do not know the number of copies sold for each issue of *Battle Front Weekly,* we can gauge from the sale of *Suara Rakyat,* the organ of Parti Rakyat, an opposition party in the 1960s that was supposedly another communist front organization. The *Suara Rakyat* sold well in Malaya, about 15,000 copies of every issue (Lee 1976: 33). We can infer that opposition publications such as *Suara Rakyat, Battle Front Weekly,* and *Fan Xin Pao* reached out to the masses in Singapore and attempted to shape their opinions.

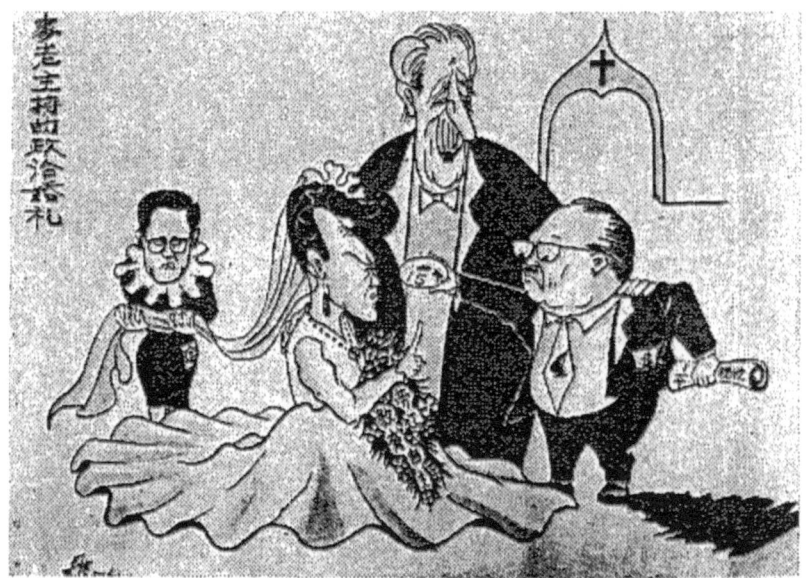

麥老主持的假合併政治婚禮

**"Political Marriage," artist unknown (using pen name),** *Battle Front Weekly,* **August 31, 1962.**

The confrontational characteristic of Chinese cartoonists is applicable to both camps in Singapore politics. Propaganda cartoons were important to the ruling party, as well as the oppositions. Just like the Barisan Sosialis, the PAP employed cartoons on the front page of their publications to demolish their opponents. Full-page cartoons were run to expose the suspected conspiracy between the Barisan and the Indonesian agitators during the period of the Indonesian confrontation in order to discredit the Barisan.[16]

It is not possible to identify the Barisan cartoonists of this period as very few of them would dare to admit that they drew the present Minister Mentor Lee Kuan Yew (a post Lee took after stepping down as prime minister in 1990) in such derogatory terms. Sometimes, not even Barisan members knew the identity of their cartoonists. Artist Ng Kim Choon used to secretly contribute cartoons to *Battle Front Weekly*; he would drop them off in the Barisan mailbox at night, unseen. Ng was not a party member, and the Barisan did not have his name or contact

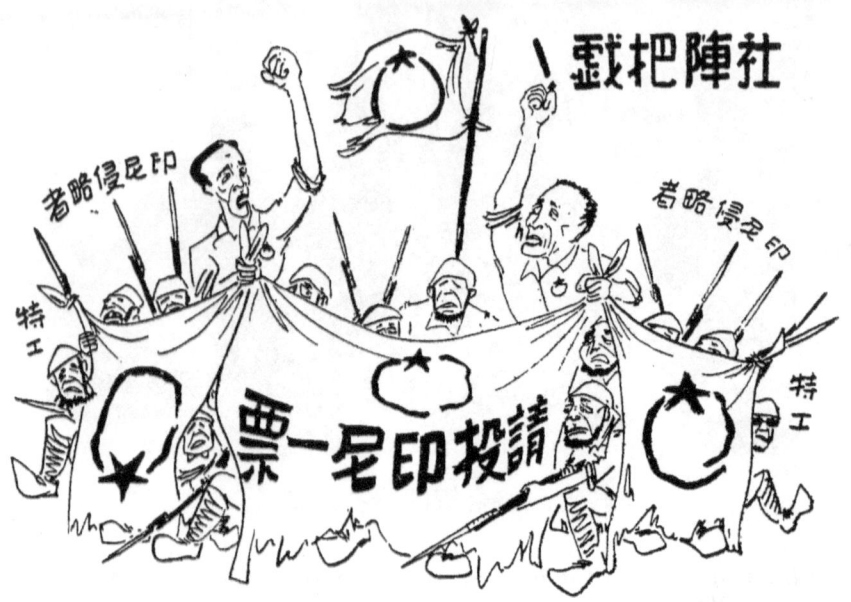

**"Indonesian Conspiracy," artist unknown (using pen name), *Petir*, organ of the People's Action Party, July 1965.**

details as all the cartoons were signed under different pen names. There was no payment, and Ng had no idea the fate of his cartoon until he picked up the next issue of *Battle Front Weekly*. He contributed those cartoons, because he disagreed with the actions of the ruling party. Such secrecy was necessary because of the rampant arrests of suspected communist subversives under the Internal Security Act in the 1960s. While Ng was willing to share with me his experience of having contributed cartoons to *Battle Front Weekly*, he was reluctant to identify the cartoons he drew for the publication (Ng, interview, 2001).

Thus, the relationship between cartoonists and politics was not so straightforward. In the case of Ng, he was using the space provided by *Battle Front Weekly* to express his views, and not necessarily as a member of the party or a communist sympathizer.[17] A cartoon from November 30, 1969, edition of *Battle Front Weekly* illustrates my point.

The late theatre pioneer of postwar Singapore, Kuo Pao Kun, was detained for four years under the Internal Security Act between 1976 and 1980 for being a member of the Malayan People's Liberation League, an underground organization of the MCP (Jit 1990: 17; Nair 1976: 16, 239). However, as seen in one cartoon he was perceived as a traitor to the socialist cause in 1969. Kuo had started working freelance with Radio and TV Singapore in 1967 and was appointed TV producer the following year, while still involved in socially conscious productions at his own Practice Performing Arts School (Kuo 2000: 391). The cartoonist who drew this cartoon obviously thought something was suspicious about Kuo's actions and wanted to expose him. Such were the cartoon "debates" in political publications in the 1960s.[18]

## 1966–80: Retreat and Compromise

After 1965, when Singapore separated from Malaysia, the Barisan cartoonists turned to regional concerns, such as the Vietnam War, as

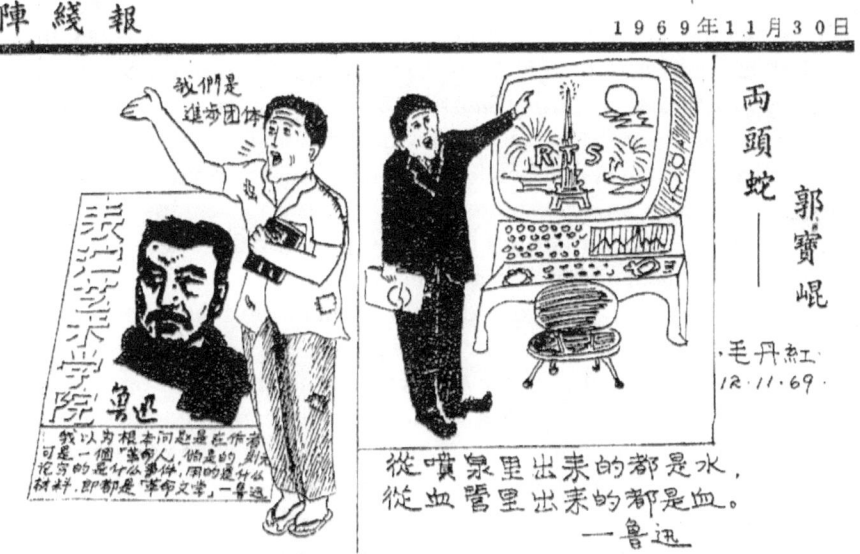

"Two Headed Snake—Kuo Pao Kun," artist unknown (using pen name), *Battle Front Weekly*, November 30, 1969.

well as excursions into local politics, such as the cartoons mentioned above. However, the party itself abandoned the parliamentary route when all its members in Parliament resigned in 1966 to take political action to the streets. The PAP swept the 1968 general elections, and no opposition stepped into Parliament till 1981.

The mood changed for Chinese cartoons. While cartoons critical of the government continued to appear in oppositional publications such as the *Battle Front Weekly*, their reach and influence was not as strong as when the party was at its peak in the early 1960s. The majority of the people rallied behind the PAP after 1965 when faced with the issue of political survival in the international arena. Partisan politics was out in order to achieve national needs of cohesion and stability.

These were reflected in the mainstream Chinese press, which was not as controversial or political. The owners of *Nanyang Siang Pau*, for example, did not want to hurt their profit margins by running anti-government cartoons. The 1960s were a tumultuous time for Singapore, and the Chinese papers wanted to stay away from party politics as much as possible. In *Nanyang Siang Pau*, the cartoons mostly dealt with social and economic issues, as well as international incidents such as the India-Pakistan conflict.

By the mid–1960s, *Nanyang Siang Pau*, like *The Straits Times*, had become pro-establishment in its views. A cartoon from the September 5, 1965, edition of *Nanyang Siang Pau* gave the government's side of the story with regard to Chinese education. It showed that the PAP was supportive of Chinese education by pumping more money into it. However, the cartoon missed the point of the strikes and demonstrations by Nanyang University students in 1965, who protested the lack of job opportunities for them once they graduated (Pereira 2003: 193). Thus, this cartoon presented a rather skewed argument in favor of the government.

Cartoons dealing with hard-core political issues in Singapore were avoided. For example, cartoons by woodcut artists, See Cheen Tee and Lim Mu Hue in 1968 and 1969, were more social and humorous. One, by See Cheen Tee, who drew the cover of *Selection of Woodcuts and Cartoons* in 1955, was one of the best drawn social cartoons from that period. Appearing in *Nanyang Siang Pau* two days after Christmas 1968, it showed old Santa presenting a new electric fan to a working-class household (as identified by their clothes) living in a Housing Development Board flat. The blades of the fan were in the shape of 6s or 9s, depending on how

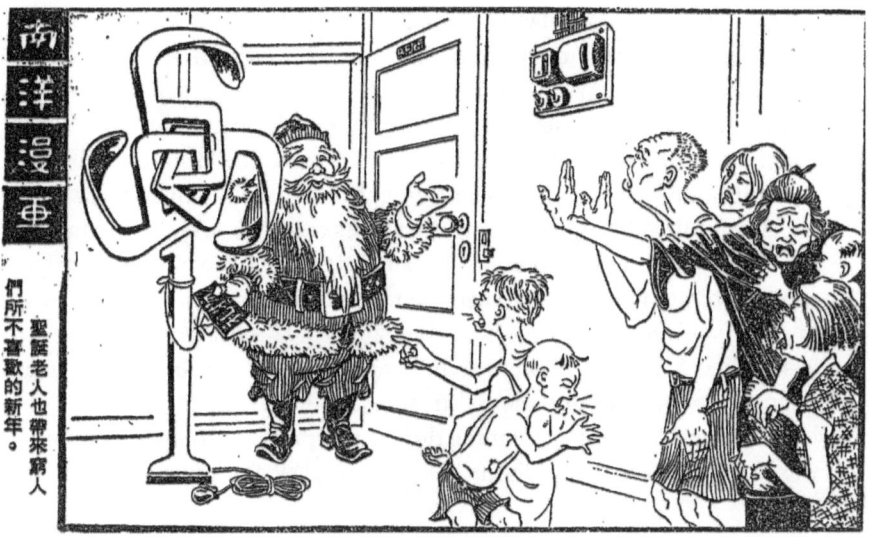

"Christmas, 1968," See Cheen Tee, *Nanyang Siang Pau*, December 27, 1968.

one looked at them. It cleverly symbolized the new year, 1969, that was arriving in a few days' time. However, the family was seen rejecting the gift, the clue to why they were doing so lies in the central positioning of the electricity reading meter in the cartoon. It hinted that this rather huge household was too poor to afford the increase in electric bills if they kept the fan. Furthermore, the younger child placed just below the meter looks like he was coughing his guts out, showing that the family was too poor to see the doctor, much less be able to afford the luxury of a new electric fan. See's cartoon was a brilliant subtle cartoon about the social realities of blue-collar life in the late 1960s, especially when the British had announced in 1968 that they would be withdrawing their naval base, affecting thousands of jobs in Singapore (Turnbull 1989: 293–94).

However, even when these cartoonists steered clear of local politics, they still got into trouble, simply because of the inherent satirical and subversive nature of the medium in which they were dealing. Artist Lim Mu Hue joined *Nanyang Siang Pau* as an art editor in 1969. Knowing how sensitive the public was to being satirized, Lim modeled his cartoon character, "Lao Lao," after himself. But he still received flack when readers called up the newspaper to complain about his cartoons, especially those that made fun of self-proclaimed artists in Singapore (Lim, interview, 2001). "I Am the Master Artist!" is interesting as it was a collaboration between Lim and Ong Yih, the co-editor of *Selection of Woodcuts and Cartoons*. The cartoon showed both of them fighting it out to determine who was the master artist in Singapore. Even though both cartoonists caricatured themselves in this cartoon, it offended the sensibilities of other artists, who thought they were the ones made fun of. This resulted in complaints against Lim's cartoons, which were taken seriously by the newspapers. In exasperation, Lim drew his last strip, showing himself on all fours, surrendering. He stopped drawing cartoons in *Nanyang Siang Pau* (Lim, interview, 2001).[19] This is a pity as cartoonists such as See and Lim were trained artists who were able to produce quality cartoons, despite the political restrictions.[20]

The problems for cartooning during this period were two-fold. One was the "us versus them" divide between the PAP and the opposition. It

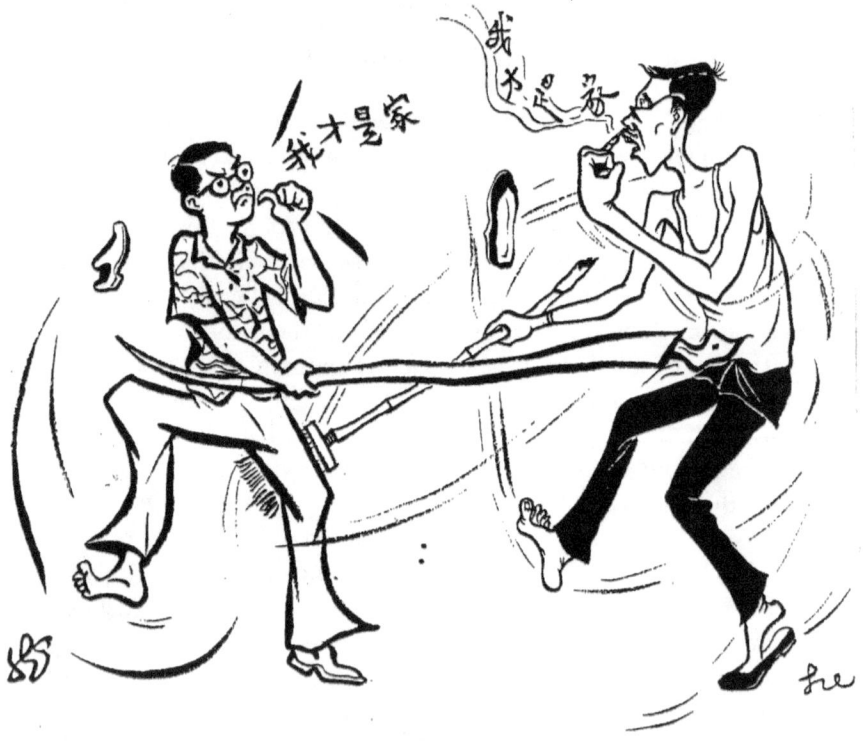

**"I Am the Master Artist!" Lim Mu Hue and Ong Yih, *Nanyang Siang Pau*, 1969.**

170

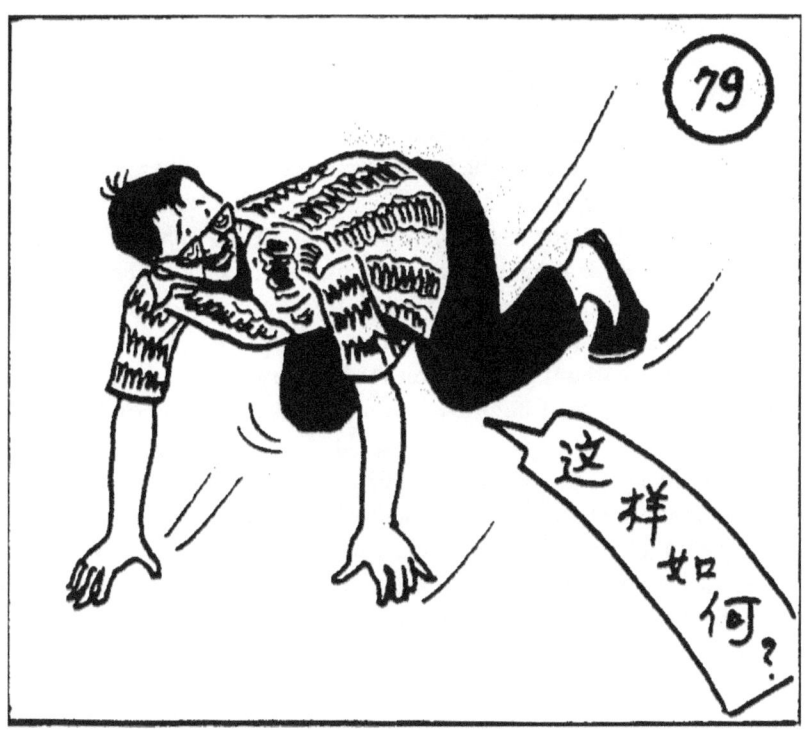

**"Surrender," Lim Mu Hue, *Nanyang Siang Pau*, 1969.**

became a case whereby, if you were not for the ruling party, you were against it.[21] Not everyone wanted to take the chance of commenting on the policies of the day out of civil consciousness and be punished, especially when one was a professional artist with a career and family to think about. Thus, with the decline of the political pluralism allowed in cartoons, many good cartoonists left the field. Those who continued were cartoonists willing to work with the limitations imposed by drawing only cartoons that were socially-acceptable (to the state) for the mainstream Chinese press, or cartoonists who only drew cartoons in service of party politics, such as those drawing for the PAP or the Barisan Sosialis. These cartoonists did not see cartooning as an artform, and most of their works were hastily executed with very little craft or attention to the potential of the medium. Their cartoons did not have the kind of complexity found in those that appeared in *Shidaipao* or *The*

*Literary Post* in the 1950s, which combined political convictions with a certain amount of artistry.

By the 1970s, a consensus in the mainstream press was reached that cartoonists would not do local works of a political nature. This is confirmed in the cartoons of the artist, Koh Sia Yong, that appeared in *Nanyang Siang Pau* between 1979 and 1980. A social realist artist and member of the Equator Art Society since the 1950s, Koh's works were political cartoons dealing only with foreign events, such as the oil crisis and the fundamentalist threats posed by the Ayatollah Khomeini. Even a veteran like him stayed away from local issues.

It was not without good reason for Koh to avoid the topic of local politics. Just three years before, prominent artists such as Kuo Pao Kun and his wife Goh Lay Kuan were arrested for communist activities. Furthermore, in 1974, the new Newspaper and Printing Presses Act was enacted. It retained the existing licensing laws and introduced a mandatory system of management shares, which could be held only by approved shareholders. These management shares, which conferred voting rights two hundred times greater than ordinary shares, were only to be allotted by the Minister of Culture, who also controlled the appointment and dismissal of directors and senior staff. This unique set of laws allowed the government to control all newspapers without having to nationalize them or take over their daily operations (Turnbull 1995: 308). In 1977, the press laws were further tightened, barring anyone from holding more than three percent of ordinary shares (Lent 1982: 164).

The relationship between art and politics was not encouraged in the 1970s. Only the university periodicals still had some bite as seen in a publication of the University of Singapore Chinese Society, depicting the suppression of student activism. But by the end of the decade, the suppression was complete. "Pulling the Strings" sums up the state of cartooning in Singapore in the 1970s; controlled by the state, the younger/student artists were resisting in futility. However, the drawing was just not up to par, when compared to the imaginative works of the 1950s and 1960s, especially the cartoons in *University Tribune*. The quality of the draftsmanship suffered when some of the better artists such as See Cheen Tee and Lim Mu Hue left cartooning because of restrictions and the need to make a living. While cartooning continued well into the 1980s, the standard of craft and level of intensity were lost. The works of cartooning collectives such as Cartoon Bun and Cartoon Fast Food

从哈侖貪污谈 5·13 事件

读〈小说中的妇女形象〉有感

《大学专栏》

哲学：人扁环境

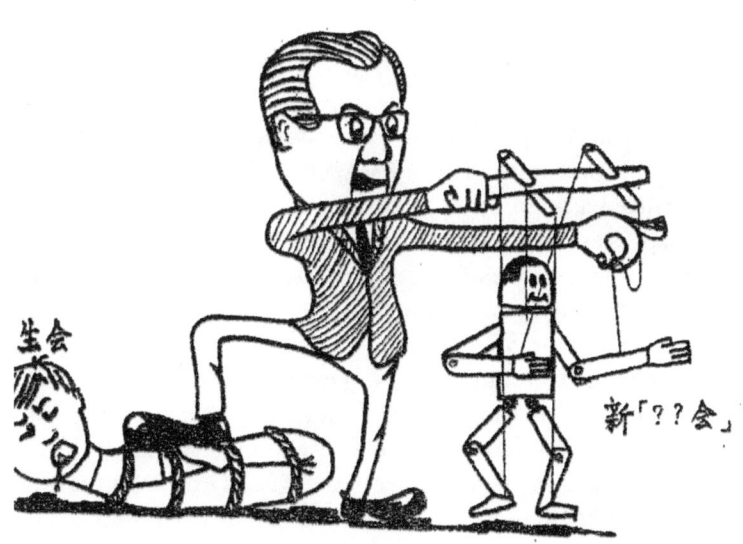

"嘿嘿！看，它还活着．説話呀！唖吧！"

"Pulling the Strings," artist unknown (using pen name), *Wind*, December 8, 1975.

in *Lianhe Zaobao* were more amateurish and gag-based, not political or social conscious.

But there is a price to be paid for the ruling party in demanding such social complicity in the public and cultural spheres of Singapore life. They have effectively "shot themselves in the foot" by dismantling the vibrant civil society of the 1950s and 1960s (of which cartoons were a part), to the point that when they need a more active citizenry now, that is not forthcoming from a population inculcated otherwise. Such public activism and service is not instilled or encouraged among the younger generation.

The time frame for this essay ends in 1980, the year in which Nanyang University, the institution of hope for the Chinese-educated in Singapore, ceased to exist. Its closing marked the end of the many concerns and activism that Chinese intellectuals and cartoonists were associated with (Chua 2001: 120). From that point onwards, gag cartoons and editorial cartoons about foreign politics dominated the medium in both English and Chinese press (Lim 2000).

## Conclusion: Co-opted and Abandoned

Idealism had to give way to professionalism as space was taken away from the cartoonists. The newspapers no longer ran their cartoons on a freelance basis. In order to continue drawing, cartoonists had to join the papers as full-time artists and steer clear of political issues. The 1970s saw the emergence of professional cartoonists such as Kefu, Lin Xizhong, and Man Tianfei, who had other editorial duties in their respective media jobs.[22]

Perhaps the cartooning career of Ong Yih, co-editor of *Selection of Woodcut and Cartoons* in 1955, is an illuminating example. Ong Yih was clearly an idealist who fought on the side of civil society for Chinese education and against yellow culture in the 1950s. Growing up as a member of the minority in Indonesia, he was well aware of the need for racial harmony. He was a Malayan, who drew cartoons promoting the cooperation of different races, even producing a Chinese comic book of Malay folklore. He was a regular contributor to *The National Language Monthly* in the early 1960s, a bilingual magazine that introduced Malay customs to Chinese readers.

From the late 1960s onwards, Ong Yih drew cartoons for government publications such as those of the People's Association and other magazines put out by the Educational Publication Bureau. He also conducted numerous cartooning classes at community centers and worked hard to promote public appreciation of cartoons in Singapore in his writings for the Chinese press.[23] However, over the years, he drew fewer cartoons about the social conditions of Singapore and concentrated more on foreign issues and events. The local topics he touched upon were in line with the moralistic cartoons encouraged by the government in the 1970s.

I suspect Ong Yih was disillusioned and frustrated with the state of cartooning in Singapore, especially with the compromise he had to make to the demands of nation-building and consolidation, by not drawing political cartoons. He had experienced and participated in the power of the medium to shape public opinion about Chinese education and the building of a more just Malayan society. But, twenty years on, all that was lost. Although he continued giving cartooning classes in community centers into the 1980s, he discouraged his students from going into political cartooning. Instead, he told them to stick to drawing children's books. This was related to me by one of his students from that period, artist Amanda Heng (Heng, interview, 2002).

The PAP frowned on activism when the 1961 split happened. A large number of PAP branch activists went over to the Barisan Sosialis. The PAP had enough of strikes and demonstrations by students and unionists in the 1960s and 1970s. The fallout of that was a pragmatic approach to politics and everyday life in Singapore, or what Chua Beng Huat (1995) termed as communitarian ideology, an ideology of pragmatism formulated by the ruling party to serve its needs of building the nation.

Pragmatism has led to anti-idealism. Instead of thinking for themselves, artists, cartoonists, and intellectuals have left much of the thinking to the state, to find solutions to the current social and economic problems resulting from globalization faced by Singapore. From being organic intellectuals, cartoonists sold themselves short, resulting in a situation that has been described by Julien Benda as the "treason of intellectuals."[24]

In a forum on Singapore's national museums in 1998, Kuo Pao Kun raised the question of why Singaporeans were able to laugh at other countries' leaders in local cartoons, but were not allowed to do so at their own politicians. I would like to suggest that Kuo already had the answer to that in his 1995 play, *Descendents of the Eunuch Admiral*:

To keep my head
I must accept losing my tail
To keep my faith
I must learn to worship others' gods
To please my lord
I must eliminate his enemy
To serve his pleasure
I must purge my own
[Wee and Lee 2003: 54].

## NOTES

1. An example of this is *Selves: The State of Arts in Singapore*, a book published by the National Arts Council of Singapore in 2002.

2. As early as 1959, the year Singapore gained self-government from the British, the then Prime Minister, Lee Kuan Yew, reminded members of Nanyang University of this fact in a speech he made to them on October 28 that year.

3. All interviews were conducted in Mandarin, except those with Heng, Ho, and See, conducted in English.

4. "Sanmao" was the popular cartoon character created by Zhang Leping of China in the 1930s.

5. However, key ministries such as internal security and defense were still controlled by the British with the governor retaining his power to veto legislation.

6. The Chinese High School and Nanyang Girls' High School students also participated in this event.

7. Ho became a PAP member of Parliament before retiring from politics to be the principal of his alma mater, Nanyang Academy of Fine Arts. Ong pursued his interest in cartooning till his death in 1993 at the age of fifty-eight.

8. See the following graduation catalogues: *Nanyang Academy of Fine Arts 3rd Anniversary of Reopening After the War* (1948); *First Painting Collection of The Nanyang Fine Art Academy by the 6th Graduates* (1951); *Nanyang Academy of Fine Arts Special Issue of Art Exhibition* (1954); *The Art of Young Malayans* (1955).

9. After the PAP came to power in 1959, it continued with the bilingual policy in education.

10. Chua was a member of the Equator Art Society who contributed cartoons to *Nanyang Siang Pau* in the early 1950s, while he was studying and teaching part-time at the Nanyang Academy of Fine Arts. He was also an ex-student of Qiu Gao Peng at Chung Cheng High School.

11. Similar "brothers-in-arms" cartoons can be found in *Malayan Student (Chinese Edition)*, 1 (November 1955), p. 5, and *The Literary Post*, 2, 4 (April 1956), cover. The *Malayan Student* was a publication of the University of Malaya.

12. See the following articles in the *University Tribune*: Chiu Po, "Malayan Culture and the Recent Book-ban," Li Chuan-Shou, "The Malay Course at Nanyang" (December 1958); "The Culture of Malaya" (November 1959); Luk Tsien, "On Establishing a Malayan New Culture" (March 1960); Ma Tak, "The Need of a Department of Malay Studies in Nantah" and Jo Fang, "Some Thoughts on Malayan Cultural Development" (November 1960).

13. Zhang Tuan Yang, "Talking about Cartoons," *University Tribune* (November

1959); Fuen Yuen, "Writers Must Remain Part of the Living Society Around Them," *University Tribune* (August 1960).

14. The Barisan Sosialis and the Singapore General Employees' Union were listed as communist front organizations by Lee Ting Hui (1976: 121–22).

15. This cartoon was printed as a bookmark to be given away to people who attended the Barisan rallies. This shows the extent and importance political parties placed on cartoons to influence the public and to get their political messages across to the people.

16. Other political parties that ran cartoons in their publications include the right wing party of Ong Eng Guan's United People's Party, who won the Hong Lim by-election in 1961.

17. Ng said that *Battle Front Weekly* was one of the few publications that welcomed all contributions, and he also drew cartoons about international politics and events. However, he admitted that many of the cartoons were done very quickly to capture the political mood of the day, and might not be very well drawn.

18. The possible context for the appearance of this cartoon could be that in July 1969, key Barisan member, Lim Chin Siong, who had been detained by the government since 1963, gave up politics and renounced communism. He was released and soon left for studies in London. The Barisan expelled him from the party and denounced him as a "spineless and barefaced renegade traitor" (Lee 2000: 135).

19. For more on Lim Mu Hue, see Ong Yih's article on "Lim Mu Hue—Forgotten Artist" (1994: 242–49) and Ong and Tan 1990. Lim died in 2008.

20. See stopped drawing cartoons by the early 1970s to concentrate on his professional art career. See died in 1996 (See, interview, 2000). Also see Chia (2001). Both See and Lim were students, and later teachers at Nanyang Academy of Fine Arts in the 1950s and 1960s.

21. Lee Kuan Yew had made this very clear in his 1961 May Day speech: "It is not possible to tell the PAP 'do this, do that, do the other,' knowing well that the objective and realistic conditions have to be faced by any government in power with the interests of the people at heart. Therefore to those who say 'seek concord amidst or whilst maintaining the differences' I say to them and to their supporters: the PAP has clearly stated where it stands. Seek concord if you will with the PAP on the PAP stand. Maintain your differences and seek no concord if you find that the PAP stand is against your stand" (Josey 1968: 135).

22. Kefu worked as an in-house artist with the state television corporation.

23. See the following for examples of Ong Yih's writings on cartooning: "1950s Singaporean Cartoons" and "The Satirical Factor in Cartoons" in *Essays on Art* (Singapore: Pachui Art Singapore, 1991), 139–48 and 195–204; "The Social Value of Comics" in *Essays on World Art* (Singapore: Thomson Cultural Centre, 1994), 233–41.

24. I borrowed the term from Julien Benda's (1969) *The Treason of the Intellectuals* (New York: W.W. Norton & Company). Benda's original treatise from 1928 was an attack on the European intellectual establishment of the 1920s for abandoning disinterested intellectual activity and for allowing its talents to be used for political and nationalistic ends. There are some similarities here between 1920s Europe and 1970s Singapore.

# Political Cartoons and Burma's Transnational Public Sphere

LISA BROOTEN

This study analyzes contemporary Burmese political cartoons produced in exile, focusing on those involving two recent crisis events in Burma, also known as Myanmar,[1] the 2007 protests dubbed the "Saffron Revolution," and the 2008 tropical Cyclone Nargis and its aftermath. These two events produced "critical discourse moments," periods of public discussion sparked by crisis events that stimulate media commentary reasserting preferred interpretations of unfolding events (Gamson and Stuart 1992). Critical discourse moments of such magnitude also promote the emergence of a transnational public sphere, where people worldwide debate the same questions provoked by the same events.

The goal of this study is to analyze how cartoon commentary on crisis events contributes to the transnational public sphere, in this case, by reproducing or challenging understandings not only of Burma and its leaders, but also of the local, national, and international players involved. The cartoons analyzed here were published in *The Irrawaddy*, a magazine founded by Burmese dissident students who fled to Thailand after a violent crackdown on massive uprisings in Burma in 1988. In targeting international policymakers, academics, and activists along with Burmese peoples inside and outside the country, *The Irrawaddy* has played a role in expanding the Burmese national public sphere into a transnational, "porous public sphere." The highly political nature of the cartoons examined here is a response to the extreme circumstances on which they are commenting; yet they also build on a long history of vibrant Burmese comic art.

## A Brief History of Burmese Comic Art

Comic art in Burma began during the British colonial period with the publication of the country's first cartoon by a British railroad official in 1914 in the *Rangoon Times,* and the first by a Burmese, Shwe Ta Lay, the following year (Lent 1995). Shortly after this, Burmese cartooning took on pro-independence themes until Burma's independence in 1948. The parliamentary period of the 1950s saw the flowering of a free and lively press, including cartoonists who saw themselves as watchdogs sniffing out corruption and abuses of power (Lent 1995; Leehey 1997). Things changed drastically in 1962, when a coup ushered in General Ne Win's Burma Socialist Programme Party (BSPP) and its twenty-six years of authoritarian government. A restrictive press act established a censorship body, the Press Scrutiny Board, and political cartooning gave way to cartoons focused on harmless topics such as nutrition and agriculture (Leehey 1997). Political cartooning reappeared during Burma's democracy movement of 1988, when for a brief time even hard-hitting political topics and ridicule of General Ne Win and the BSPP were the subject of cartoons appearing in the more than forty independent newspapers and magazines that emerged (Leehey 1997). After massive street protests in 1988 were met with a violent crackdown, a bloody coup led to the formation of a new military regime that shut down all independent periodicals and reestablished the strict censorship system.

Since 1988, cartoonists inside Burma have steered clear of overtly political topics, focusing instead on popular subjects such as children's humor, science fiction, and stories featuring famous cartoon characters, which while ostensibly apolitical, often carry important social messages (Lent 1995). Due to the unpredictability that makes "the mercurial standards of the Press Scrutiny Board shift with small changes in the political atmosphere," cartoonists have difficulty navigating the landscape of acceptable discourse (Leehey 1997: 154). Yet cartoons have continued to play an important political role in Burma, at times passing through the strict censorship system by virtue of the genre's potential for multiple interpretations (Lent 1995; Leehey 1997).

While Burmese cartoonists have relied primarily on comic books as their medium (Lent 1995), cartoons have also been self-published, and have appeared in government periodicals and daily newspapers, private weekly and monthly magazines, and more recently, in the publications of the Burmese media in exile established in the border areas after the 1988 crackdown. It is in exile that Burmese cartoons have again taken on a highly political role, functioning to support the democratic movement and ridicule the various manifestations of military rule, including the current State Peace and Development Council (SPDC). In addition, political cartoons produced in exile have also played a key role in extending the Burmese public sphere, which is no longer contained by the boundaries of the state but is rather increasingly transnational.

The power of cartoons lies in their ability to simplify highly complex events by using easily understood symbols, relying on and perpetuating mythical images of bad guys and victims. In commenting on the two crisis events examined here, cartoons clearly perform this function. Yet, in simplifying these events, they also leave key players out of the picture, an absence which functions to promote international solidarity within the transnational public sphere in support of change in Burma and victims of the crises.

## The Saffron Revolution

The protests that caught the world's attention in September 2007, dubbed the Saffron Revolution in reference to the robes worn by the monks who led them, began in August in response to unannounced cuts in fuel subsidies by the Burmese regime, the SPDC. These cuts caused the price of diesel and petrol to double and natural gas to increase five-fold (*BBC News*, August 15, 2007), leading to sharp increases in transport and food prices, and the first street protests in Burma in at least a decade. In mid–September, the protests grew to an estimated fifty thousand to one hundred thousand participants, and spread to over twenty-five cities (*BBC News*, September 25, 2007). When a group of monks and their sympathizers marched to the home of revered opposition leader Aung San Suu Kyi, held under house arrest for twelve of the previous eighteen years, she was briefly permitted to greet them before they dispersed peacefully. As reports emerged of arrests and beatings, international condemnation was swift. U.S. President George W. Bush, for example, announced unilateral sanctions against the Burmese leaders and encouraged others to do the same (*BBC News*, September 25, 2007), and the Dalai Lama expressed his support for the monks (*Philippine Inquirer*, September 24, 2007).

The regime imposed curfews in the two biggest cities of Yangon and Mandalay, and reports emerged of monasteries being barricaded, monks and protestors beaten and arrested, and several deaths (*The Australian*, September 27, 2007). The shooting of Japanese photojournalist Kenji Nagai at close range by a Burmese soldier and other acts of violence against unarmed protestors were captured by amateur mobile phone footage, sent out via the Internet, then reported by international news agencies. The regime cut off Internet access in an attempt to stem the flow of information, and soldiers reportedly began targeting those with cameras. October began with a heavy troop presence and the protests subsided, although at least one thousand monks had reportedly been forcibly disrobed and detained (Montlake 2007). The total number arrested, beaten, wounded, and killed between August and October 2007 is still disputed and will likely never be verified. In December, however, after a visit to Burma, UN envoy Paulo Sergio Pinheiro reported that more than six hundred people were still being detained, seventy-four were listed as missing, and at least thirty-one people had been killed, adding that these figures might "greatly underestimate the reality" (*BBC News*, December 7, 2007).

## Constitutional Referendum and Cyclone Nargis

On May 2 and 3, 2008, tropical Cyclone Nargis hit Burma, the deadliest natural disaster in the country's recorded history, bringing heavy winds that ripped off roofs, downed trees and power lines, and collapsed buildings. Huge waves followed, sweeping away entire villages in the Irrawaddy Delta region. The official government death toll was grossly underestimated as the regime tried to reduce the disaster's political impact by keeping foreign aid workers from reporting on the full extent of the damage. The UN estimates that 2.4 million people were affected by the cyclone, and as of early June 2008, only 1.3 million of these people had received basic assistance which they consider inadequate and below minimum requirements (United Nations Office, 2008). Estimates are that as many as 130,000 may have been killed in the cyclone, and two to three million left homeless. Aid workers critiqued the regime's secrecy, obsession with security, and restrictions that led to delays in relief efforts and many more deaths than might have otherwise occurred (*New York Times*, June 18, 2008).

The Burmese regime's suspicions about the motives of outsiders and its desire to project an image of successful democratic reform caused it to both close its doors to outsiders and to push ahead with a planned constitutional referendum, despite the cyclone's devastation. The regime did accept bilateral aid from neighboring Thailand and India a few days after the storm hit, but other planes loaded with relief goods were not permitted into the country. For several weeks, foreign aid workers waited for visas after the Burmese regime stated it was "not ready to receive search and rescue teams as well as media teams from foreign countries" (*BBC News*, May 9, 2008). Despite calls to postpone the scheduled May 10 national constitutional referendum, the regime postponed the vote until May 24 only in the five hardest hit regions it had declared disaster areas, but went ahead as scheduled in the rest of the country. Heavily criticized for this decision, the regime nevertheless announced an overwhelming "yes" vote in favor of the new constitution, as was widely expected.

As the days passed, little aid was getting to the victims, abandoned bodies were scattered throughout the country, and concerns were raised about sanitation and disease. On May 23 the regime finally agreed to allow in all foreign aid workers (Kazmin 2008), yet refused to allow relief supplies to be delivered from U.S., British, and French military ships waiting offshore. On June 5, U.S. Navy ships sailed away from Burma's coast, their relief supplies undelivered (*CBC News*, June 5, 2008). Reports emerged of authorities confiscating aid from private donors, arresting aid workers for refusing to hand the aid over, offering aid on the condition that recipients provide labor in return, and forcing survivors out of emergency camps and back to their destroyed villages (*CBC News*, June 5, 2008). Many governments were outspoken in their criticism of the regime's handling of the situation. For example, the United States accused the regime of "criminal neglect" (*New York Times*, June 18, 2008), and French Foreign Minister Bernard Kouchner urged the U.N. Security Council to force the regime to allow aid delivery to cyclone victims (*International Herald Tribune*, May 19, 2008). And while the regime allowed foreign aid workers into the country, it restricted and monitored their movements.

These two crisis events, while quite different, also share key similarities. The 2007 Saffron Revolution and the Burmese regime's violent response were provoked by an internal crisis, while Cyclone Nargis was a natural disaster. Yet, the regime's bungled response in both cases was heavily criticized by the Burmese as well as outside observers, who debated the need for international intervention in the transnational public sphere that emerged during both crisis events.

## Crisis, the Porous Public Sphere, and the Transnational Dialectic

In times of crisis, humor does not disappear, but functions instead to bind the beleaguered together, to release tension and help people cope with what are often exhausting or overwhelming circumstances (Holman and Kelly 2001). Especially in crisis situations, cartoons help with cognitive reframing of the events and clearly define the opposition. By framing violence as mundane, the cartoonist can bring its horror to the everyday level and make it bearable (Levin 2007).

Perhaps, especially for those communities in exile from a crisis-afflicted homeland, identity involves a form of antagonism, an identification *against* something "other."

> Persons and communities which perceive themselves as displaced construct their "authentic" identities in terms not of some sort of originary culture but with defensive reference to experiences in exile which they consider antagonistic against a threatening other and that antagonism—although nominally to be purged when the full identity it impedes is realized—remains fundamental to identity [Bowman quoted in Najjar 2007: 260].

This identity against a threatening "other," however, becomes especially complicated when that "other" comes from *within* one's native land, or when the "collective" being constructed excludes some elements of the national while including external elements. Especially in the search for international solidarity, a form of transnational collective identity emerges, contributing to and reshaping the "porous public sphere."

Olesen (2007) introduces the concept of the porous public sphere in order to escape the dichotomizing assumption that the public sphere is *either* transnational or national in nature. In his analysis, a public sphere is defined more productively as having degrees of porosity, often determined by two interconnected parameters: media and people. The media constitute an important infrastructure of communication in the public sphere, and are increasingly transnational and interconnected (Olesen 2007). The increased movement of peoples across borders has also increased the porosity of public spheres, which receive issues and information from outside the nation, and, in turn, affect other national contexts.

Porous public spheres contribute to the transnational public sphere that emerges during crises and their resulting critical discourse moments. The transnational public sphere is not a consistent state of affairs but rather a temporary phenomenon provoked by events that resonate widely. It is transitory, "a social space created when individuals, organizations, media, politicians, and officials at local and national levels around the world, aware of 'voices' in other places, debate the same questions at the same time with reference to the same events, statements and actions" (Olesen 2007: 305).

Burma introduces a further complexity, in that its national public sphere is obstructed by the state, and is thus created and maintained largely in exile, with contributions from inside and outside the state. Into this public sphere also flow the perspectives of non-governmental organization (NGO) workers, advocacy groups, academics, policymakers, and politicians from many countries. In addition, dissidents, refugees, and migrant workers from Burma are especially key in bringing news both into and out of the country as they move across its borders. This Burmese public sphere, then, is transnational and especially porous in nature, contributing to the transnational public sphere that emerges during crises.

## The Analysis

The cartoons analyzed here were all published in *The Irrawaddy*, a prime vehicle in the creation and maintenance of the Burmese public sphere, and among the most developed and professional of the Burmese exiled media, having widened its scope since its founding to include Southeast Asia and world news that affects the region. While the magazine is printed in English, *The Irrawaddy* online has both English and Burmese-language versions. It is thus both a nationally and regionally focused media outlet targeting an international audience. A glance at its letters to the editor makes clear that its readers include diplomats, aid agency and NGO staff, politicians, academics, and activists. *The Irrawaddy* also contributes to and reprints stories from other media. Its stories and interviews with its editor have been quoted in various international media, and its cartoons have been printed in the Thai English-language daily *The Nation* as well as other Thai media.

*The Irrawaddy*'s cartoons are published online, and are therefore accessible around the world, including in Burma, where people always manage to find ways around the regime's blocking of the Internet. The cartoons examined here, with one exception, were produced by two cartoonists living outside of Burma: Harnlay, a Burmese in exile, and Stephff, a French expatriate, both of whom have lived in Thailand for years, producing cartoons primarily about Burma, although they both also comment on the regional political scene. This reinforces the transnational nature of both *The Irrawaddy* and the international discourse community it has helped to produce, which like the cartoons examined here, addresses both local realities and global politics, with a focus on Burma and its relationship with international organizations, other countries, and international media. They thus comment on and simultaneously contribute to the transnational dialectic provoked by the two crisis events examined here, which brought Burma into the international news more than any other events in the country's recent history.

The majority of the cartoons examined here were published in October 2007 and May 2008, the two months with the largest number of cartoons in *The Irrawaddy*'s online cartoon archive, which dates back to June 2004. This unusually high number of cartoons, three to four times the monthly average published during 2007 and 2008, indicates the importance of these two events. I examined a total of forty-nine cartoons, twenty-five of which comment on the events leading up to the protests beginning in mid–September 2007 and their aftermath, and twenty-four of which comment on the May 2008 Cyclone Nargis and the national referendum on Burma's new constitution on May 10.[2]

To assess how these cartoons contributed to the transnational public sphere provoked by these crises, I analyze them to determine the perspective presented, to whom they are addressed, and their main messages. I look at the main actors and the frequency of their appearance, who is the brunt of the joke, and who is not. As the presence or absence of characters can also be telling (Levin 2007), I examine who is left out of these cartoons and what that may signify and how these cartoons may function as a call to action. In addition, I study their symbolism, including the cartoonist's "amplification through simplification," in which the focus on specific details amplifies their meaning (McCloud 1994: 30).

No claim is made here that the patterns revealed represent the intent of the artists who drew these cartoons or the editors who approved them. The process of deriving meaning is complex, and only partially dependent on the intentions of the message creator. Reading strategies also contribute to meaning in a process of intertextuality, in which the repetition of symbols, images, and ideas are understood or decoded in multiple ways by readers responding based on individual experiences and, especially in the transnational public sphere, varying cultural norms (Fiske 1992; Gamson 1992). My intent is thus not to claim a single set of symbolic meanings as "true," but rather to identify patterns of representation that function in symbolic ways to shape understandings of Burma and those involved in these crisis events.

## The Cartoons

These cartoons complement the editorial line of *The Irrawaddy* in its analysis of regional politics and its focus on the Burmese regime, its actions, and the potential for its downfall. Some elements of the international community are a focus, especially the UN, the Association of Southeast Asian Nations (ASEAN), and China, and with the cartoons on the cyclone, the international aid community. The military is featured in a majority of the cartoons, while ordinary Burmese civilians appear less often. In the cartoons examined from the 2007 protests, the monks feature heavily, represented as the most threatening human element to the regime's power. Opposition leader Aung San Suu Kyi is a surprisingly rare figure in these depictions, as are the Burmese in exile.

Overall, the butt of the jokes is the regime, with the UN, ASEAN, and China close behind. Given the gravity of the situations commented on, it is perhaps not surprising that ordinary Burmese, Aung San Suu Kyi, and the exiled Burmese community seem off limits to humorous treatment in these cartoons. Criticisms found in some of the Burmese media in exile of the attempt by some donors to attach conditions to their aid also do not appear here. Neither do major national actors such as the U.S., France, or other key European nations, despite the important roles they played in international debates about how to get the regime to respond more effectively to the crisis. The majority of representations of the international community, with the exception of the UN, ASEAN, China, and Thailand, show them as thwarted in their attempts to offer aid.

These cartoons reinforce images of the regime as violent, greedy, corrupt, and lacking compassion, and of international organizations, especially the UN and ASEAN, as either ineffective in motivating the regime to change or complicit in their greed. The cartoons paint a very unflattering picture of China, the primary international ally of the junta, and of the junta itself as using brute force to control the Burmese peoples or cunning strategy with the international community. They also, however, emphasize times when the regime is under threat, such as by protestors, the strength of the cyclone, and possible revolt within its own ranks. The cartoons also contribute to Burmese national iconography, especially, in this case, Buddhism and the *sangha* or order of monks, and surprisingly less so with Aung San Suu Kyi. They thus reinforce several stereotypes, calling upon what Dodds (2007: 158) describes as a form of "common sense" shared by their audience in order to define the opposition, release tension provoked by the unprecedented events, and elicit a desire for action. What follows is a summary of how the key actors in these cartoons are represented, followed by greater detail regarding the cartoons and their commentary on each of the two crises.

## THE SPDC AND THAN SHWE

The Burmese generals share a set of consistent characteristics in the work of the artists represented here. They are generally dressed in olive green, with a large military cap featuring a skull in its center front. Skulls are a key symbol in these cartoons; they are also featured on the multicolored medals that adorn the generals' chests, their shoulder epaulettes, and their belt buckles. Other key symbols are the shiny black military boots, compared with the civilians' bare feet or simple flip-flops, and the generals' big bellies, compared with skinny civilians. Representing the Burmese military regime is then top Senior General Than Shwe, adorned with the telltale hat and chestful of skull-medals, and identifiable by his spectacles.

The regime appears in forty-seven of the forty-nine cartoons examined here, or 96 percent. Thirty-one of these (66 percent) show a regime in control of the situation represented. Nine cartoons (19 percent) show a regime nervous, taken by surprise, or in some way threatened, while seven (14 percent) are ambiguous. The majority of those representations of the regime as nervous or threatened occur during the 2007 protests, while only two of these occur during the Cyclone Nargis cartoons, showing the regime surprised at the strength of the storm and its possible derailing of the constitutional referendum. During the early days of the protests, the regime's soldiers appear nervous or surprised by protestors and monks. In October, two cartoons also represent the possibility of internal military revolt. Another shows General Than Shwe overcome by the power of the international "Panties for Peace" campaign, discussed below.

## The Burmese People

Ordinary citizens appear in twenty-three of the cartoons, or 47 percent of the time, fairly evenly represented as active or passive. The Union Solidarity and Development Association (USDA), a paramilitary organization used to attack civilian protestors, is represented clearly in two cartoons as puppets of the regime. During the Saffron Revolution, representations of active citizen protestors appear mostly at the start, while passive portrayals of wounded or dead citizens appear in the aftermath. Monks appear in 40 percent of the cartoons dealing with protest events, and of these ten cartoons, appear active in seven and wounded or dead in the remaining three. Burmese people appear as victims of the storm in thirteen (54 percent) of the cyclone cartoons, about half the time struggling to stay alive or get at food held back by the regime, and half the time as dead, wounded, or sitting passively in shock or exhaustion. Aung San Suu Kyi appears in only four of the cartoons, one showing her in a standoff with a tank, one as watching while UN Envoy Gambari struggles to bridge the gap between herself and General Than Shwe, and two as a caged or chained prisoner.

## THE INTERNATIONAL COMMUNITY

Key players in the international community are represented in about 60 percent of these cartoons, yet not uniformly. On the one hand are representations of international organizations, specifically the UN and ASEAN, and national actors such as China and Thailand, represented as weak in the face of regime demands or complicit with the regime. Different players in the international community emerge, such as international aid agencies or media, on the other hand, who offer assistance but are thwarted in their attempts.

Prior to the September 2007 protests, several cartoons provide simplified versions of the geopolitical context, reflecting the sentiment among many political commentators that the UN and ASEAN are ineffective in promoting change in Burma. In one cartoon, Than Shwe blows out a flame atop a pedestal labeled "ASEAN Human Rights Commission," while three ASEAN officials stand by looking worried. Another cartoon

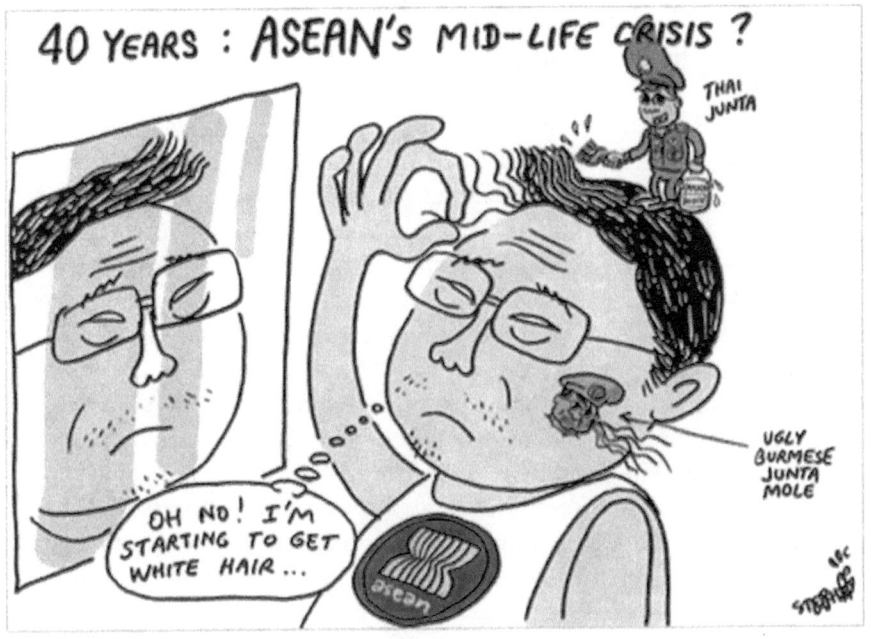

"ASEAN's Mid-life Crisis," Stephff, August 9, 2007 (courtesy Stephff and *The Irrawaddy*).

entitled "40 Years: ASEAN's Mid-life Crisis?" features a middle-aged man with the ASEAN logo on his undershirt, frowning into the mirror and thinking, "Oh no! I'm starting to get white hair." On his head a miniature military man, labeled "Thai junta" is painting his hair white. On one cheek is Than Shwe's face, labeled "ugly Burmese junta mole." These cartoons emphasize the discomfort within ASEAN regarding the Burmese junta and the military junta installed by the September 2006 coup in Thailand, a discomfort that nevertheless offers hope for the Burmese democratic movement. The UN and its Special Envoy to Myanmar, Ibrahim Gambari, are the subjects of a September 5 cartoon entitled "Gambari Bridging the Gap," depicting Gambari struggling to position a bridge between the two banks of a dry riverbed. A frowning General Than Shwe stands on one bank, a frowning Aung San Suu Kyi on the other. The bridge is clearly not long enough to connect the two banks, and Gambari is sweating and shaking with the effort of his clearly impossible task.

## Rising Fuel Prices, Increasing Unrest, and the Saffron Revolution

Two cartoons in August 2007 refer to the rising fuel prices in Burma, as well as the regime's use of force to react to popular discontent, specifically through the Union Solidarity and Development Association (USDA). A cartoon entitled "Fueling Protest," for example, shows two Burmese peasants hanging from the top of a graph shooting upward from a gas pump, controlled by one of two large hands protruding from olive green military sleeves. The graph represents the rising price of fuel, and while the peasants try to pull it downward, the other of the two large hands holds up a puppet shooting a slingshot at the peasants, a clear reference to the USDA. In another reference to the USDA, the cartoon entitled "The Brain Behind the Mindless Bullies" features a general holding a video game console, with two wires attached in turn to two thug-like figures holding wooden clubs with nails protruding from them. They are clearly on the lookout for a fight, while the general controlling them sits calmly with a satisfied grin, holding his remote control. These cartoons challenge the regime's claim of civilian support by representing the USDA as puppets of the generals, their violence orchestrated by the regime.

## CALM VERSUS PANIC

The September 2007 protest cartoons depict a struggle between a calm *sangha*, or order of Buddhist monks, representing a threat to the regime, and a clearly disconcerted military. A September 20 cartoon entitled "A Bold Step Forward" shows a monk calmly stepping his bare foot on the armor-toed boot of General Than Shwe, who reacts with surprise. A cartoon published the next day entitled "Tsunami Warning for the Generals" features a startled Than Shwe lying on a beach in his exaggerated military cap, its skull insignia reacting in surprise to the line of calm but stern monks in wine-colored robes forming a wave-like force bearing down on the general.

Once the protests gain strength, the junta's violent responses become the focus of ridicule. One cartoon quotes a Burmese official saying, "We will deal with the protests in a correct manner," and shows three soldiers baring their teeth and armed with weapons as their tense officer shouts into a walkie-talkie. They are all pointing their fingers and weapons at a group of monks, eyes closed or downcast as they calmly stand their ground. There is a stark contrast between the military men in angry, nervous motion and the still, determined monks. Even the misty smoke surrounding the soldiers is symbolic, as is the clear air surrounding the monks.

A similar theme of calm versus panic characterizes "Cornered but Unbeaten—The True Leader," featuring a crowd of soldiers aiming their guns at a seated Buddha image. A military officer leads the group, shouting into a megaphone as two helicopters and two large tanks back them up. The potentially violent military is contrasted here with the moral authority of the lone, seated Buddha, acknowledged by the caption as the "true leader." Yet, the officers in these two cartoons do not have skulls on their uniforms and are unadorned by medals, their caps featuring only a yellow insignia. Perhaps this distinction from the top generals is intended to demonstrate that much of the military, including many of its officers, are merely following orders from more devious and violent leaders.

## BLOOD AS DEATH AND BRUTALITY

Death becomes the focus and blood a key symbol in the aftermath of the regime's attacks on civilians. Although the first reports of beatings and deaths emerge on September 26, the use of blood in these cartoons begins on September 28, with a cartoon referring not to Burmese protestors, but to Japanese journalist Kenji Nagai, killed by a Burmese soldier the day before. This cartoon shows a chalk outline of a body next to a pool of blood and a camera. Standing above this is a Burmese soldier, his finger still on the trigger and his gun still smoking. White skulls adorn his helmet, chest, belt buckle, and shoulder epaulettes, and his expression is solemn. The cartoon is captioned, "A Picture Is Worth a Thousand Guns." The publication of this image as the first commentary on the deaths during the 2007 protests reflects the importance of non–Burmese participants in the Burmese public sphere in exile and the outreach function of *The Irrawaddy*.

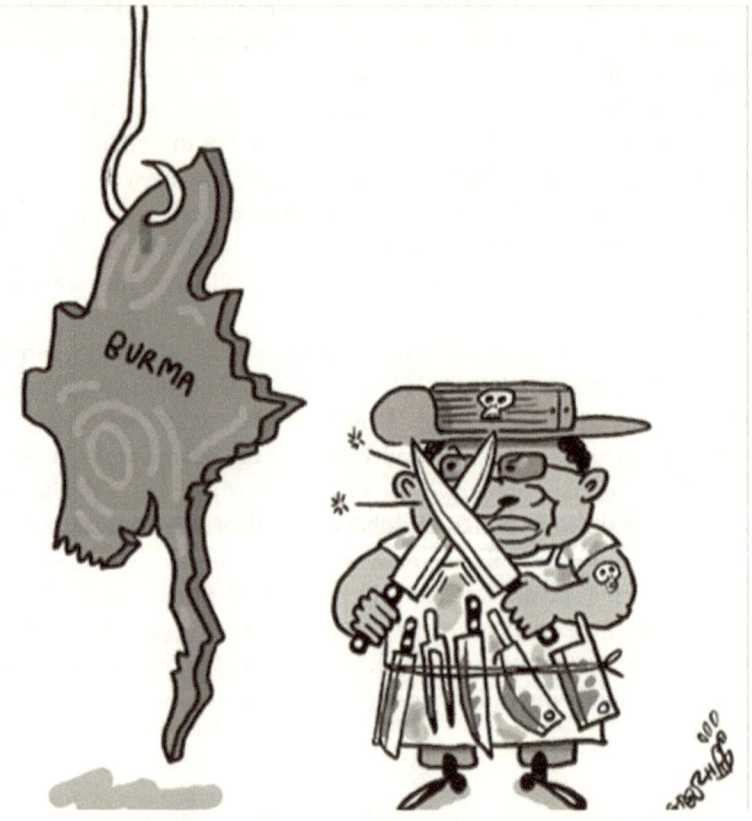

"Butcher of Burma," Stephff, October 2, 2007 (courtesy Stephff and *The Irrawaddy*).

Several cartoons published after this one continue to use blood in a symbolic way to avoid direct representation of the deaths occurring in the country. A cartoon published on October 1 entitled "Boots, Beatings, Blood," refers to a photograph circulating at the time of abandoned flip-flops lying on a blood stained road. The cartoon adds military boots to the image, and personifies both the boots and flip-flops with faces. The boots look mean; the flip-flops appear dead or wounded, with Xs for eyes, grimaces, or tongues hanging out. Only the boots are untouched by blood, except for the bloody flip-flop one is stepping on. A cartoon on the following day, captioned "Butcher of Burma," portrays Burma as a piece of meat on a hook. Than Shwe, with skull-adorned military hat and bloody apron, a skull tattoo on his upper arm, stands sharpening two clean knives, with other blood-stained knives tucked under the apron string around his waist. With military boots, bloody flip-flops, and a butcher carving a hunk of meat as symbols for the actors in these events, the cartoons bring the horror to a bearable level, yet also emphasize its extremes in what Levin (2007: 215) calls the "scenario of the absurd."

One cartoon makes more explicit reference to the shocking nature of the violence against monks and the hypocrisy of the Burmese state-run media. Blood seeps from a pile of dead monks that compose the base of a sparkling gold temple. General Than Shwe stands nearby, untouched by the blood and singing, his face partially hidden by a newspaper with the logotype "The New Lies of Myanmar," and the headline "Crackdown on Protestors: Two Dead and Half!" Above Than Shwe are written the words "'utmost' restraint from Burmese soldiers" with an arrow pointing to the pile of dead, grimacing monks. The caption reads "The Heights of Brutality."

## International Organizations, Regime Allies, and Foreign Investment

A strong theme throughout these cartoons is outsiders' complicity with the regime, through inaction, foreign investment, or direct military support, such as provided by China. One of the first cartoons to comment on the protests was published September 19, and depicts a crowd of surprised and angry monks and a civilian supporter being confronted by an angry soldier and a civilian reminiscent of the USDA. Somewhat removed but taking in the scene are two smug-looking Asian men, one labeled "ASEAN" and the Other "China." They sit relaxed and smiling, and the caption reads, "As Always, We Are Closely Watching Events." The only cartoon not drawn by Harnlay or Stephff, but rather by South African cartoonist, Zapiro, published in *The Irrawaddy*, emphasizes China as a regime ally. It is entitled "The Real Test of Strength" and features Aung San Suu Kyi and a group of monks facing down the barrel of a gun protruding from a tank driven by Than Shwe and labeled "Myanmar Junta." Behind it is a much larger tank, labeled "China's Backing." Aung San Suu Kyi is saying "Stop!" and from the large tank behind Than Shwe comes the order "Go."

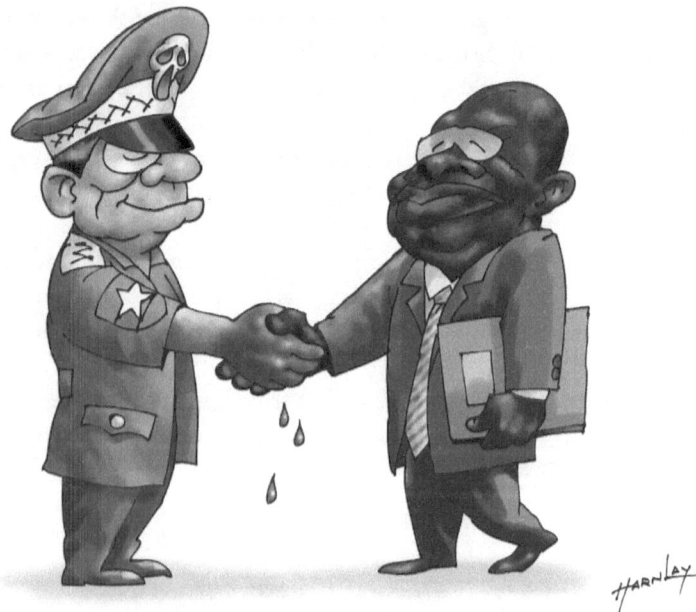

"I am in blood stepp'd in so far that, should I wade no more, returning were as tedious as go o'er." --"Macbeth" by William Shakespeare

"I am in blood stepp'd...," Harnlay, October 4, 2007 (courtesy Harnlay and *The Irrawaddy*).

The blood eventually stains those outside the country as well as within, in a powerful commentary on the role of international actors. On October 4, a cartoon comments on UN Special Envoy Gambari's visit to Burma, which began on September 29, by depicting Than Shwe and Gambari shaking hands and grinning. Than Shwe's hand drips blood, and the caption features a line from *Macbeth*: "I am in blood stepp'd in so far that, should I wade no more, returning were as tedious as go o'er." The use of Shakespeare further emphasizes the transnational nature of the public sphere addressed here.

These portrayals consistently depict China as backing the Burmese regime, despite a UN Security Council statement on October 11, strongly deploring the regime's violent response to protestors, seen by some analysts as a shift in China's position. A cartoon published the day after this Security Council statement shows a frowning, globe-headed man facing a Chinese man who has one arm raised in a gesture of no, the other lowered to protect a basket labeled with a Burmese flag and filled with a dripping gas pump and hardwood logs. The caption reads, "No Thanks, We'll Handle This Our Way." A small Than Shwe wielding a stick and a smoking gun smiles deviously and says "Thank you" to the large Chinese man he is hiding behind, and behind him, a pile of monks and civilians lie on the blood stained road. That China's position may have shifted, or that China may itself be under great international pressure is not a focus of commentary here, indicating that China functions as a key threat against which Burmese in exile and their allies define themselves.

A call to action against the complicity of foreign investors, especially those in the energy sector, is the focus of a cartoon featuring a nervous-looking Than Shwe, who has four pipelines running out from the back of his pants, each labeled to represent a major foreign investor in the energy sector. A devious looking cat holding a huge pair of scissors appears ready to cut one of the lines. The caption reads, "Cutting the Lifeline of the Than Shwe Region, It's Your Choice." A similar theme is found in the cartoon captioned "Business as Usual," which shows a smug-looking Than Shwe filling an oil can from a hose supplied with blood from a pile of dead civilians. Jumping over the dead civilians, a Chinese-looking man and a Middle Eastern-looking man both seem eager to get their hands on the blood/oil.

## The International Campaign

Only two of the forty-nine images examined here make reference to the Burmese in exile and their transnational campaign against the regime. A cartoon entitled "Disarming the Opposition" features Than Shwe inside a high wall topped by a Burmese flag, wearing a pig mask and wielding a chainsaw, mowing down, as though young trees, the raised fists emerging from the ground, leaving bloody stumps and fallen yet still-clenched fists in his wake. Outside the wall is another forest of raised and clenched fists. From behind his mask, the grimacing general glances over the wall at the fists beyond, his chainsaw dripping with blood.

The second reference to the transnational Burma campaign appears in November, closing out the commentary on the 2007 protests. Captioned "Up to His Neck in Knickers," the cartoon refers to a campaign dubbed "Panties for Peace," which began in October. The campaign focused on the Burmese traditional belief in *pone*, a form of male power supposedly weakened by physical contact with women's garments, especially their lower garments. Calling on women worldwide to send their underwear to Burmese embassies, the campaign spread to Australia, Europe, Singapore, and Thailand, as reported by *The Irrawaddy* (October 18, 2007). The cartoon depicts Than Shwe drowning in a sea of women's underwear, and targets the transnational Burmese public sphere, rather than a wider, international audience. For those who knew about or participated in the campaign, it showcases a small victory in otherwise difficult circumstances.

In both cases, the commentary on the Burma campaign is positive. The external opposition remains standing despite the regime's violence, as it is outside the reach of the regime mowing down protestors inside Burma. The "Panties for Peace" cartoon depicts this campaign as successfully overwhelming Than Shwe. Perhaps the Burmese in exile and this broader transnational campaign are not a focus of more of the cartoons or of critique, because they also form the core of *The Irrawaddy*'s audience, the "we" *against* which the regime and the ineffective or complicit international organizations are defined. This is also the audience appealed to for continued action against the regime.

# Cyclone Nargis and the Constitutional Referendum

Cyclone Nargis interrupted a planned May 10 vote on Burma's military-drafted constitution, itself a subject for cartoons as early as February 2008, when the first referendum-related cartoon shows a Burmese civilian standing before a ballot box marked "No." Above and astride this box are two enormous military boots, flanked on one side by a pair of handcuffs labeled "3 years in jail," and on the other, a rifle barrel. A cartoon in a similar vein published in April is captioned, "The Government Expects the Referendum Will Go Like Clockwork" and features a civilian with a large key protruding from his back holding up a sign that says "Yes." And in a May 3 cartoon, Than Shwe stands at a doorway marked "Burma," holding up a large sign saying "No" to three people outside holding video cameras, cameras, and microphones. The caption reads "The Junta Votes 'No' to International Media." These cartoons reinforce the overwhelming perception that the Burmese people would be coerced to vote yes in the referendum by a regime

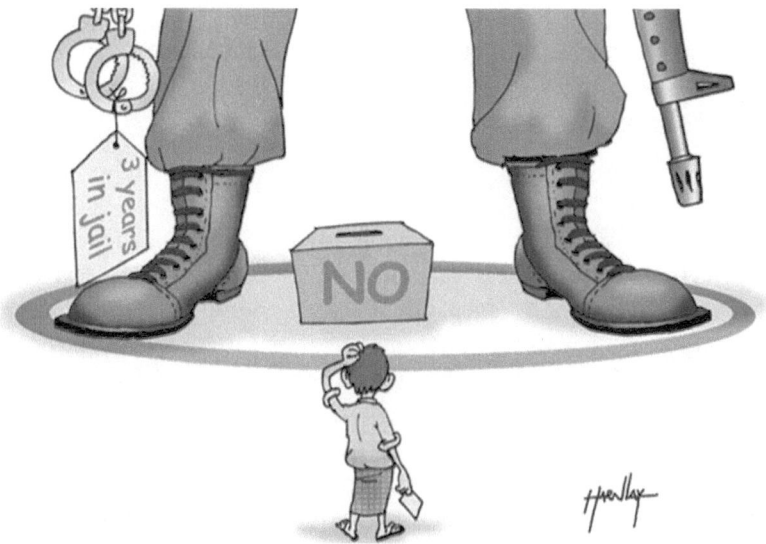

"**Voting on the Draft Constitution,**" Harnlay, February 28, 2008 (courtesy Harnlay and *The Irrawaddy*).

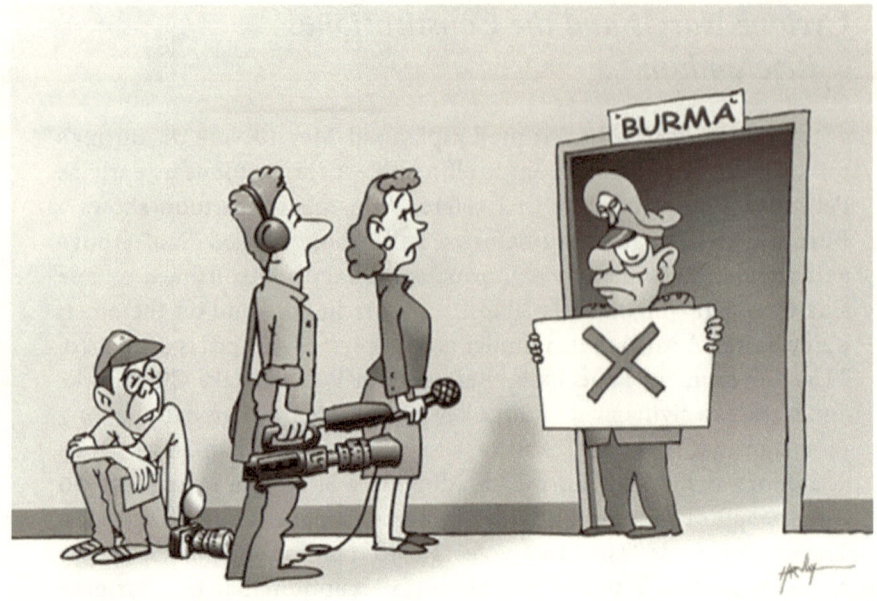

**"The Junta Votes 'No' to International Media," Harnlay, May 3, 2008 (courtesy Harnlay and *The Irrawaddy*).**

that would report a "yes" vote regardless of the actual outcome, as independent observers and international media were not permitted to observe events.

## CONTROL AT A COST

In the most prolific month represented in *The Irrawaddy* cartoons archive, there were nineteen cartoons published in May 2008, seventeen of which focus on the cyclone and the regime's handling of the situation. While the first few depict a regime surprised by the strength of the cyclone's devastation, the majority focus on the regime's greed in handling the crisis, first by using it to get the "yes" vote they desired in the referendum. The May 11 cartoon captioned "You Want Supper?—Then, Just Vote 'Yes,'" like several others, contrasts a destitute civilian with a well-dressed, portly general, in this case holding a box of aid out of the man's reach, while also thrusting toward him a ballot box. Another shows Than Shwe appealing to the international community for aid, because "my daughter has lost a U.S. $10 million diamond necklace in the tropical

198

storm," a reference to the heavily critiqued, lavish wedding of his daughter, in which she wore diamonds worth millions of dollars.

Many cartoons focus on the regime's attempts to keep international aid and aid workers out of the country, and employ symbols such as cobwebs and beard stubble to indicate the long wait of these aid workers and of the cyclone victims for the aid kept from them. Another technique is the representation of emaciated villagers to emphasize victims' hunger. To demonstrate the regime's tactics in keeping out aid, cartoons include representations of the generals literally tying aid boxes with red tape; holding the door shut against aid workers pushing to get in; and denying visas to waiting aid workers sporting beard stubble and cobwebs. One particularly graphic cartoon captioned, "Everything Is under Control" shows a Burmese general physically pushing a drowning man back in the water while waving away an aid worker in a nearby boat attempting to throw the man a life buoy. In the water nearby floats a naked body.

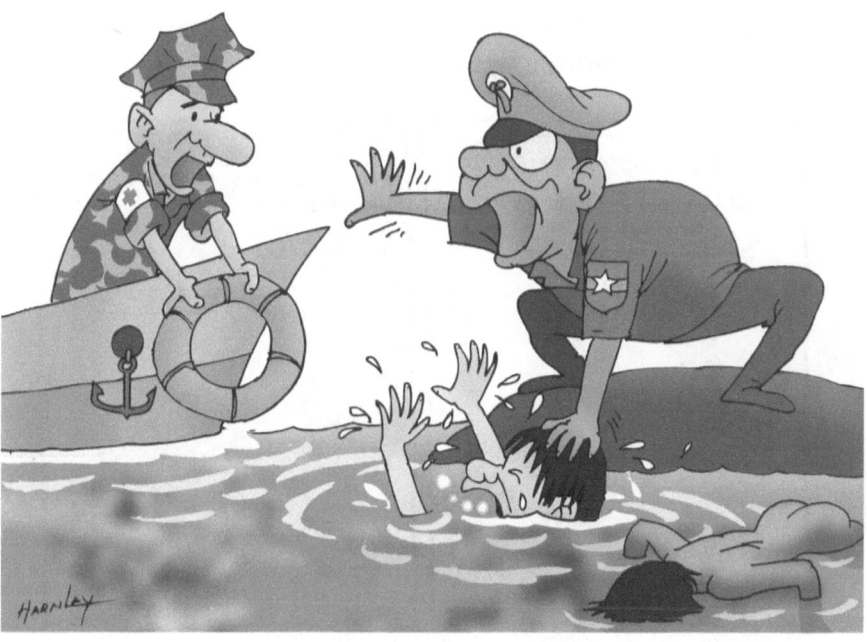

**"Everything Is under Control," Harnlay, May 20, 2008 (courtesy Harnlay and** *The Irrawaddy*).

These cartoons at times respond directly to the regime's claims. For example, a May 30 cartoon refers to the regime's statement that people from the Irrawaddy delta could "survive on their own, even without bars of chocolate donated by the international community" by living on "fresh vegetables that grow wild in the fields and on protein-rich fish from the rivers" (*The Age,* May 30, 2008). It depicts a military officer saying to aid workers, "Our people are self sufficient. We don't need your help," and handing to an emaciated woman and her two children a small bunch of wild vegetables, a small fish, and a frog. With his other hand, he clutches a chocolate bar. Only a few buttons hold the officer's big belly from popping out of his straining shirt, and his cheeks are swollen with chocolate. The foreign aid providers stand wide-eyed, clutching their aid packages, including a box of chocolates.

## THE IMPOTENCE OF THE INTERNATIONAL COMMUNITY

The international community is a target of biting humor here, ridiculed as weak in the face of regime demands, especially the UN, represented in these cartoons by Secretary General Ban Ki-moon. In one

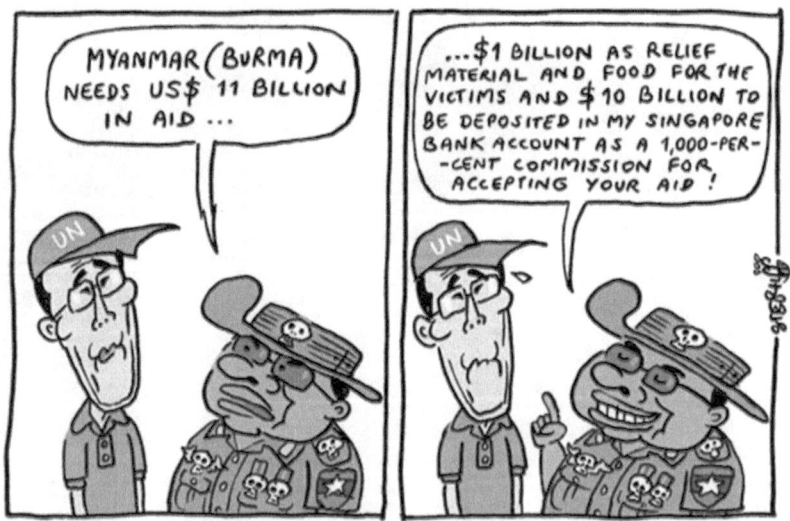

"Ban Meets the Aid Broker," Stephff, May 23, 2008 (courtesy Stephff and *The Irrawaddy*).

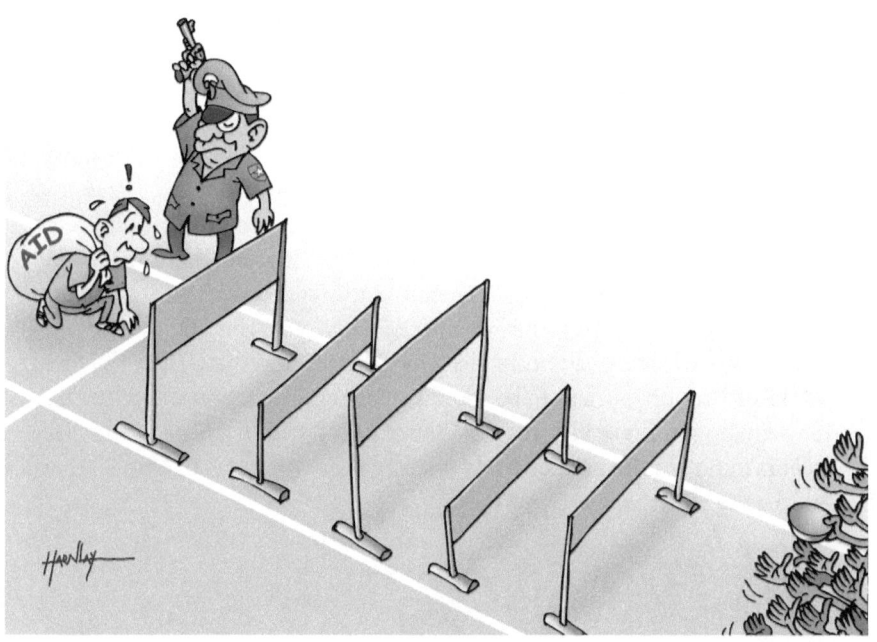

**"The Race to Save Lives," Harnlay, June 12, 2008 (courtesy Harnlay and *The Irrawaddy*).**

cartoon, for example, Than Shwe says to Ban Ki-moon, "Myanmar (Burma) needs $11 billion in aid. $1 billion as relief material and food for the victims and $10 billion to be deposited in my Singapore bank account as a 1000 percent commission for accepting your aid!" Another depicts the international community, led by ASEAN and the UN, meeting with Than Shwe, who is holding up a long list and saying, "All right, now listen up! Here are my tough conditions for allowing aid into Myanmar," to which Ban Ki-moon answers, "Wait! When we said 'tough conditions attached' we meant OUR conditions!!!"

Debates by the international community on how to deal with the regime's intransigence are not a focus of the commentary here; what is emphasized are efforts to get aid into Burma. Cartoons depict an international aid community sweating with the effort to assist the Burmese people, in one case having to literally jump over hurdles to reach starving Burmese in a cartoon captioned "A Race to Save Lives." In another captioned "Handicapped Helping Hands," aid workers are trying to slip boxes of aid through holes in a fence topped by barbed wire, a military watchtower nearby.

A few cartoons suggest that the UN and ASEAN are not just impotent, but complicit with the regime. One captioned "Food for Thought" shows an uncomfortable-looking Ban Ki-moon sitting down to a sumptuous meal with Than Shwe. As they eat, hands hold out aid boxes covered in cobwebs from one side of the frame, while from the other, stretch out skeletal arms and hands. Another caption suggests that the UN and ASEAN are characterized by "A General Indifference." The image depicts three men representing the regime, ASEAN, and the UN sitting on a flood bank while a dead body floats by. ASEAN and the UN, in the form of Ban Ki-moon, appear to be scolding the regime, represented by Than Shwe, who sits there idly, paying them little attention. None of the three seems to notice the bloated body floating past, or the destruction apparent in the landscape around them.

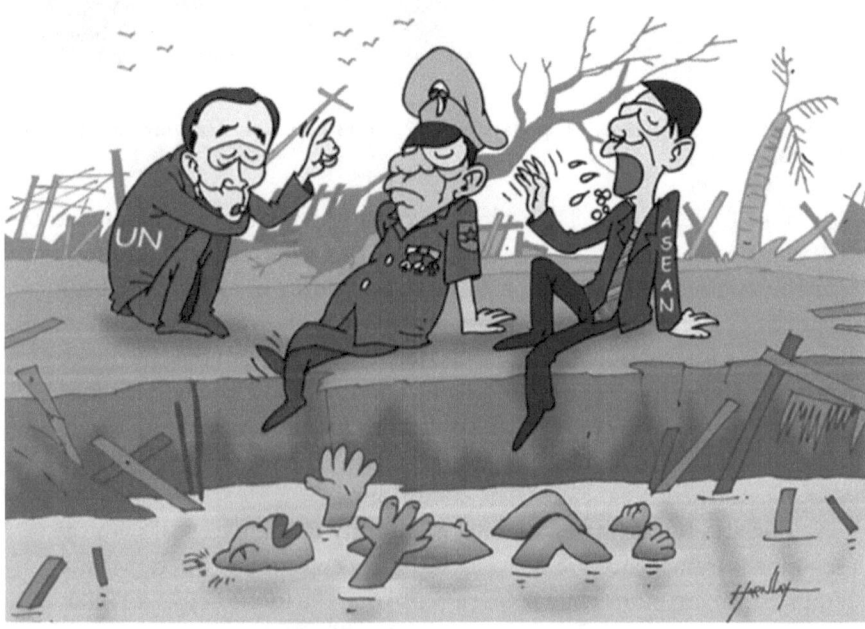

"A General Indifference," Harnlay, May 22, 2008 (courtesy Harnlay and *The Irawaddy*).

## Political Cartoons and Crisis Events

The messages of the cartoons commenting on these two crisis events are fairly consistent. Given the porous nature of the Burmese public sphere, these cartoons may function to keep key international actors such as the U.S., France, and even Burmese opposition activists off limits for ridicule and to build solidarity during crisis. This suggests that a key function they play is to clearly define the opposition, and in turn, the collective identity of those supporting the victims.

The complexities of the situation facing international actors such as the UN, ASEAN, and China are not reflected here, indicating not only frustration at their impotence, but also that these images function more to reinforce the stereotypes against which the Burmese and their allies define themselves than to challenge them. Yet, the cartoons do suggest that the UN and ASEAN are harmed by the intransigence of the regime, perhaps as a call to action and solidarity among those UN and ASEAN leaders who might be readers of *The Irrawaddy*. Likewise, the complicity of foreign investors is a focus of a few of these cartoons, but their target is most often China. Only one cartoon focuses on other foreign investors in the energy sector, and is an obvious call to action through its caption, "Cutting the Lifeline of the Than Shwe Region. It's Your Choice." The international aid community is represented primarily in a positive light, as generous donors whose efforts are thwarted by the regime.

Symbols found throughout these cartoons, including skulls on military uniforms, military boots, blood stains, cobwebs, and facial stubble representing the long wait for aid, and emaciated villagers, all function to emphasize the horror of the regime's actions, while also making it bearable by ridiculing its absurd extremes. While many of these cartoons are dark, hope can be found in representations of active civilian protestors, of a calm and organized order of monks, and of the threat both present to the regime. Once the protests gained strength, the junta's violent response becomes the focus of ridicule, suggesting their weakness in comparison with the calmness of the monks, and in one cartoon, Aung San Suu Kyi.

That the majority of the cartoons represent a regime in control reflects the frustrating, drawn out struggle of the Burmese democratic opposition both inside and in exile. Nevertheless, two cartoons here directly imply a possible split within the military, and the symbolism of the regime's uniforms also allows for distinctions between the most ruthless generals and the rest who are acting on orders, yet are perhaps more humane. The lack of skulls on some military uniforms, and the nervousness of the soldiers offer signs of hope for change within the military ranks.

While a variety of critical commentary on both the Saffron Revolution events and the aftermath of Cyclone Nargis does appear in Burmese exiled media, including *The Irrawaddy*, there is less of it in these simplified cartoons. One consequence of a transnational, porous public sphere on political cartoons, then, especially in times of crisis, is to reduce the variety of critique that might otherwise emerge. The need for solidarity intensifies the simplification already characteristic of political cartoons, so that they paint an unambiguous picture of the bad guys and the good guys, and promote within the transnational public sphere a collective call for action in support of the victims. So while the cartoonists within Burma must remain cautious and negotiate the unpredictability of the censors, hard hitting political cartoonists carry on in exile, working toward the day when political cartooning can again flourish inside Burma in the next, freer phase of commentary on national, regional, and international affairs.

## NOTES

1. The name "Burma" has taken on political connotations since the military government changed the country's name in 1989 to the Union of Myanmar. While the government claimed the new name is ethnically neutral and would provide a greater sense of national unity, the opposition movement opposed the name change, since it was made without consulting the people through a referendum. While the UN has accepted the name change, the U.S. has not, and the terms are generally understood to indicate one's position in the struggle over control of the country.

2. The total number of cartoons examined focusing on the Saffron Revolution included five in August 2007, seven in September 2007, eleven in October 2007, and one in November 2007. The total number focusing on the national constitutional referendum, the cyclone, and its aftermath include one in February 2008, one in April 2008, nineteen in May 2008 and three in June 2008.

# 8

# Cartoonist Lat and Malaysian National Identity

## An Appreciation

### MULIYADI MAHAMOOD

The name Lat, or Dato' Haji Mohd Nor Khalid, has become synonymous with the history of Malaysian cartoons. Working in a variety of genres and broaching many themes, Lat is considered to be a mirror of society, an institution, and a cultural hero because of the Malay and Malaysian values that he upholds. In other words, Lat's works reflect the face of Malaysia.

In addition to the enthusiastic reception given to his works at the local and global level, the recognition of Lat's popularity has been demonstrated by the various awards he has received, such as the Dato' Paduka Mahkota Perak award granted by His Royal Highness the Sultan of Perak (1994); the 13th Asia Fukuoka Cultural Award, in Fukuoka, Japan (2002); the Visual Art Award (Fine Art) in conjunction with the National Art Award (2006); and an Honorary Doctorate in Anthropology and Sociology from the National University of Malaysia (UKM) (2007). Indirectly, this also serves as recognition of the field of cartoons in general.

The questions of national identity and multi-ethnicity in Malaysia represent two important themes in Lat's works; indeed, it can be said that these issues serve to make Lat's works stronger and unique. In this context, the questions of identity are not only seen from the perspective of bringing a personal style to his works, but rather from the point of view of reflecting the national quest for a collective identity. This is approached by Lat through the depiction of various themes that have a

205

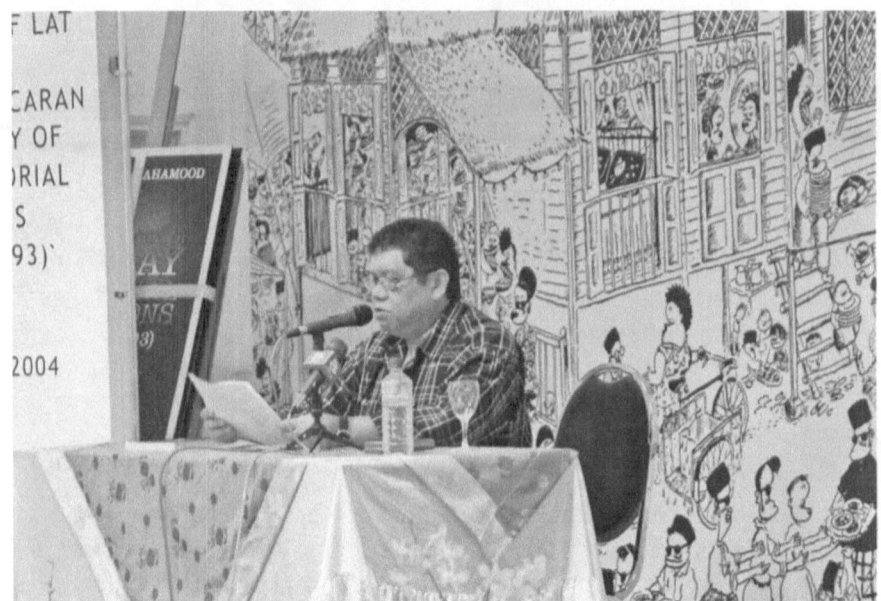

**Lat in the 2000s.**

strong Malay and Malaysian flavor. As a matter of fact, Lat is quite seri-ous when discussing the theme of identity in contemporary Malaysian cartoons, which for him is strongly influenced by Japan and Taiwan.

This essay surveys Lat's contribution to the building of a Malaysian identity through an appreciation of his works. This is achieved through a study of the style and themes in his works, including strip and editorial cartoons, and comic novels. Lat's cartoons form part of Malaysia's artistic heritage.

## An Appreciation of Lat's Works: A Reflection of Culture and Identity

Several factors contribute to the strength of Lat's cartoons. First, his sensitivity to the various customs and traditions of multi-racial Malaysia, together with his interest in aspects of the national culture that are fast disappearing have served to enhance the Malaysian elements in his works, thus raising readers' awareness toward the question of national identity. Lat's choice to deal with political and social themes in a neutral manner enables his works to be accepted by all. His approach of presenting international issues in a Malaysian context also enables the local readers to appreciate his works in a more meaningful manner. However, the most important factor of Lat's popularity is that through his humor, he manages to poke fun at the flaws of society and the government and criticize them in a subtle way. Lat's comments comply with the ethical and aesthetic criteria of Malay criticism that is subtle, metaphorical, and symbolic. Lat's style of criticism reflects his Malay identity.

Lat conveys his criticisms and jokes through images and text. The images are presented either directly, metaphorically, or symbolically through scenes of daily life that comprise human figures, objects, animals, and caricatures. In this context, metaphors are constructed either based on traditional or contemporary issues. The Malay aesthetic values that are expressed in Lat's cartoons can be evaluated in relation with the principles of Malay aesthetics outlined by Zakaria Ali, and that consist of six points, namely refined, useful, united, contrasted, symbolic, and meaningful (1989).

Lat's interest in the creation of a national identity has been obvious since his earliest works, particularly the strip cartoon series "Keluarga Si Mamat" published in *Berita Minggu* first in 1968. In addition to his interest in capturing his environment, he also created the series as a result of his unease in view of the large number of imported comics and cartoons in the Malay newspapers at the time, for instance "Ferd'nand" by Mik, "Nancy" by Ernie Bushmiller, and "Tok Misai" by Rousen. According to Lat (1994),

> I drew the chicken coop, I drew chicken, I drew my teachers ... things that were within reach, things that I knew about. Anyway, in the newspapers there were so many foreign comics, so I knew I should concentrate on local things.
> I sent off five pieces of "Keluarga Si Mamat" to *Berita Minggu* saying it would be good to have more local cartoons. They were using a lot of foreign cartoons at the time, like "Ferd'nand" [17–18].

In this context, Lat's emergence has had an impact on balancing the number of foreign cartoons in addition to addressing the lack of local cartoons at the time. After 1973, *Berita Minggu* only published local cartoons submitted by Lat, Lazuardi, and Raja Hamzah. According to

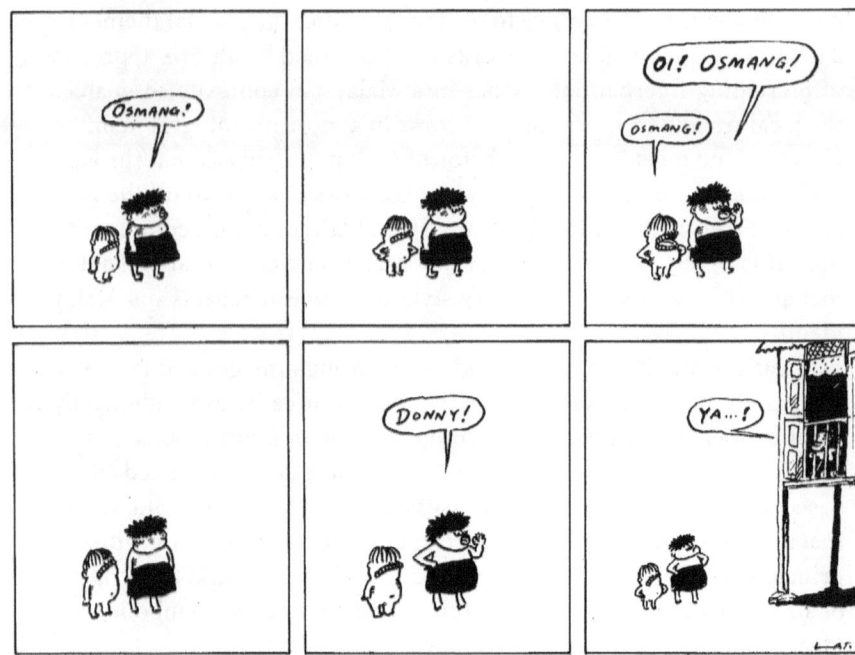

**Lat's "Keluarga Si Mamat," *Berita Minggu*, 1979 (courtesy Lat).**

famed editor A. Samad Ismail, the decision to stop publishing imported comics and cartoons corresponded to the newspaper's policy to encourage the development of local themes and cartoons (Muliyadi 2004: 126). In other words, Lat's original act of submitting cartoons with a local theme preceded the newspaper's aspiration and corresponded to the search for a national identity that was advocated in the National Cultural Policies (1971).

"Keluarga Si Mamat" features characters such as Mamat, Dolah, Osmang, Epit, Mastura, Yati, father, mother, and granny. The cartoon series that explores the theme of childhood is quite funny, especially when showing the naughtiness of Mamat's younger brother Epit, the relationships between boys and girls (for instance, Mamat's unrequited love for Yati), and their encounter with a Singaporean girl called Mastura. Humor arises from the fact that children experience adult situations. The adult characters' dialogues are usually quite serious, but are nonetheless interjected with cynical remarks. In addition to the draw-

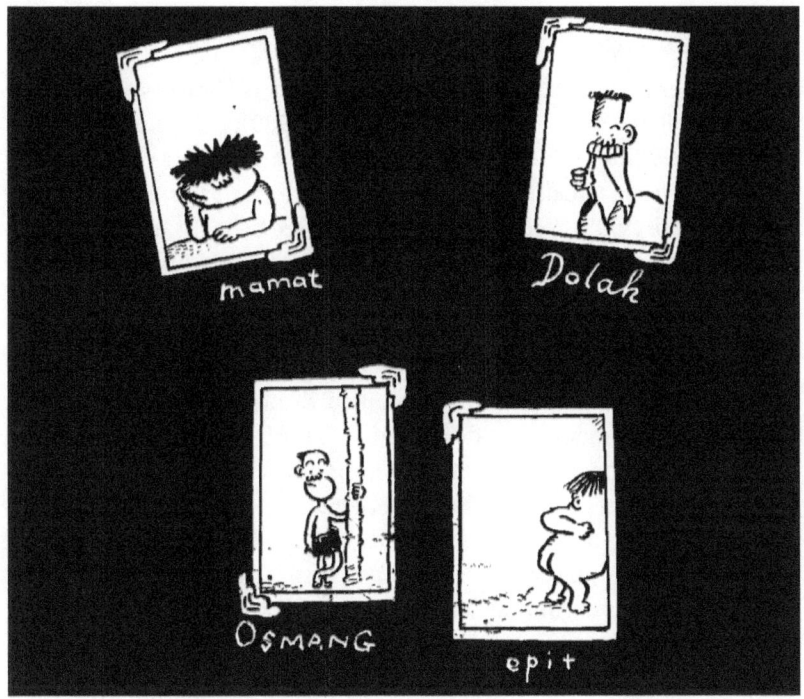

**Lat's "Keluarga Si Mamat," *Berita Minggu,* 1979 (courtesy Lat).**

ings, the texts also play an important role in this cartoon series. "Si Mamat" corresponded to local taste and has remained popular to this day. Lat's desire to create a work with local characteristics reflects his stand on constructing a local and personal identity in cartoons.

Unlike previous strip cartoons by Raja Hamzah, namely "Dol Keropok dan Wak Tempeh" (*Utusan Zaman*) and "Keluarga Mat Jambul" (*Berita Harian*), that only revolved around the daily life of their main characters, Lat's "Keluarga Si Mamat" broached broad subjects that touched on current issues. Topics such as music, polygamy, technological change, unemployment, the clash between eastern and western cultural values, and the loafing culture were explored through the use of the characters in realistic settings. This shows that Lat's awareness of local and contemporary issues already existed in his strip cartoons, long before spreading to his editorial cartoons. Lat's interest in local cultural issues is clearly reflected in his works on traditional weddings, as well as on cultural aspects of multi-racial Malaysia that he depicted in "Scenes of Malaysian Life" published in the *New Straits Times*.

Furthermore, Lat has published major works in books such as *Kampung Boy* (1979), *Town Boy* (1980), *Mat Som* (1989), *Kampung Boy—Yesterday and Today* (1993), and over twenty anthologies of editorial cartoons, among which are *Lat As Usual* (1990); *Be Serious!* (1992); and *Lat Was Here* (1995). Scenes of village life were brought to life through the depiction of the villagers' daily activities, such as working in rubber plantations or tin mines, weeding orchards and vegetable gardens, putting the laundry out to dry, riding their bicycle, buying groceries, and chatting in coffee-shops. The children's naughty behavior brightens the atmosphere. Lat records it all in detailed drawings from a variety of angles using cinematographic techniques. This is enhanced by his treatment of figures that are rich in expressions and emotions, well-matched with the characters and environment depicted.

In *Kampung Boy*, village scenes are captured in fine detail through images of houses and vegetation. In addition to capturing Lat's childhood experience, *Kampung Boy* also reflects the cultural values of rural Malay life. Loving family ties and friendships are explored effectively through a sensitive drawing style. Lat also incorporates Islamic values through the aspect of the education he received during his childhood, such as learning to read the Qur'an and to pray. Meanwhile, in his strip series "Ayuh Ke Masjid" (Let's Go to the Mosque) published in *Berita Harian* in 2001, Lat used cartoons directly as a vehicle of moral and religious education directed at children.

*Kampung Boy* evokes a strong feeling of nostalgia among readers who grew up with Lat's works or in a village. However, and more importantly, Lat also addresses the issue of the definition of the identity that exists in the Malay culture, and advocates that sacred values such as love and respect for family, ancestral origins, and traditional culture be maintained and cultivated. For Malay society, going back to the village for each celebration or long holiday reflects the people's loving commitment not only to their parents or relatives, but also to the essence of Malay culture that is inherent in their lives: politeness, respect for elders, and cooperation.

In *Kampung Boy—Yesterday and Today*, published in 1993, Lat drew all types of games that he played in his childhood, and compared them with the games played by children today. Like *Kampung Boy*, the strength of this work depends on the refined and compact quality of his style in

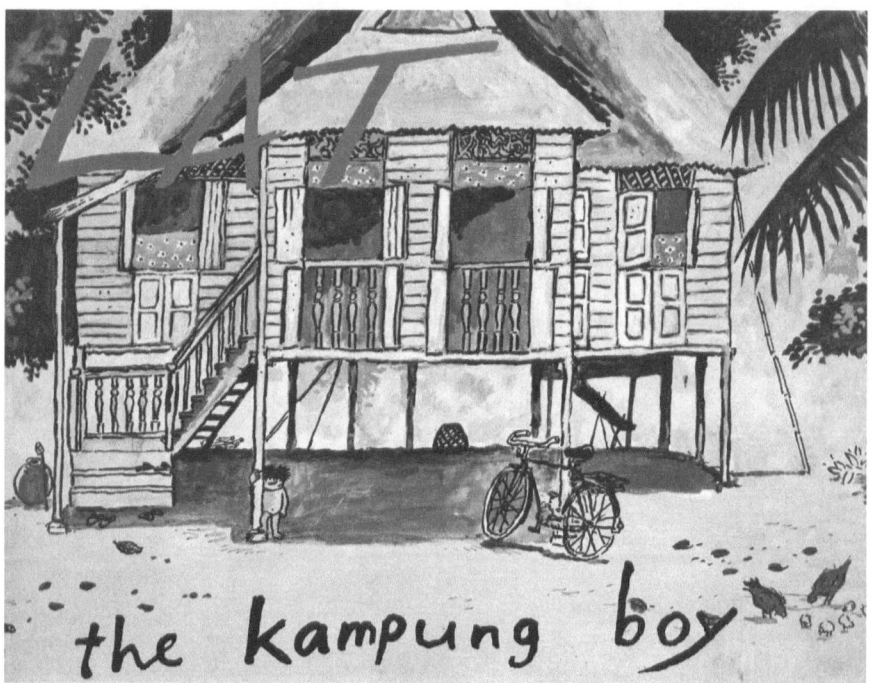

**Lat, front cover of *Kampung Boy*, 1979 (courtesy Lat).**

capturing the elements of his surroundings, as well as in presenting the issue of the cultural identity crisis as a result of the clash between culture and technology. Lat makes society realize how much we need to look back in order to see what we have lost in our modern life.

In addition to his books and strip cartoons, Lat manages to infuse his editorial cartoons with a Malaysian identity as well. He started being known as an editorial cartoonist working on socio-political themes in 1975, through his "Scenes of Malaysian Life" series in the *New Straits Times.* An analysis of these editorial works reveals that, in addition to self-portraits and caricatures of well-known figures, several characters regularly recur in his works, namely the old Chinese woman, the bald Chinese man, the chubby bespectacled Indian man, the Sikh man and the Malay couple riding a scooter.

These characters have become trademarks in his cartoons. However, unlike the characters in the strip cartoons that possess particular functions, the characters in the editorial cartoons vary in function of

211

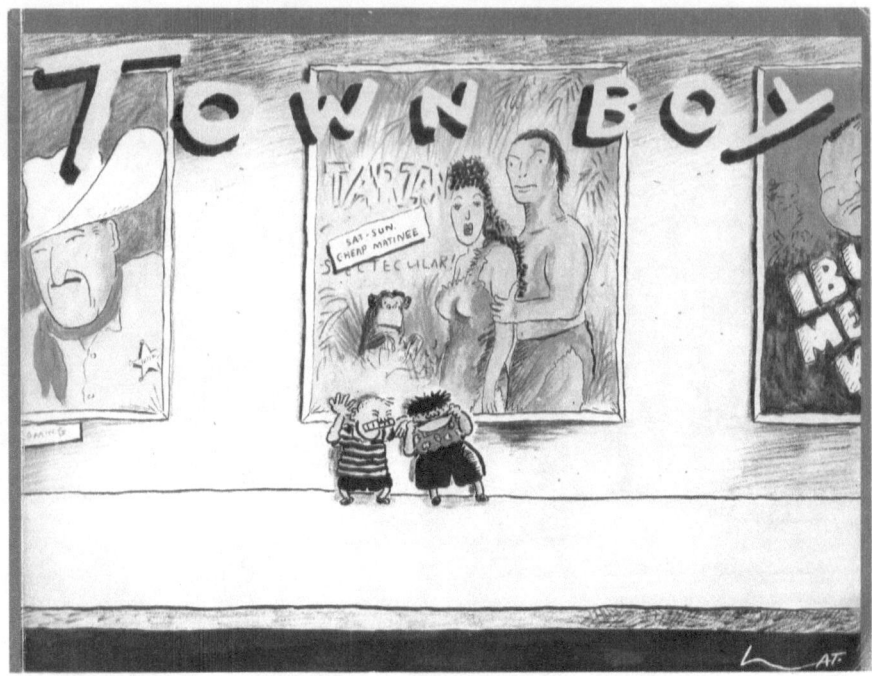

**Lat, front cover of *Town Boy*, 1980 (courtesy Lat).**

the issues depicted. Generally, they serve to represent the ethnic variety of the country, as well as Lat's awareness of the various racial and cultural groups in Malaysia. The depiction of these multi-racial characters also clearly reflects the unique features of Malaysian society that values moderation, politeness, civility, tolerance, respect, understanding, and racial harmony. Lat's awareness of interracial relations can also be seen in earlier works based on personal experience, for instance *Town Boy* (1980). The politeness and moderation that form part of the Malaysian identity can also be seen in Lat's focus on the moral, educational, and constructive aspects of his criticisms.

## Conclusion

A study of Lat's works shows that as an artist, he is deeply aware of such issues as current developments, national identity, as well as cultural

212

and traditional variety in a multi-racial country. Ever since the beginning of his artistic involvement, Lat has dealt directly with questions of national identity by creating works revolving around local issues, reminding readers of their cultural roots.

Through a variety of cartoon genres, Lat encompasses unique elements that form the core and symbolize the essence of Malaysian society: a multi-racial society living in racial harmony and unity, who values compromise, understanding, respect, and moderation. Lat also translates the essential traditional values of Malay society that upholds Islam as the core of its identity through works with social or personal themes that depict elements of a life revolving around society, customs, culture, traditions, respect, cooperation, family values, and social relationships. Lat reminds his readers about their roots, their current situation, and their future.

Lat's perspective has given birth to a form of cartoon with a strong Malaysian identity. In the context of the identity crisis experienced by comics and cartoons that are strongly influenced by Japonism, Lat has managed to stay on and succeed, because he has found a Malaysian form and identity since his early artistic involvement. He has answered the quest for a national identity and has become an inspiration for many cartoonists and artists in the country.

Lat's artistic sophistication, gentle satire, and subtle criticism in treating contemporary and cultural issues form part of the most important aesthetic elements in his works. His approach that targets an audience comprising Malaysian society as a whole enables his works to be appreciated by readers, regardless of race, religion, age, profession, or social position. Lat's cleverness in expressing both the evident and hidden meanings of his works through depictions of daily activities strengthens the role of his works, not just as a form of documentation or even commentary on life, but more importantly, as a vehicle for society to express its dissatisfaction with situations or political systems.

After over forty years as a cartoonist, Lat still continues to draw. This can be related to the speech he delivered when he was awarded the Fukuoka Art and Cultural Award in 2002, in which he said: "Cartoon is the most effective medium of communication in the world. Through cartoon, we try to understand one another in a positive and honest way."

## Appendix: Lat's Works

Lat. 1979. *The Kampung Boy*. Kuala Lumpur, Malaysia: Berita Publishing Sdn. Bhd.

Lat. 1979. *Keluarga Si Mamat*. Kuala Lumpur, Malaysia: Berita Publishing Sdn. Bhd.

Lat. 1980. *With a Little Bit of Lat*. Kuala Lumpur, Malaysia: Berita Publishing Sdn. Bhd.

Lat. 1983. *Lat and His Lot Again*. Kuala Lumpur, Malaysia: Berita Publishing Sdn. Bhd.

Lat. 1985. *Entahlah mak...!* Kuala Lumpur, Malaysia: Berita Publishing Sdn. Bhd.

Lat. 1985. *It's a Lat Lat Lat Lat World*. Kuala Lumpur, Malaysia: Berita Publishing Sdn. Bhd.

Lat. 1987. *Lat and Gang*. Kuala Lumpur, Malaysia: Berita Publishing Sdn. Bhd.

Lat. 1989. *Better Lat than Never*. Kuala Lumpur, Malaysia: Berita Publishing Sdn. Bhd.

Lat. 1990. *Lat as Usual*. Kuala Lumpur, Malaysia: Berita Publishing Sdn. Bhd.

Lat. 1992. *Be Serious!* Kuala Lumpur, Malaysia: Berita Publishing Sdn. Bhd.

Lat. 1994. *Lat 30 Years Later*. Petaling Jaya, Malaysia: Kampung Boy Sdn. Bhd.

Lat. 1995. *Lat Was Here*. Kuala Lumpur, Malaysia: Berita Publishing Sdn. Bhd.

Lat. 2004. *Dr. Who?* Kuala Lumpur, Malaysia: Berita Publishing Sdn. Bhd.

# About the Contributors

Lisa **Brooten** is an associate professor in the Department of Radio-Television at Southern Illinois University Carbondale. She has published on local and global social movement media, indigenous media, and human rights, among other subjects. Her work has been published in the *Asian Journal of Communication*, the *International Journal of Media and Cultural Politics*, the *Journal of Children and Media*, and the *International Journal of Comic Art* as well as in several books.

Warat **Karuchit** received a Ph.D. in mass media and communication from Temple University in Philadelphia. He is the associate dean in the School of Communication Arts and the director of the Master of Arts in Communication Arts program at Sripatum University in Bangkok, Thailand.

John A. **Lent** was a professor for 51 years. He taught at De La Salle College (Philippines), Universiti Sains Malaysia, the University of Western Ontario and Temple University, and he was also a visiting professor at Shanghai University, Communication University of China, Jilin College of the Arts Animation School, and Nanjing University of Economics and Finance. He publishes and edits *International Journal of Comic Art*.

**Lim** Cheng Tju is a history teacher in Singapore who has written extensively about history, popular culture, and the arts. His articles on comic art have appeared in the *Southeast Asian Journal of Social Science*, *Journal of Popular Culture*, *International Journal of Comic Art*, and *Print Quarterly*. He is also a country editor (Singapore) for *International Journal of Comic Art*.

**Muliyadi** Mahamood is a professor of the history of art in the Liberal Studies Department, Faculty of Art and Design, Universiti Teknologi

MARA, Malaysia. He received a Ph.D. in cartoon studies from the University of Kent. He is the founding president of PEKARTUN, the Malaysian Cartoonists' Association. He has written books on art and cartooning, including a history of Malaysian political cartoons.

# Works Cited

## Print Sources

Abraham, Yamila. 2010. "Boys' Love Thrives in Conservative Indonesia." In *Boys' Love Manga: Essays on the Sexual Ambiguity and Cross-Cultural Fandom of the Genre*, edited by Antonia Levi, Mark McHarry, and Dru Pagliassotti, 44–55. Jefferson, NC: McFarland.

*The Age.* 2008. "Burma's Generals Blast 'Chocolate Bar' Aid." May 30.

Ahmad, Hafiz, Benny Maulana, and Alvanor Apalanzahi. 2006. *Histeria! Komikita.* Jakarta: Elex Media Komputindo.

Ajidarma, Seno Gumira. 2002. "Doyok: A Portrait of Jakarta's Lower Class." *Kompas.* November 1. Reprinted by *Karbon.* http://karbonjournal.org.

Alanguilan, Gerry. 2006. "Remembering Lastikman." August 23. http://alanguilan.multiply.com/journal/item/5.

_____. 2007a. "The Death of a Once Great Industry." In *Komiks. Sa Paningin ng mga Tagakomiks*, edited by Randy Valiente and Fermin Salvador, 57–60. Quezon City: Central Book Supply.

_____. 2007b. "The Filipino Comics Artist and Manga." In *Komiks. Sa Paningin ng mga Tagakomiks*, edited by Randy Valiente and Fermin Salvador, 98–105. Quezon City: Central Book Supply.

*AMCB.* 1978. "Comics Sale Soars." December: 12–13.

Anderson, Benedict R. O' G. 1978. "Cartoons and Monuments: The Evolution of Political Communication under the New Order." In *Political Power and Communications in Indonesia*, edited by Karl D. Jackson and Lucien W. Pye, 283–321. Berkeley: University of California Press.

Ang, Hwee Suan, ed. 1991. *Dialogues with Rajaratnam.* Singapore: Shin Min Daily News.

*Australian, The.* 2007. "Attacks on Monks a 'Great Wrong,'" September 27.

*Baan Moeng.* 1999. "Pra Mahajanaka Dai Rang Wan Cartoon Dee Den" [Pra Mahajanaka wins best cartoon award]. December 12: 6.

Bach Lien. 2007. "Cartoon, Video Take on Modern Life in Ha Noi." *Viet Nam News.* May 26. Accessed May 28, 2007. http://vietnamnews.vnagency.com.vn/Life-Style/164975/Cartoon-video-take-on-modern-life-in-Ha-Noi.html.

Badrudin, Ramli. 1988. "Indonesian Cartoonists Cannot Have Authoritative Opinions." *WittyWorld International Cartoon Magazine,* no. 5 (August): 34–36.

Barley, Tasa Nugraza. 2010a. "Fighting Terror Through Comics." *Jakarta Globe*, September 27. http://www.thejakartaglobe.com/entertainment/fighting-terror-through-comics/398319.

_____. 2010b. "Indonesian Comic Books Showcase Local Color." *Jakarta Globe*, March 5. http://www.thejakartaglobe.com/artsandentertainment/indonesian-comic-books-showcase-local-color/362175.

*BBC News*. 2007. "Burma Toll at Least 31, UN Says." December 7.

_____. 2007. "US to Impose New Burma Sanctions." September 25.

_____. 2008. "Burma Shuns Foreign Aid Workers." May 9.

Bejo, Noel B. 1986. "'Komiks' in the Philippines: A Medium That Seeks Recognition." *Communicatio Socialis Yearbook* 5: 155–70.

Benda, Julien. 1969. *The Treason of the Intellectuals*. New York: W.W. Norton & Company.

Berman, Laine. 1998. "LAINE BERMAN Sheds a Tear for the Late Great Indonesian Comic." *Inside Indonesia*, July-September. http://insideindonesia.org/content/view/761/29.

_____. 2001. "Comics as Social Commentary in Java, Indonesia." In *Illustrating Asia: Comics, Humor Magazines and Picture Books*, edited by John A. Lent, 13–36. Honolulu: University of Hawaii Press.

_____. 2005. "Comic Heyday! Indonesia's Comic Scene Is in a Golden Age but the Industry Remains Marginal and Plagued by Self-doubt." *Inside Indonesia*, July-September. http://www.insideindonesia.org/edition-83/comic-heyday.

Bonneff, Marcel. 1976. *Les Bandes Dessinées Indonesiennes; Une Mythologie en Image*. Paris: Puyraimond.

Brandon, James. 1967. *Theatre in Southeast Asia*. Cambridge: Harvard University Press.

Brillon, Cherish Aileen A. 2007. "*Darna* and Intellectual Property Rights." *Plaridel* 4 (1): 97–114.

Buban, Charles E. 2008. "Tackling Teen Pregnancy with Animé-Inspired Comics." *Philippine Daily Inquirer*. August 8.

Budiyanto, A. 2006. "Converting Icons: Indonesian Muslim's Conquering the Icons." Paper presented at ARI 4th Graduate Workshop on Religion and Technology in Contemporary Asia, Singapore, January 18–24.

Bundoc-Ocampo, Nene J. 1983. "Komiks-Magasin: The PNA's Link to the Common Tao." In *Asean Editors Conference, Manila, 18–22 January*, 1–3. Manila: Philippine News Agency.

*Business Thai*. 2004. "Yuk Low Cost Talad Cartoon" [The age of low cost cartoon market]. April 15.

Caber, Michael. 2007. "Filipino Artists Place High in Japan Cartoon Contest." *Manila Standard Today*. August 9: 5.

Cabling, Mario S. 1972. *May Sining, Tagumpay at Salapi sa Pagsulat ng Komiks* [Art, Success and Money in Writing Comics]. Manila: National Book Store.

Calingo, Melvin. 2007. "Filipino Comics and Everything in Between." In *Komiks. Sa Paningin ng mga Tagakomiks*, edited by Randy Valiente and Fermin Salvador, 107–12. Quezon City: Central Book Supply.

Callueng, Ronan. 2007. "Who Wants to Make a Superhero? Comic Book Artists Take Time off from Their Drawing Boards to Tell Us How It's Like to Bring Life to Heroes." *T3 The World's No. 1 Gadget Magazine*. August. http://alanguilan.com/komikero/interview19.html.

Capino, José B. 2005. "Learning from *Darna, Dyesebel, Barbi*, and *Vampira*: Notes on the Hybridity of Philippine National Cinema." *Ideya* 6 (2)/7 (1): 45–58.

_____. 2006. "Philippines: Cinema and Its Hybridity." In *Contemporary Asian Cinema*, edited by Anne Ciecko, 32–44. Oxford: Berg.

"Cartoon Thai." 2008. *Wikipedia*. Accessed August 21, 2008.

Cartoonthai Institute. 2008. Kamnodkarn Kiddee Project No 3 [Schedule of Kiddee Project No. 3]. [Leaflet]. Bangkok: Cartoonthai Institute.

*Catalogue: Koloni Komik Indonesia*. Jakarta: P.T. Gramedia m&c!.

*CBC News*. 2008. "Burmese Junta Forcing

Cyclone Victims out of Emergency Camps: Amnesty." June 5.

"Chai Ratchawat Lai Sen Mee Chee Wit" [Chai Ratchawat, lively drawing]. 1999. *Praew* (October): 135–47.

Chaiyapruk Cartoon. 2008. Accessed September 8. http://www.bangkok bookclub.com/product.detail_44994_ th_392603.

Chan, Fadli. 2009. "The Popularity of Manga Culture." *Dunia Perspektif*, February 22. http://fadlinx.blogspot. com/2009/02/popularity-of-manga-culture.html.

Chan, Yonina. 2005. "Amazing Fabulists: Comic Book Creators, and an Abiding Passion." *Manila Bulletin*. December 2: E-5.

Chen, Elena. 1989. "A Pilot Study on the Use of Comics for Evangelism Among Female Factory Workers." In *Case Studies in Christian Communication in an Asian Context*, edited by Ross W. James, 137–59. Manila: OMF.

Chen, Mong Hock. 1967. *The Early Chinese Newspapers of Singapore (1881–1912)*. Singapore: University of Malaya Press.

Chi (Do Huu Chi). 2010. "Comics in Vietnam: A Brief History." Unpublished paper.

Chia, Wai Hon. 2001. *See Cheen Tee: Artist Extraordinaire*. Singapore: Raffles Avenue Editions.

Chongkitthawon, Kawi. 1990. "Editor Comments on Political Cartoonists." *The Nation* (Bangkok). January 2: 6.

Chu, Chenfa. 2004. *Red Wave: Cultural Revolution-inspired Chinese Literature in Singapore*. Singapore: Lingzi Media Pte Ltd.

Chua, Beng Huat. 1995. *Communitarian Ideology and Democracy in Singapore*. London and New York: Routledge.

Chua, Joel. 2007. "Japanese Manga Style and Its Influence on Pinoy Komiks." In *Komiks. Sa Paningin ng mga Tagakomiks*, edited by Randy Valiente

and Fermin Salvador, 106. Quezon City: Central Book Supply.

Chudori, Leila. 1991. "R. A. Kosasih: Di Tengah Pandawa dan Kurawa." *Tempo*, December 21: 41–67.

Chulasak Amornwej. 1997. "Rak Kaew Cartoon Thai Than Utthakanon" [A Root of Thai Cartoon Than Utthakanon]. *Krungthep Turakij*. June 6: Jor 3.

_____. 1998a. "Sa-Ngob Jampat Jaak 'Sibgree Jam' Tueng 'Kon Nuea Lok'" [Sa-Ngob Jampat, from 'Lance Corporal Jam' to 'Out-of-This-World Man']. *Krungthep Turakij*. August 23: Jor 5.

_____. 1998b. "Witt Sutthasatien Jaak Cartoon Tai Lem Soo Samnuan 'Swing'" [Witt Sutthasatien, from cartoon at the end of the book to 'Swing' style of writing]. *Krungthep Turakij*. September 6: Jor 5.

_____. 1999a. "Wan Wela Nang Sue Cartoon" [Time of cartoon books]. *Krungthep Turakij*. May 30: Jor 6.

_____. 1999b. "Kon Ja Pen Nak Kien Cartoon" [Before becoming a cartoonist]. *Krungthep Turakij*. June 6: Jor 5.

_____. 2001a. "Nak Kien Cartoon Ying" [Female cartoonist]. *Krungthep Turakij*. May 12: Por 5.

_____. 2001b. Tamnan Cartoon [The legend of cartoon]. Bangkok: Sangdow.

Darmawan, Ari. 1992. "Citra Audivistama: Kreativitas, Menajemen dan Bonafiditas." *Cakram*, June: 32–33.

Darmawan, Hikmat. 2009. "The Naïve City: Sketches of the '60s and '70s' Jakarta in Romance Comics." *Karbon*, February 5. http://karbonjournal.org.

David, Joel. 1990. *The National Pastime: Contemporary Philippine Cinema*. Manila: Anvil Publishing.

_____. 1995. *Fields of Vision: Critical Applications in Recent Philippine Cinema*. Quezon City: Ateneo de Manila University Press.

del Mundo, Clodualdo, Jr. 1986. "KOMIKS: An Industry, a Potent Medium, Our National 'Book,' and

Pablum of Art Appreciation." In *Philippine Mass Media: A Book of Readings*, 180–85. Manila: Communication Foundation Association.

De Vera, Ruel S. 2008. "Ninoy in a Nutshell." *Philippine Daily Inquirer*. October 13.

Dodd, Mark. 1993. "Cambodia Cartoonists Celebrate New-Found Freedom." *Reuter Wire Service Report*. July 19.

Dodds, Klaus. 2007. "Steve Bell's Eye: Cartoons, Geopolitics and the Visualization of the 'War on Terror.'" *Security Dialogue* 38 (2): 157–77.

Elliston, Jon. 1997. "Counterinsurgency Comics." *ParaScope*. Accessed December 9, 2002. http://www.parascope.com/articles/0497/phoenix.htm.

Fang, Xiu, ed. 1991. *Selection of Malayan Chinese Literature Vol. 7: Essays (1945–1956)*. Singapore: Persekutuan Persatuan-Persatuan Lembaga Pengurus Sekolah China Malaysia.

Feldman, Edmund B. 1994. *Practical Art Criticism*. Princeton, NJ: Prentice Hall.

Fernie, Eric. 1995. *Art History and Its Methods: A Critical Anthology*. London: Phaidon.

Fiske, John. 1990. *Introduction to Communication Studies*. London: Methuen.

Flambojan. n.d. "Meski Sudah 22 Kali Bercinata Tak Pernah Sampai Kejenjang Perkawinan." No. 79: 22–23.

Flores, Emil Francis M. 2004. "Super Pinoy: The Concept of the Superhero in Filipino Films." Paper presented at the Conference on New Southeast Asian Cinema: Where Big Budget Meets No Budget. Singapore, May 3–4.

Fondevilla, Herbeth L. 2007. "Contemplating the Identity of Manga in the Philippines." *International Journal of Comic Art* 9 (2): 441–54.

Fortuna. n.d. "Kalau Johnny Hidayat Bercinta." no. 38: 4–7.

Gamson, William. 1992. *Talking Politics*. New York: Cambridge University Press.

Gamson, William, and David Stuart. 1992. "Media Discourse as a Symbolic Contest: The Bomb in Political Cartoons." *Sociological Forum* 7 (1): 55–86.

Garcia, Angelo T. 2008. "The Rise (Again) of Local Comics." *Manila Bulletin*. June 14. http://www.mb.com.ph/issues/2008/6/14/YTCP20080614127280.html.

Gombrich, E. H. 1963. *Meditations on a Hobby Horse and Other Essays on the Theory of Art*. London: Phaidon Press.

Hara, Fujio. 1997. *Malayan Chinese and China: Conversion in Identity Consciousness, 1945–1957*. Tokyo: Institute of Developing Countries.

Harper, T. N. 1999. *The End of Empire and the Making of Malaya*. Cambridge: Cambridge University Press.

Heimann, Rolf. 2007. "Cartooning in Indonesia." *Inkspot*, Autumn: 8–9.

Hertanto. 1992. "Karyawan Boleh 'Berkemah' di Kantor." *Tiara*, no. 56 (July 5): 82–83.

Ho, Kah Leong, and Yih Ong, eds. 1955. *Selection of Woodcuts and Caricatures by Singapore and Malayan Artists*. Singapore: Life Society Publishers.

Holman, Valerie, and Debra Kelly. 2001. "Introduction. War in the Twentieth Century: The Functioning of Humour in Cultural Representation." *European Studies* 31: 247–63.

Horn, Maurice, ed. 1981. *The World Encyclopedia of Cartoons*. New York: Chelsea House Publishers.

Indarto, Kuss. 2004. "RI Comic Strips a Stranger in Their Own Country." *The Jakarta Post*, March 20. http://www.thejakartapost.com.

*International Herald Tribune*. 2008. "France Urges UN to Force Myanmar to Allow Foreign Aid." May 19.

Islip, Aklas. 2007. "How Do You Revive the Filipino Komiks Industry?" In *Komiks. Sa Paningin ng mga Tagakomiks*, edited by Randy Valiente and Fermin Salvador, 63–67. Quezon City: Central Book Supply.

*Jakarta Post, The.* 2004. "Festival to Hold Comic-Making Class." August 29.

Jit, Krishen. 1990. "Introduction: Kuo Pao Kun —The Man of the Future in Singapore Theatre." In *The Coffin Is Too Big for the Hole ... and Other Plays*, 7–28. Singapore: Times Books International.

Jones, Clayton. 1987. "Filipino Comics Are More Than Laughing Matter." *Christian Science Moniter*, August 12: 1, 8.

Josey, Alex. 1968. *Lee Kuan Yew Vol. 1.* Singapore: Times Books International.

Juiartha, I. Wayan. 2003. "History Introduced to Children Through Comics." *The Jakarta Post*, May 1. http://www.thejakartapost.com.

_____. 2004. "Young Cartoonists Skilled in Biting Satire." *The Jakarta Post*, December 16. http://www.thejakarta apost.com.

*Junior.* 1975. "Kartun-Kartun Kita. Yang Ha..Ha dan Yang Astaga." no. 45 (February 7):8–9, 64–65.

Karna, Mustaqim. 2007. "Mumbling Our Comic: An Overview of Indonesian Comic Books' Condition." *International Journal of Comic Art* 9 (1): 311–31.

Karnjariya Sukrung. 2000. "Rebirth of 'Toons." *Bangkok Post*, July 1. Accessed April 16, 2003. http://www.bangkok post.com.

Kazmin, Amy. 2008. "Burma to Admit 'All Aid Workers.'" *Washington Post*, May 23.

Kee, Pookong, and Kwai Keong Choi. 1997. *A Pictorial History of Nantah.* Singapore: Chinese Heritage Centre.

Keenan, Faith. 1997. "Licensed to Laugh." *Far Eastern Economic Review.* September 4: 44–45.

Kenley, David. 1998. "Publishing the New Culture: Singapore's Newspapers and Diaspora Literature, 1919–1933." *Explorations in Southeast Asian Studies* 2, 2 (Fall). Accessed June 5, 2009. http://www.hawaii.edu/cseas/pubs/explore/kenley.html.

Koendoro Br., Dwi. 2007. "The Root of Indonesian Comic and Animation Tree." Paper presented at first Annual Asian Youth Animation and Comics Contest (AYACC), Guiyang, China. September 7.

Koh, Sia Yong. 1995. *A Mirror of Our Times 1979–1980: A Story in Cartoon.* Singapore: Self-published.

Kong Tun. 1997. "'Prayoon Chanyawongs' Kor Kerd 'Pipittapant Cartoon Thai' Sueb San Lai Sen Arom Dee" [The Prayoon Chanyawongs Foundation leads to the Thai Cartoon Museum, maintaining humor arts]. *Matichon.* April 28: 9.

Kor Moon Boeng Ton [Basic information]. 2003. Accessed March 5. http://www.geocities.com/toonclick/intro.htm.

Kosasih, R. A. 1977. "Pandawa Diperdaya 1." *Seri Mahabharata*, Vol. 12, *Antara Baju Tamsir dan Senjata Konta.* Jabar: Langlangbuwana.

Kuo, Pao Kun. 2000. *Images at the Margins: A Collection of Kuo Pao Kun's Plays.* Singapore: Times Books International.

Kwok, Kian Woon, Arun Mahizhnan, and T. Sasitharan, eds. 2002. *Selves: The State of the Arts in Singapore.* Singapore: National Arts Council.

Lat. 1979a. *The Kampung Boy.* Kuala Lumpur, Malaysia: Berita Publishing Sdn. Bhd.

_____. 1979b. *Keluarga Si Mamat.* Kuala Lumpur, Malaysia: Berita Publishing Sdn. Bhd.

_____. 1990. *Lat as Usual.* Kuala Lumpur, Malaysia: Berita Publishing Sdn. Bhd.

_____. 1992. *Be Serious!* Kuala Lumpur, Malaysia: Berita Publishing Sdn. Bhd.

_____. 1994. Lat on Lat. In *Lat 30 Years Later.* Petaling Jaya, Malaysia: Kampung Boy Sdn. Bhd.

_____. 1995. *Lat Was Here.* Kuala Lumpur, Malaysia: Berita Publishing Sdn. Bhd.

Lee, Kuan Yew. 1959. "Address to members of the Nanyang University, at 7.30

p.m. on Wednesday, October 28." Accessed May 8, 2004. http://www.a2o.com.sg.

_____. 1998. *The Singapore Story: Memoirs of Lee Kuan Yew.* Singapore: Times Editions Pte Ltd and the Straits Times Press.

_____. 2000. *From Third World to First: The Singapore Story: 1965-2000.* Singapore: Times Editions Pte Ltd and the Straits Times Press.

Lee, Ting Hui. 1976. *The Communist Organization in Singapore: Its Techniques of Manpower Mobilization and Management, 1948-66.* Singapore: Institute of Southeast Asian Studies.

Leehey, Jennifer. 1997. "Message in a Bottle: A Gallery of Social/Political Cartoons from Burma." *Southeast Asian Journal of Social Science* 25 (1): 151-66.

Lent, John A., ed. 1982. *Newspapers in Asia: Contemporary Trends and Problems.* Hong Kong: Heinemann Asia.

_____. 1993a. "Antonio Velasquez, Father of Philippine *Komiks.*" *Philippines Communication Journal* (March): 47-50.

_____. 1993b. "Southeast Asian Cartooning: Comics in Philippines, Singapore and Indonesia." *Asian Culture* (Winter): 11-23.

_____. 1995. "Cartooning in Myanmar and Bangladesh." *The Comics Journal* 178: 35-38.

_____. 1997. "The Uphill Climb of Thai Cartooning." *Southeast Journal of Social Science* 25: 93-109.

_____. 1999a. "Bun Lour Sarn (Thailand)." In *The World Encyclopedia of Comics,* edited by Maurice Horn, 165-66. Philadelphia: Chelsea House Publishers.

_____. 1999b. "Chai Rachawat (1941- )." In *The World Encyclopedia of Comics,* edited by Maurice Horn, 193-94. Philadelphia: Chelsea House Publishers.

_____. 1999c. "Comics Controversies and Codes: Reverberations in Asia." In *Pulp Demons: International Dimensions of the Postwar Anti-Comics Campaign,* edited by John A. Lent, 179-214. Cranbury, NJ: Associated University Presses.

_____, ed. 2001. *Animation in Asia and the Pacific.* London: John Libbey.

_____. 2003. "Cartooning in Malaysia and Singapore: The Same, but Different." *International Journal of Comic Art* 5 (1): 256-89.

_____. 2004. "The First 75 Years of Philippine Komiks." *Comic Book Artist* (September): 74-95.

_____. 2009. "Strips in Zuiddost-Azië: Terug van Weggeweest." *Stripschrift* (March): 28-33.

Levin, Florencia Paula. 2007. "Politics Seen through the Prism of Humor in the Argentinean Democratic Transition of 1973: Landrú and Ian." *International Journal of Comic Art* 9 (1): 198-230.

Levy, Mark. 1989. "Wayang Kulit: Indonesia's Shadow Puppet Plays as a Model for Performance." *High Performance* (Summer): 38-41.

Lim, Cheng Tju. 1997. "Singapore Political Cartooning." *Southeast Asian Journal of Social Science* 25 (1): 125-50.

_____. 2000. "Political Cartoons in Singapore: Misnomer or Redefinition Necessary?" *Journal of Popular Culture* 34 (1): 77-83.

_____. 2001."Sister Art—A Short History of Chinese Cartoons and Woodcuts in Singapore." *International Journal of Comic Art* 3 (1): 59-73.

Lim, Ronald S. 2008. "Trese Gets Lucky." *Manila Bulletin Online,* November 1. http://www.mb.com.ph/YTCP2008 1101139546.html.

Liquete, Karen Anne C. 2007. "The Comic Quest." *Manila Bulletin,* October 10.

Liu, Kang. 1991. *Chop Suey.* Singapore: Global Arts & Crafts Pte Ltd.

Loh, Kah Seng. 1998. "Within the Singapore Story: The Use and Narrative of History in Singapore." *Crossroads* 12 (2): 1–21.

Lok Wannee. 2001. "86 Pi Kab Cartoon Ti Yang Mee Chee Wit Kong 'Prayoon Chanyawongs'" [86 years and cartoons that still live of Prayoon Chanyawongs]. December 28: 13.

Maglalang, Demetrio M. 1976. *From the Village to the Medium: An Experiment in Development Communication.* Manila: Communication Foundation of Asia.

Magsaysay Awardees. 2003. Accessed May 8. http://www.rmph.org.ph/frames.html.

Mahr, Krista. 2008. "Comic Relief." April 10. Accessed April 13, 2008. http://www.time.com/time/magazine/article/0,9171,1729550,00.html.

*Manager Online.* 2007. "Yee Poon Kluen Talad Cartoon Thai 90% Tong Pattana Kon Prub Witee Kid Kon Arn" [Japanese comics own 90% of Thai cartoon market; must develop cartoonists and change the way readers think]. April 4. http://www.manager.co.th/Business/ViewNews.aspx?NewsID=9500000038664.

*Manila Times.* 1998. "Let's Get Stone(d). Pinoy Comic Book for International Release This Month." August 1. http://alanguilan.com/komikero/interview04.html.

Manuel, Marlon. 2004. "Unfunny War in Iraq Comes to the Funny Pages." Accessed August 5. http://www.azcentral.com/arizonarepublic/ae/articles/0425politicaltoons25.html.

Maragay, Fel V. 2007. "Komiks Makes a Comeback." *Manila Standard*, February 26.

Marcelo, Nonoy. 1980. "Komiks: The Filipino National Literature?" *Asian Culture* (January): 18–20.

Marston, John. 1996. "Cambodian Satirical Cartoons and the Representation of Hierarchy." Paper presented at Association for Asian Studies annual meeting, Honolulu, Hawaii, April 12.

———. 1997. "Em Sokha and Cambodian Satirical Cartoons." *Southeast Asian Journal of Social Science* 25 (1): 59–77.

Maslog, Crispin C. 2007. *Philippine Communication Today.* Quezon City: New Day Publishers.

Matawaran, Ely. 1987. "Larry Alcala: Foremost Filipino Cartoonist." *Witty-World International Cartoon Magazine* (Autumn): 30–31.

*Matichon.* 1999. "Pu Ying Nai Cartoon Kong 'Prayoon Chanyawongs'" [The women in Prayoon Chanyawongs' cartoons]. August 29: 16.

———. 1999. "'Toon Mahajanaka' Taloo 2 Lan Lem" ['Mahajanaka Cartoon' surpasses 2 million copies]. December 12: 19.

Matienzo, Ros H. 1979. "Ravelo, Iconoclast." *Philippine Comics Review* (October-December): 16–23.

McCloud, Scott. 1994. *Understanding Comics.* 2nd ed. New York: Harper Collins.

McCoy, Alfred, and Alfredo Roces. 1985. *Philippine Cartoons: Political Caricature of the American Era 1900–1941.* Quezon City: Vera-Reyes.

McDougall, Bonnie S., ed. 1980. *Mao Zedong's "Talks at the Yan'an Forum on Literature and Art": A Translation of the 1943 Text with Commentary.* Ann Arbor: Center for Chinese Studies, The University of Michigan.

Meed Tee 13 [The 13th Dagger]. 2008. *Wikipedia.* Accessed August 28.

*Metro.* 1972. "Johnny Hidejet. er." no. 27 (October-November): 5–7.

Mijares, Lawrence. 2007. "Industiya: What Really Killed the Filipino Komiks Industry?" In *Komiks. Sa Paningin ng mga Tagakomiks,* edited by Randy Valiente and Fermin Salvador, 52–56. Quezon City: Central Book Supply.

Montlake, Simon. 2007. "Monks Flee Crackdown in Burma." *Christian Science Monitor,* October 5.

Muliyadi Mahamood. 1997. "The Development of Malay Editorial Cartoons." *Southeast Asian Journal of Social Science* 25 (1): 37–58.

_____. 2001. "The History of Malaysian Animated Cartoons." In *Animation in Asia and the Pacific*, edited by John A. Lent, 131–52. London: John Libbey.

_____. 2003. "An Overview of Malaysian Contemporary Cartoons." *International Journal of Comic Art* 5 (1): 292–304.

_____. 2004. *The History of Malay Editorial Cartoons (1930s–1993)*. Kuala Lumpur: Utusan Publications and Distributors Sdn Bhd.

Nair, CV Devan. 1976. *Socialism That Works: The Singapore Way.* Singapore: Federal Publications.

Najjar, Orayb Aref. 2007. "Cartoons as a Site for the Construction of Palestinian Refugee Identity." *Journal of Communication Inquiry* 31 (3): 255–85.

Nasco. 1977. "Johnny Hidayat. Pacar Sudah Ke 23, Belum Kawin Kawin Juga!" *Adam & Eva*, no. 0011 (July 17): 10–11, 38.

*New York Times.* 2008. "Burmese Endure in Spite of Junta, Aid Workers Say." June 18.

Nguyen, Mai Lynn Miller. 2010. "Cambodian Comics: A New Leaf?" *AsiaLife Guide*, September: 30–35.

*NhanDan Online.* 2009. "Cartoonists' Works Light Up City." November 10. Accessed March 22, 2010. http://www.nhandan.com.vn/.../culture_car.htm.

Nugroho, Id. 2009a. "Comic Strip Campaigns Against Nuclear Power." *The Jakarta Post*, June 30. http://www.thejakartapost.com/news/2009/06/30/comic-strip-campaigns-against-nuclear-power.html.

_____. 2009b. "Indonesian Comic Strips: Drowning but Not Dying." *The Jakarta Post*, December 14. http://www.thejakartapost.com/news/2009/12/14/indonesian-comic-strips-drowning-not-dying.html.

_____. 2009c. "Old Comic Strips Enjoy a Creative Revival." *The Jakarta Post*, March 5. http://www.thejakartapost.com/news/2009/03/05/old-comic-strips-enjoy-a-creative-revival.html.

Odios. 1987. "Johnny Hidayat: Kartunis Yang Gagal Berwiraswasta." *Wawasan*, March 8.

Olesen, Thomas. 2007. "The Porous Public and the Transnational Dialectic: The Muhammed Cartoons Conflict." *Acta Sociologica* 50 (3): 295–308.

Olivares, Patrick Raymond. 1996. "Comic Book Artists[sic] Marvels at His Ethnic Superheroes." *Philippine Daily Inquirer*, October 2. http://alanguilan.com/komikero/interview02.html.

Ong, Wincy. 2005. "Stretching the Concept of the Pinoy Superhero." *The Philippine Star*, March 11. http://alanguilan.com/komikero/reviews08.html.

Ong, Yih. 1991a. "1950s Singaporean Cartoons." In *Essays on Art*, 139–48. Singapore: Pachui Art Singapore.

_____. 1991b. "The Satirical Factor in Cartoons." In *Essays on Art*, 195–204. Singapore: Pachui Art Singapore.

_____. 1994a. "The Social Value of Comics." In *Essays on World Art*, 233–41. Singapore: Thomson Cultural Centre.

_____. 1994b. "Lim Mu Hue—Forgotten Artist." In *Essays on World Art*, 242–49. Singapore: Thomson Cultural Centre.

Ong, Yih, and Fucheng Tan, eds. 1990. *Works by Lim Mu Hue*. Singapore: Siqiang Publishers.

Ou, Qing Chi. 1998. "Fang Xiu and Malayan Chinese Literature." *Tropical Journal* 1 (December): 12–31.

Parinya Changsawek. 1994. "Chai Ratchawat Rachan Hang Tung Ma Mern (1)" [Chai Ratchawat, the king of Tung Ma Mern (1)]. *Naew Na.* December 22: 5.

Paulino, Roberto G. 1995. "A Slice of Larry." *Starweek (The Philippine Star)*, August 20: 4–5.

_____. 1998. "The Filipino According to Comics of Larry Alcala." *The Philippine Star*, August 2: L-6.

Peacock, James L. 1968. *Rites of Modernization*. Chicago: University of Chicago Press.

Pereira, Alexius. 2003. "Triads and Riots: Threats to Singapore's Social Stability." In *Past Times: A Social History of Singapore*, edited by Chan Kwok Bun and Tong Chee Kiong, 182–97. Singapore: Times Editions.

Pham, Holly. 2009. "Cambodian Comic Book Challenge: Phnom Penh's Up-and-Coming Cartoonists Create a 24-Page Comic Book within 24 Hours, from Concept to Final Production...." *Phnom Penh Post*, June 8. Accessed June 10, 2009. http://www.phnompenhpost.com.index.php.

Pham, Thanh Ha. 2008. "Press Cartoons, Not Only for Fun." *NhanDan Online*, April 3. Accessed April 3, 2008. http://www.nhandan.com.vn/english/culture/030408/culture-p.htm.

*Philippine Daily Express*. 1977. "*Superaide* Comic Book Launched." September 12: 28.

*Philippine Daily Inquirer*. 2007. "Dalai Lama Offers Support to Myanmar Monks." September 24.

Ploenpit Sriburin. 2006. "'Bancha-Kamin' Koo Hoo Cartoon Karn Mueng" [Bancha-Kamin, political cartoonist duo]. *Positioning*, July. Accessed August 27, 2008. http://www.gotomanager.com/news/details.aspx?id=50184.

*PMM*. 1977. "Johnny Hidayat Ar." No. 28 (December 30): 10–11.

Pontenila, Roberto J. 1992. "From Kenkoy to Zuma: A Look at Filipino Values in Komiks." In *Communication Values and Society*, edited by Crispin Maslog, 267–80. Los Baños: Philippine Association of Communication Educators.

"Pop Culture China." 2001. *Singapore Journal of Tropical Geography* 22 (2): 113–21.

Pramono, SH. 1985. "Wadah Kartunis Bukan Untuk Bikin Kartu Nama." *Sinar Harapan*, October.

Prieng [pen-name]. 2000. "Chai Ratchawat—Wanich Jarungkitanant Kui Foeng Roeng Kien Lae Cartoon" [Chai Ratchawat—Wanich Jarungkitanant talk about writing and cartoon]. *Thai Post*, January 16: 21.

Pulumbirit, Oliver M. 2007. "Rediscovering the 'Komiks' Wellspring. Escapism, from Page to Screen and Beyond." *PDI Monday*, June 25. http://alanguilan.com/komikero/interview18.html.

Putranto, Sugathi, and Nita Purwanti. n.d. ca. 2010. "Indonesian Alternative Comics from Yogjakarta, Indonesia." *SEAsite Indonesia*.

Rafael, Vicente L. 1995. "Taglish, or the Phantom Power of the Lingua Franca." *Public Culture* (Fall): 101–26.

Rana (pen-name). 1997. "Vithit Usahajit Pu Hai Kam Nerd 'Kai Hua Roh'" [Vithit Usahajit, the creator of 'Kai Hua Roh']. *Dichan*, January: 142–55.

Redondo, Dando. 1979. "Rizal, Inventor of the Comics." *Philippine Comics Review* (October-December): 50–53.

Redondo, Sisenando P. 1979. "The First Philippine Comicbook Editor: Isaac Tolentino." *Philippine Comics Review* (October-December): 24–29.

Redza Piyadasa. 1994. "The Cartoonist—An Appreciation and Tribute." In *Lat 30 Years Later: Compilation of Lat Cartoons*. Art Printing Works Sdn. Bhd.

Renan, Ernest. 1996. "What Is a Nation?" In *Becoming National: A Reader*, edited by Geoff Eley and Ronald Grigor Suny, 41–55. New York and Oxford: Oxford University Press.

Rentjoko, Antyo, and Rudy Badil. 1992. "Penyulam Kitik Dwi Koendoro." *Jakarta Jakarta*, no. 293 (February 8–14): 28–39.

Reyes, Emmanuel A. 1989. "Black and White in Color: The Lure of the 'Komiks' Movie." In *Notes on Philip-*

*pine Cinema*, 71–78. Manila: De La Salle University Press.

Reyes, Soledad S. 1980. "The Philippine Komiks." *International Popular Culture* 1 (1): 14–23.

_____. 1985. "Romance and Realism in the Komiks." In *A History of Komiks of the Philippines and Other Countries*, edited by Cynthia Roxas and Joaquin Arevalo, Jr., 47–52. Quezon City: Islas Filipinas Publishing Co.

Rizal, J. J., and Rani Elsanti. 2008. "Benny and Mice's Exploit in Jakarta." *Karbon*. http://karbonjournal.org.

Roxas, Cynthia, and Joaquin Arevalo, Jr. 1985. *A History of Komiks of the Philippines and Other Countries*. Quezon City: Islas Filipinas Publishing Co.

Rudolph, Jurgen. 1996. "Amusements in the 'Three Worlds.'" In *Looking at Culture*, edited by Sanjay Krishnan, Sharaad Kuttan, Lee Weng Choy, Leon Pereira, and Jimmy Yap, 21–33. Singapore: Self-published.

Sabarini, Prodita. 2010. "Comic Artists Reach for a Wider Audience." *The Jakarta Post*, January 18. http://www.thejakartapost.com/news/2010/01/18/comic-artists-reach-a-wider-audience.html.

Sacerdoti, Guy. 1986. "Philippines: Comics in a Campaign." *Far Eastern Economic Review*, January 9: 31.

Salazar, Marlet D. 2008. "Komiks from the Heart: The Art of Illustrator Gilbert Monsanto." *Philippine Daily Inquirer*, April 6.

Salvini, Milena. 1971. "Performing Arts in Indonesia." In *the Performing Arts in Asia*, 49–54. Paris: Unesco.

San Diego, Bayani, Jr. 2007. "'Andong Agimat' to the US Film Mart." *Philippine Daily Inquirer*, October 7.

Saran Thongpan. 2000. Hem Vejakorn Jitrakorn Rai Samnak Rien Chang Kien Nok Sataban [Hem Vejakorn, artist with no training, drawer without institute]. Accessed April 16, 2003.

http://www.sarakadee.com/feature/2000/10/hem.htm.

Sataban Cartoon Thai Moolaniti Dek [Cartoonthai Institute, Foundation for Children]. n.d. [Booklet]. Bangkok: Cartoonthai Institute.

Schechner, Richard. 1990. "Wayang Kulit in the Colonial Margin." *The Drama Review* (Summer): 25–61.

Sears, Laurie. 1996. *Shadows of Empire: Colonial Discourse and Javanese Tales.* Durham, NC: Duke University Press.

Sherzer, Dina, and Joel Sherzer. 1987. *Humor and Comedy in Puppetry.* Bowling Green, OH: Popular Press. See chapters by Sherzers and by Fredrik E. de Boer.

Shiddiq, Ariel Ash. 2009. "Seeking Jakarta in Senggol Jakarta." *Karbon*, February 5. http://www.karbonjournal.org.

Siahaan, Armando. 2009. "Koloni Brings More Color to Indonesia's Comic Scene." *Jakarta Globe*, September 17. http://www.thejakartaglobe.com/artsandentertainment/koloni-brings-more-color-to-indonesia-comic-scene/330470.

Singh, Daljit, and V. T. Arasu, eds. 1984. *Singapore: An Illustrated History 1941–1984.* Singapore: Information Division, Ministry of Culture, Singapore.

Siregar, Arif. 1989. "Panji Koming, Pailul, dan Walt Disney." *Matra* (October): 143–46.

Sitthiporn Gulawarottama, and Chanansiri Maksampan. 2000. "Prawat Cartoon Thai" [The history of Thai cartoon]. Accessed March 5, 2003. http://www.geocities.com/toonclick/history.htm.

Soedarmo, Darminto M. 1987. "Kartun Tenggang Rasa GM Sudarta." *Minggu Ini* (May): 93.

Soth Polin, and Sin Kimsuy. 1982. "Kampuchea." In *Newspapers in Asia: Contemporary Trends and Problems*, edited by John A. Lent, 219–37. Hong Kong: Heinemann Asia.

*The Straits Times* (Singapore). 1995. "Indonesian Comics Industry Crippled by Poor Quality, Costs." September 28.

Sudarmo, Darminto M. 1987. "Kartunis Pramono ya Kartunis ya Journalis." *Kartika Minggu*, July 26.

_____. 1989. "Merentang Sayap Pergaulan Budaya." *Jayakarta*, January 26.

Sukree Manchainimit. 2006. "Sen Cheevit Cartoon Chai Rachawat" [The cartoon drawing of Chai Rachawat's life]. *Positioning*. July. Accessed August 22, 2008. http://www.positioningmag.com/Magazine/PrintNews.aspx?id=50182.

Sumartana, Th. 1980. "Bayangan 13 Tahun Indonesia di Mata Kartunis G. M. Sudarta." In *Indonesia 1967–1980*, by G. M. Sudarto, xi–xxv. Jakarta: Penerbit P. T. Gramedia.

Surewicz, Anita. 2008. "Comic Artist Chan Pisey Thinks Outside the Box." *Phnom Penh Post*, August 20. Accessed August 21, 2008. http://www.phnompenhpost.com/index.php.

Suroto, Surjorimba. 2010. "Indonesian Comics: 80 Years On." In *Liquid City, Vol. 2*, edited by Sonny Liew and Lim Cheng Tju, 176–83. Berkeley, CA: Image Comics.

Sy, Marvin. 2007. "Darna, Dyesebel Creators Cited." *The Philippine Star*, March 1.

Tan, Budgette. 2007. "The Secret Origins of Alamat." In *Komiks. Sa Paningin ng mga Tagakomiks*, edited by Randy Valiente and Fermin Salvador, 48–49. Quezon City: Central Book Supply.

Tan, Chong Kee, and Tisa Ng, eds. 2004. *Ask Not: The Necessary Stage in Singapore*. Singapore: Times Editions.

Tejokusumo, Andrea. 2008. "Manga Wields Strong Influence over Local Comics." *The Jakarta Post*, August 4, sec. Supplement.

*Tempo*. 1976. "Johnny Hidayat, Kartunis Laris." January: 24–26.

Thammakiat Gunari. 2000. "Chai Ratchawat Kub Rang Wan Mor Ror Wor Ayumongkol" [Chai Ratchawat and the Highness Ayumongkol Award]. *Thai Post*, January 16: 5.

*Thanh Nien Daily*. 2008. "Teenagers Tempted by Sex Comics." Accessed October 4, 2008. http://www.thanhniennews.com/education.

Thee, Marcel. 2009. "Lotif Is a Comic Slice of Indonesian Life." *Jakarta Globe*, September 7. http://www.thejakartaglobe.com/arts/lotif-is-a-comic-slice-of-indonesian-life/328502.

Thuc-Sinh. 1984. "Choe—Detained Cartoonist." *Index on Censorship*, no. 6: 8–9.

Thum, Ping Jin. 2010. "Chinese Newspapers in Singapore, 1945–1963: Mediators of Elite and Popular Tastes in Culture and Politics." *Journal of the Malayan Branch of the British Royal Asiatic Society* 83 (1): 53–76.

Tiu, Linus Velasco. 2001. "Tales of the Big Gerry." *The Daily Tribune*, September 2. http://alanguilan.com/komikero/interview09.html.

Tran Dinh Thanh Lam. 2002. "Foreign Comics Rule the Roost in Vietnam." *Asia Times Online*, March 6. http://www.atimes.com/se-asia/DC0LAE01.html. Accessed November 14, 2010.

Tran Van Can, Huu Ngoc, and Vu Huyen. 1987. *Vietnamese Contemporary Painters*. Hanoi: Red River.

Tuc, Ho-Dac. n.d. "Choe: The Vietnamese Best Known Cartoonist." *On Vietnam & Asia*. http://home.vicnet.net.au/~thodac/tucchoe.htm.

Turnbull, C. M. 1995. *Dateline Singapore: 150 Years of The Straits Times*. Singapore: Singapore Press Holdings.

Ubonrat Siriyuvasak. 2001. *Rabob Wittayu Lae Toratat Thai: Krong Sang Tang Settakij Karn Meung Lae Pon Kratob Tor Sitti Seri Parp* [Thailand's radio and television system: Econopolitical structure, and effects on rights and freedom]. Bangkok: Chulalongkorn University Press.

United Nations Office for the Coordination of Humanitarian Affairs. 2008.

*Cyclone Nargis OCHA Situation Report No. 27*, June 4.

Valiente, Randy, and Fermin Salvador. 2007. *Komiks. Sa Paningin ng mga Tagakomiks*. Quezon City: Central Book Supply.

Vann, Michael G. 2009. "Caricaturing 'The Colonial Good Life' in French Indochina." *European Comic Art* 2, 1 (Spring): 83–108.

*VietNamNet*. 2007. "First Cartoon Contest Announced." December 12. Accessed December 13, 2007. http://english.vietnamnet.vn/lifestyle/2007/12/759358.

_____. 2008. "Racy Foreign Comics Worry Parents." September 22. http://english.vietnamnet.vn/lifestyle/2008/09/804902.

_____. 2008. "Erotic Comics Hurt Growing Kids." October 31. Accessed November 14, 2010. http://www.lookatvietnam.com/2008/10/erotic-comics-hurt-growing-kids.html.

_____. 2009. "VN Cartoons Search for the Key to Popular Esteem." May 12. Accessed June 10, 2009. http://english.vietnamnet.vn/reports/2009/05/847098.

*VietNamNet/Viet Nam News*. 2009. "Cartoons to Help Preserve Culture." August 4. http://www.lookatvietnam.com/.../cartoons-to-help.

Villegas, Dennis. 2007. "On Reviving the Filipino Komiks Industry." In *Komiks. Sa Paningin ng mga Tagakomiks*, edited by Randy Valiente and Fermin Salvador, 61–62. Quezon City: Central Book Supply.

Wang, Ru Min, ed. 1997. *Tan Lark Sye 100th Anniversary*. Singapore: Nantah Business Co. and Hong Kong Nanyang University Alumni.

Wang, Zhen Chun. 1992. "Four Cartoonists—Talking about Their Past." In *The Roots Series 3*, 69–79. Singapore: Seng Yew Book Store.

Ward, A. H. C., Raymond Chu, and Janet Salaff, eds. 1994. *The Memoirs of Tan Kah Kee*. Singapore: Singapore University Press.

WD, WS. 1992. "Dunia Impian Dwi Koendoro." *Mode*, no. 11 (June 7): 54–58.

Wee, C. J. W-L, and Chee Keng Lee, eds. 2003. *Two Plays by Kuo Pao Kun: Descendants of the Eunuch Admiral and the Spirits Play*. Singapore: SNP Editions.

Weeks, John. 2011. "Economics and Comics: Khmer Popular Culture in Changing Times." *International Journal of Comic Art* 13(1):3–31.

Widyawanti, Wiwin. 2003. *The Spirit of Creativity: Dar! Mizan*. Bandung: Dar! Mizan Publishing House.

Wilmott, J. R. 1989. "Lat: Malaysia's Favourite Son." *Reader's Digest*. Hong Kong: Reader's Digest Association Far East Ltd.

Wisut Pornnimitr. 2008. Accessed September 9. http://www.typhoonbooks.com/web/typhoon_thai.html.

Yap, Koon See. 1996. *The Press in Malaysia and Singapore (1806–1996)*. Kuala Lumpur: Self-published.

Yeo, Kim Wah, and Albert Lau. 1991. "From Colonialism to Independence, 1945–1965." In *A History of Singapore*, edited by Ernest Chew and Edwin Lee, 117–53. Singapore: Oxford University Press.

Yong, C. F. 1991. "The British Colonial Rule and the Chinese Press in Singapore, 1900–1941." *Asian Culture* 15 (June): 30–37.

Yunanto, Ardi. 2009. "The Driver Is Male, but the Voice Is Female." *Karbon*, February 5. http://www.karbonjournal.org.

Yunanto, Ardi, and Hikmat Darmawan. 2009. "Tracing the City in Indonesian Comics." *Karbon*, February 5. http://www.karbonjournal.org.

Zakaria Ali. 1989. *Seni dan Seniman*. Kuala Lumpur: Dewan Bahasa dan Pustaka.

## Interviews

Alanguilan, Gerry. 2008. Personal interview with John A. Lent, Manila, Philippines, July 10.

Alcala, Larry. 1988. Personal interview with John A. Lent, Manila, Philippines, September 26.

Atmojo, Kemala. 1992. Personal interview with John A. Lent, Jakarta, Indonesia, July 28.

Badrudin, Ramli. 1992. Personal interviews with John A. Lent, Jakarta, Indonesia, July 25, 28.

Brocka, Lino. 1986. Personal interview with John A. Lent, Quezon City, Philippines, August 21.

Chai Rachawat and Sia. 2008. Personal interview with Warat Karuchit, Bangkok, Thailand, August 18.

Chan Pisey. 2010. Personal interview with John A. Lent, Phnom Penh, Cambodia, June 22.

Chí (Dó Huú Chí). 2010. Personal interview with John A. Lent, Ho Chi Minh City, Vietnam, June 27.

Chua, Mia Tee. 2001. Personal interview with Lim Cheng Tju, Singapore, December 12.

Cinco, Manuel "Fyke." 1986. Personal interview with John A. Lent, Quezon City, Philippines, August 22.

Duong Thanh Hoai. 2010. Personal interview with John A. Lent, Ho Chi Minh City, Vietnam, July 2.

Fabregas, Jimmy. 1986. Personal interview with John A. Lent, Quezon City, Philippines, August 21.

Gallaga, Peque. 1986. Personal interview with John A. Lent, Quezon City, Philippines, August 20.

Gomez, Pablo S. 2008. Personal interview with John A. Lent, Manila, Philippines, July 14.

Ha, Phuong. 1993. Personal interview with John A. Lent, Hanoi, Vietnam, August 11.

Heng, Amanda. 2002. Personal interview with Lim Cheng Tju, Singapore, December 18.

Hidajat, Johnny. 1992. Personal interview with John A. Lent, Jakarta, Indonesia, July 29.

Ho, Kah Leong. 2001. Personal interview with Lim Cheng Tju, Singapore, December 7.

Klo. 2010. Personal interview with John A. Lent, Phnom Penh, Cambodia, June 22.

Koendoro, Dwi. 1992. Personal interview with John A. Lent, Jakarta, Indonesia, July 27.

_____. 2004. Personal interview with John A. Lent, Petaling Jaya, Malaysia, September 14.

Kong Ngoan. 1993. Personal interview with John A. Lent, Hanoi, Vietnam, August 11.

Lacaba, Jose "Pete." 1986. Personal interview with John A. Lent, Quezon City, Philippines, August 22.

Lee, Ricky. 1986. Personal interview with John A. Lent, Quezon City, Philippines, August 22.

Lim, Edi. 2004. Personal interview with John A. Lent, Petaling Jaya, Malaysia, September 12.

Lim, Mu Hue. 2001. Personal interview with Lim Cheng Tju, Singapore, December 19.

Lopez, Oscar. 1964. Personal interview with John A. Lent, Manila, Philippines, September 29.

Mahtum. 1992. Personal interview with John A. Lent, Jakarta, Indonesia, July 28.

Marcelo, Nonoy. 1988. Personal interview with John A. Lent, Manila, Philippines, September 29.

_____. 1992. Personal interview with John A. Lent, Manila, Philippines, July 17.

Martinez, Emmanuel. 1992. Personal interview with John A. Lent, Manila, Philippines, July 18.

Masdiono, Toni. 2008. Personal interview with John A. Lent, Manila, Philippines, July 13.

_____. 2010. Correspondence with John A. Lent, August 16.

Moeu Diyadaravuth. 2010. Personal interview with John A. Lent, Phnom Penh, Cambodia, June 22.

Ng, Kim Boon. 2001. Personal interview with Lim Cheng Tju, Singapore, December 15.

Nguyen Thanh Chung. 1993. Personal interview with John A. Lent, Hanoi, Vietnam, August 10.

Nhek Sophaleap. 2010. Personal interview with John A. Lent, Phnom Penh, Cambodia, June 22.

Poomchai Boonsinsook. 2008. Personal interview with Warat Karuchit, Bangkok, Thailand, August 26.

Pramono R. Pramoedjo. 1992. Personal interview with John A. Lent, Jakarta, Indonesia, July 26.

Prom Vorleak. 2010. Personal interview with John A. Lent, Phnom Penh, Cambodia, June 22.

Purwono, S. (Non-o). 1992. Personal interview with John A. Lent, Jakarta, Indonesia, July 28.

Qiu, Gao Peng. 2001. Personal interview with Lim Cheng Tju, Singapore, December 6.

Reyes, Soledad S. 1986. Personal interview with John A. Lent, Quezon City, Philippines, August 24.

See, Yee Wah [daughter of late artist, See Cheen Tee]. 2000. Personal interview with Lim Cheng Tju, Singapore, June 13.

Setiawan, Arwah. 1992. Personal interview with John A. Lent, Jakarta, Indonesia, July 29.

Sudarno, Darmintom. 1992. Personal interview with John A. Lent, Jakarta, Indonesia, July 28.

Sudarta, G. M. 1992. Personal interview with John A. Lent, Jakarta, Indonesia, July 28.

Sudjai Promkerd. 2008. Personal interview with Warat Karuchit, Bangkok, Thailand, September 1.

Suranit Jumsai na Ayutthaya. 2008. Personal interview with Warat Karuchit, Bangkok, Thailand, August 15.

Suzara, Romy. 1986. Personal interview with John A. Lent, Quezon City, Philippines, August 22.

Tan, Wee Huan. 1998. Personal interview with Lim Cheng Tju, Singapore, September 25.

_____. 2001. Personal interview with Lim Cheng Tju, Singapore, December 3.

Tanyaluck Trechasreesutee. 2008. Personal interview with Warat Karuchit, Bangkok, Thailand, August 26.

Try Samphos. 2010. Personal interview with John A. Lent, Phnom Penh, Cambodia, June 22.

Uth Roeun. 2010. Personal interview with John A. Lent, Phnom Penh, Cambodia, June 23.

Velasquez, Tony. 1988. Personal interview with John A. Lent, Manila, Philippines, September 26.

Weeks, John. 2010. Personal interviews with John A. Lent, Phnom Penh, Cambodia, June 19, 22.

Worawut Worawitayanont. 2008. Personal interview with Warat Karuchit, Bangkok, Thailand, August 29.

Yonzon, Boboy, and Guia Yonzon. 2007. Personal interview with John A. Lent, Guiyang, China, September 10.

_____. 2008. Personal interviews with John A. Lent, Manila, Philippines, July 11–12.

# Index

Pen names of cartoonists are included in parentheses after given names.
Translations of titles (where available) are included in brackets.
Page numbers in **bold italics** indicate pages with illustrations.

235

247